GENTRY LEADERS IN PEACE AND WAR

THE GENTRY GOVERNORS OF DEVON IN THE EARLY SEVENTEENTH CENTURY

Mary Wolffe

UNIVERSITY
of
EXETER
PRESS

First published in 1997 by
University of Exeter Press
Reed Hall, Streatham Drive
Exeter, Devon EX4 4QR
UK

British Library Cataloguing in Publication Data
A catalogue record of this book is available
from the British Library

ISBN 0 85989 513 0

Typeset in 11/14 Original Garamond
by Exe Valley Dataset Ltd, Exeter

Printed and bound in Great Britain
by Short Run Press Ltd, Exeter

For John and Catherine

Contents

Illustrations

Figures

Maps

Geneaological Tables

Tables

Preface

This county history has a firm personal imprint because I bring to it my varied experience of historical study over many years. The two strongest features of this are my long-standing interest in the seventeenth century which existed even before it was deepened by tutorials with Christopher Hill at Oxford over forty years ago and secondly, my fascination with the process of historical research, learnt through years of observing and, sometimes, assisting my late husband in his study of the fifteenth century. When I had the opportunity to pursue my own research, I had no doubt that it would be on the early seventeenth century; but even though my residence in Devon suggested a local subject, I wanted it to be one which linked the county with national affairs. The early years of Charles I were a particularly fruitful time for this purpose. It is a period for which a study of the government of Devon also provides many opportunities to assess the nature of its relations with the royal government. The trials of the leading gentry in billeting expeditionary forces led to their frequent correspondence with the Privy Council; social orders, proclamations and financial demands provided further tests of their efficiency and their loyalty. A study of gentry government could thus reach beyond purely county issues and also become a means of revealing the individual governor's experience of royal government, possible grounds for his later allegiance during the Civil War.

This book has been planned to underline the special character of the county government which lay in the quality of its gentry leaders. The first part considers their collective rule of the county, principally as justices of the peace. This grew out of my initial study of the gentry government of Devon from 1625 to 1640 which also revealed how strongly the government of the county was

influenced by the principles and personal values of the individual
gentry governors.[1] This book now builds on that foundation by
giving far greater emphasis to the careers of those gentry who
shaped the county government at this time. This fresh line of
approach also leads logically to widening the time span of the book.
It is possible to continue most of the biographical studies into the
years of civil war when the need for clear-cut decisions adds much
to our knowledge of these gentlemen. As the county records are
slight for the war years, this biographical approach also makes it
possible to give some account of the county government during the
war and to reveal something of the tension of being a county JP in
a war-torn county.

It has become inevitable that any county history since the work
of Alan Everitt on Kent has to give some consideration to the
question 'was this a county community'?[2] This book will make it
clear that I consider that the small group of gentry leaders who
governed Devon were drawn together by bonds of relationship and
long residence in the county, but primarily by their government of
the county. This collegiality of the bench made possible an effective
government of the county, but it did not turn Devon into a county
community. There were few, other than the gentry governors
themselves, who came from families long accustomed to rule the
county and it was only in their government of Devon that a sense
of county is revealed. Walter Yonge wrote of the abortive attempt
to raise ship money in 1628 and expressed the decision of the
gentry leaders as 'our county refused to meddle therein'.[3] They
occasionally wrote of the county as their country but I have found
no firm evidence that this sense of county went beyond the gentry
rulers themselves; as for the rest of the gentry, the size of the
county and its geographical features made it more likely that their
interests and influence would be centred on their neighbourhood
rather than on the county as a whole. Although I do not think that
the concept of county community fits the Devon I describe, it
has challenged me and other historians to examine the various lines
of research suggested by that debate and now led on to discussion
of county government as part of national government.[4] That is a

line which accords far more closely with my findings on the government of Devon than the idea of county community. As England was a centralized country but not a bureaucratic one, the king depended on the county gentry to raise taxes and soldiers and to enforce order; there was thus an interchange of orders and actions which drew the gentry government into the national one. As Devon's government ruled a large, populous and defensively important county, it was of particular value to the king that they ruled with great competence. The emphasis of this book on the individual gentry leaders transfers the balance of this study of county government from the institutional to the personal level. It suggests that this can be another means of providing new insights into understanding the nature of county government in the early seventeenth century.

While I have been working on this book, I have appreciated the interest shown by many members of the History Department of Exeter University. I have valued this as a continuation of the sympathetic concern they evinced during the long illness of my late husband. I owe a special debt to my two supervisors for my Ph.D: Professor Ivan Roots and Dr Jonathan Barry, who has also aided me in developing it into this book. I am grateful to Mrs Margery Rowe, John Draisey and the other members of the staff of the Devon Record Office for all their assistance. I have received many very valuable comments from those who have read earlier versions of this book, particularly Professor Conrad Russell, Dr John Morrill, Dr Richard Cust, Dr Mark Stoyle and my son, Dr John Wolffe. My family have always supported me with their encouragement and interest, my son has given me the benefit of his own experience of historical research, while my daughter and son-in-law have entertained me during my periods of research in London.

Abbreviations

APC	*Acts of the Privy Council*
BIHR	*Bulletin of the Institute of Historical Research*
BL	British Library
CCC	*Calendar of the Committee for Compounding*
CJ	*Commons Journal*
CSPD	*Calendar of State Papers Domestic*
DCNQ	*Devon and Cornwall Notes and Queries*
DNB	*Dictionary of National Biography*
DRO	Devon Record Office
E	Thomason Tracts, kept at the British Library
EHR	*English Historical Review*
Epiph.	Quarter session after feast of Epiphany (6 January)
HMC	*Historical Manuscripts Commission*
JP	Justice of the Peace
LJ	*Lords Journal*
Mich.	Quarter session after feast of St. Michael the Archangel (29 September)
Mid.	Quarter session after feast of St. John the Baptist (24 June)
PRO	Public Record Office
QS	Quarter Sessions
SRO	Somerset Record Office
TDA	*Transactions of the Devonshire Association*
TRHS	*Transactions of the Royal Historical Society*

The spelling of quotations from manuscripts has been modernized. Only the quarter-session minute books QS1/1, 3, 5, 6 are paginated.

PART I

THE GENTRY
GOVERNMENT OF DEVON
1625–1640

Chapter 1

The Setting for the Gentry Government

Devon has a clear geographical entity, it lies between sea coasts to north and south, with the river Tamar on its western border and Exmoor and the Blackdown hills straddling its eastern border. Within the county there are outstanding features, the dominating granite heights of Dartmoor, rivers rising there or on Exmoor, carving their way through beautiful narrow gorges before widening out into the fertile valleys. The highland and lowland areas dictate different kinds of farming and settlement. While the lowlands of the south were principally devoted to arable farming in the seventeenth century, those of the east concentrated on stock-rearing, and in both these regions life centred on the village. Sheep farming was the main occupation on the bare highlands to the north and west and here the scattered population lived in small hamlets or on isolated farms. Sheep farming gave rise to the principal industry of the county, the cloth trade, which was concentrated in east Devon and on the borders of Dartmoor. Dartmoor was also the area for tin-mining, but by the seventeenth century this was a declining industry. Far more important was fishing, both along the extensive coasts and stretching as far as the Newfoundland fishing grounds.

It is not surprising that a county with such clear natural borders was ruled by a single bench in the seventeenth century, the largest county in England to be so governed. It was also 'very populous and very well inhabited as no part of the realm more or better'.[1] The most recent estimate for the county's population gives a figure of approximately 234,000; to provide a contrast, that of Essex has been numbered at about 100,000.[2] It was also a prosperous county, regarded by a contemporary as superior to any other for what it 'yieldeth in sundry respects both for publyke welth and private proffites and specially for corne and cattell, for clothe and woll, for tynne and mettals and for fishe and sea commodities'.[3] However, this report does not allow for the great variation in the standard of living in the different parts of the county. A study of mortality during the famine crises of the late sixteenth century has shown that the pastoral settlements lying between Barnstaple in the north and Crediton in the centre were particularly vulnerable, while the mixed farming areas of the south were unaffected.[4] Another feature facing the administrators of such a large county would have been the problem of communications. The ride to quarter sessions or assizes in Exeter might be 'very uneven, full of hills and valleys . . . very uneasy for travellers and their horses . . . and being also very full of stones . . . troublesome to pass through'.[5]

On the one hand the county was united by its compact natural borders but on the other hand it was divided by narrow river valleys, the formidable region of Dartmoor and difficult means of communication. These natural hazards promoted differences between the varying areas but they did not impose a divided county government. This was in contrast to the situation in neighbouring Somerset where the peripatetic bench often concentrated on local rather than county issues or in Sussex where the bench was divided into east and west, with only a joint annual meeting.[6] It is one of the particular strengths of Devon's gentry administration that it developed a structure of divisions and sub-divisions which accommodated internal differences without injuring the unity of county government.[7] Unlike Somerset and Sussex, Devon had one outstanding city, Exeter, one of the major towns of England and a county in its own right. The nature of the city ensured that the county administration was drawn towards that single centre. Quarter sessions and assizes always met in the castle unless there was some unusual circumstance such as an outbreak of plague. Exeter was also the cathedral city and the centre of the Exeter

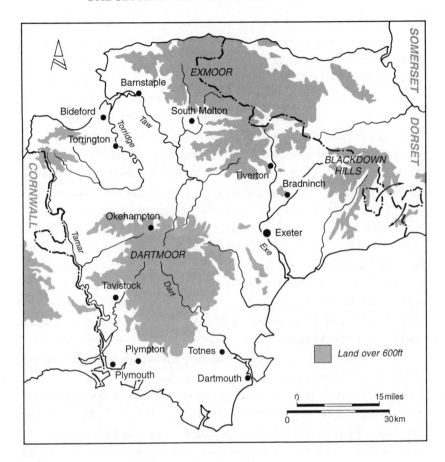

MAP 1 Relief map of Devon

diocese, covering Cornwall as well as Devon. Several JPs owned houses in Exeter; the city was very well supplied with inns which could serve for entertainment, so meetings for quarter sessions and assizes may well have been occasions for social meetings as well as administrative and judicial affairs.

None of the other twelve corporate towns of Devon could rival Exeter. These ranged from Plymouth, which had rapidly and recently developed because of its importance as a naval port, down to Plympton which had suffered from its near neighbour's sudden growth. The largest of the other corporate towns after Plymouth was Tiverton, whose wealth stemmed from the cloth trade and was maintained with its change from heavy to lighter cloths; this was also the strength of South Molton and Torrington. Barnstaple was the main port for the northern clothing towns, but it was losing ground to its smaller rival Bideford because of the silting up of the Taw river. The five other corporate towns were Totnes, whose prosperity had been somewhat affected by the decline of the heavy broadcloth trade; Dartmouth with its growing importance from the Newfoundland fisheries; Tavistock, the centre for tin-mining; Bradninch with a lace as well as a cloth industry; and Okehampton, which had only achieved its charter in 1623. All these boroughs had their own JPs and so the county JPs had no authority within their boundaries, except in Okehampton, whose charter excluded the town's JPs from making judgements over felonies.[8] The county JPs were sometimes used as intermediaries between the towns and the Privy Council and some county JPs wearing their different hats as sheriff, deputy lieutenants or commissioners did exercise some authority within the towns, but the internal affairs of the corporate towns are generally outside the scope of this study.

This chapter is concerned with setting the scene for the gentry government, but what was the nature of this body termed 'the gentry'? What would contemporaries have understood by it? Gentry was a new term which only began to be used at the end of the sixteenth century to describe the separate social groups of knights, esquires and gentlemen who all had the quality of gentility in common, as distinct from other status groups such as the yeomen. This concept of gentility was replacing the old idea of chivalry, while continuing to use the chivalric titles. Landed wealth rather than military prowess had become the criterion for knight-hood before the new order of baronet was instituted in 1611, requiring a yearly income of £1,000 from aspirants. Meanwhile, the rank of esquire was receiving formal recognition: this title might be assumed by landowners without any clear justification by birth, office holding or heraldic law. It has been claimed that, in general, counties followed their own rules on entitlement to this status.

There was also confusion over what merited the status of gentleman; birth, education and office were all means of achieving it but the essential need was to have sufficient landed income to live in the manner of a gentleman; in other words to have the leisure and independence to be capable of holding office. It was these characteristics of leisure and independence which would have marked out all the four ranks of gentry to their contemporaries as suitable to hold office at the appropriate level of local government.[9]

Turning from the general to the particular, how does one describe the gentry of Devon? Is it possible to have some idea of the number of gentry in the county? It is comparatively easy to number the higher gentry drawing largely on the subsidy roll of 1624 and the Protestation Returns of 1641. This produces a total of 379 for the period from 1624 to 1641, even though this is bound to exaggerate slightly the number alive at any one moment.[10] Although these baronets, knights and esquires are the central characters of this book, they relied heavily upon many lesser officials within the divisions, hundreds and parishes to carry out their instructions and to keep them informed of local problems and disputes. Many of these lesser officials claimed to be gentlemen but any attempt at a head count is handicapped by considerable inconsistency in recording the status of gentlemen. However, it was found that nearly all Devonians termed 'gent' or 'Mr' in the subsidy rolls or Protestation Returns had gentry status in all other documents. This provided grounds for numbering 1,129 gentlemen who will be referred to as 'established' gentlemen.[11] Yet this figure omits the many termed 'gent' in other documents; so a second count was made of all office-holders and grand jurymen described as 'gent', this produced 752 names.[12] This does not pretend to be a complete list, but when the 258 who appear in both counts are eliminated it leads to a total of 1,623 gentlemen, which with the higher gentry produces a possible total of 2,002 for the gentry of Devon between 1624 and 1641.

What were the characteristics of each of these groups of gentry? Naturally more information is available on the higher ranks and they are the ones most relevant to this study. Their most obvious feature was their landed wealth and the fact that there was a close connection between the size of their estates and their likelihood to hold county office. The subsidy rolls are the basis for that statement; between 1625 and 1641 one hundred baronets, knights and esquires were on at least one commission of the peace and 61 per cent of them, with legible subsidy rates, paid at the rate of £20 or above whereas only 11 per cent of those who did not hold any office paid at this rate. Clearly status was not enough for county office, it needed to be combined with considerable landed wealth. What of the rest of this rank, the ones with smaller estates? Only sixty-seven of them have been found aiding in the county administration as militia officers, members of commissions, collectors of subsidies and treasurers for hospitals and maimed soldiers; the rest of the higher ranks of gentry, about 200 in all, have not been found holding any administrative position in Devon.[13]

Two other major characteristics of the upper echelons of the Devon gentry were the long residence of their families in the county and their tendency to make endogamous marriages; two features which one would expect to be interlocked. The family with the longest history of pre-eminence were the Courtenays, whose Devon connection began soon after the Norman Conquest. In some cases the long-standing of a family is shown as clearly on the map as in the genealogical tables with place names such as Copplestone, Cruwys Morchard and Fowelscombe. Although few of the leading gentry of the seventeenth century were newcomers to the county, some of them had risen in status and prosperity over the previous hundred years. The causes for their rise were diverse; some families, such as the Prideaux, owed it to the success of an able lawyer.[14] Others rose in wealth with grants of monastic lands; nearly all the grants of Devon land went to men already established in the county.[15] A profitable marriage, sometimes into the family of a wealthy merchant was another stepping stone; this was the route taken by Richard Reynell of Creedy and Walter Yonge. Only ninety of the 379 higher gentry did not belong to families recorded in the heralds' visitations and some of these married into families which did. All but thirty-six of those who do appear in the visitations could trace their family's residence in the county back for at least a hundred years.[16]

The strong leaning of the gentry towards endogamous marriage is illustrated in Table 1. A further breakdown of these figures might suggest a local rather than a county approach to marriage. Of the knights marrying within the county just over a half (eleven) found their brides within twenty-five miles of their residence and among esquires the number was 131 out of the 160 whose marriages are known. This pattern of local marriages did not, however, extend over the county boundaries. Only five of the fifty brides coming from Cornwall or Somerset came from within twenty-five miles of the border. This was probably due as much to the natural deterrent to easy contact of the Tamar, Exmoor and the Blackdowns as to any inherent county loyalty. Endogamous marriage and long residence of a family within a county have both been given special attention since Everitt's description of a county community in Kent, so it is perhaps useful to consider whether a summary of the findings of other historians leads to any obvious conclusion. The trend to endogamous marriage has been found in Kent, Cheshire, Cornwall, Sussex, Dorset, Suffolk, Yorkshire, Lincolnshire, Lancashire, Leicestershire and Northants, but not in Warwickshire. Worcestershire, Herefordshire and Essex.[18] There is no common geographical feature to these two groups of counties to suggest a simple reason for this difference, nor do the counties where endogamous marriage was common inevitably have a gentry long established in the county; it was so in Kent, Cheshire, Lancashire, Sussex and

Table 1:
Marriages of 379 Baronets, Knights and Esquires[17]

		Devon	Somerset	Cornwall	Other	Unknown
13	baronets	4	4	2	2	1
54	knights	21	7	3	16	7
312	esquires	160	19	15	9	109
	Total	185	30	20	27	117

Cornwall in addition to Devon, but was not true of Lincolnshire.[19] Clearly these two features were present in many other counties but, in Devon at least, they often concerned the locality as much as the county and should not be exaggerated to suggest the existence of a county community.

Inevitably there is less information of the lower gentry but there are grounds to distinguish between the 'established' and the 'office-holding' gentlemen. Only 456 of them are known to have had armigerous status and nearly all of these were 'established' gentlemen. The genealogical tables based on the heralds' visitations include the marriages of just under 200 of them and show that they had an even more local approach than those of the higher gentry. Over half of them travelled no more than ten miles for their brides (122 out of 198). As landed wealth was so important in determining the standing of the gentry, the subsidy roll assessments are of particular value, especially as subsidy was charged on lands or goods according to which was the larger source of one's wealth. Three-quarters of the 'established' gentlemen were assessed for land whereas under half of the 'office-holding' gentlemen were so assessed. The rates paid also suggest that the 'established' gentlemen' were generally the more wealthy. One other possible distinction may be drawn between the two classes of gentlemen. In the only known example of an assize grand jury it was 'established' gentlemen or esquires who were chosen, whereas 'office-holding' gentlemen sat on the quarter-session grand jury. In most counties with assize records, the assize grand jurors were of a higher standing than the quarter-session ones, so this distinction may also have been true of Devon.[20]

Two classes of gentlemen have been defined by the terms 'established' and 'office-holding'; it remains to justify these terms as more than convenient labels. Was it only their superior birth, their greater wealth and possibly their service as assize grand jurors which distinguished the 'established' gentlemen from the rest? Can the differences in the kinds of service they rendered to the county go further? The functions fulfilled by the 'established' gentlemen bear a marked similarity to those of the less wealthy esquires. They held any of the lesser county offices not held by those esquires and about half the junior militia offices (totalling forty-five). Yet only thirty-four of them have been identified as head constables, and although 179 were empanelled as quarter-session grand jurors only fifty-one have been found sworn. So it appears that most of those recognized as a gentleman in the subsidy rolls or Protestation Returns would be willing to hold one of the lesser county offices often associated with esquires and so reinforce their gentry status, but that they were generally substantial enough to avoid being named for the time-consuming duties of head constable or quarter-session grand juror; functions which were not the clear monopoly of the gentry and so ones which would not have strengthened their gentry profile.

The rest of those who have been included among the gentlemen of the county, find their place there because they have been noted with that status in their office-holding or grand jury service. Is it possible to carry this further and suggest that they had this status because they were performing a duty; were they in fact gentlemen by service not just office-holding gentlemen? A change in the grand jury lists suggests that this might be so.[21] Until Epiphany 1631 about a quarter of those listed have no designation against their names in the list of those empanelled or of those actually sworn, but from that date some of those empanelled without any designation become gentlemen on the list of those sworn; the two lists being pinned together. In 1634, for the first time everyone named on both lists was termed gentleman, including some who were without that title earlier. This suggests that a decision had been taken in Devon that the status of gentleman was implicit in certain duties. J.S. Morrill, in his pamphlet on the Cheshire Grand Jury, has also aired the possibility of a gentility of service,[22] while M.D.G. Wanklyn also writing on Cheshire considered that the conferment of the title of 'gent' on grand jurymen was a legal fiction.[23] No county study has been found recording a similar change in status to that apparent in the Devon records. The subsidy rolls also lend some support to this idea of the order of gentleman being acquired by service. Ten listed in the 1624 subsidy roll without any status have acquired it on a later roll or in the Protestation Return after a period of service as head constable.

This discussion of the varying levels of gentry status leads to some conclusions on how they related to service in the county. All the major offices, which entailed authority over the whole county, were drawn from the foremost rank of the gentry, the baronets, knights and esquires. They were assisted by a few esquires and 'established' gentlemen in the lesser county offices. The hundred office of head constable was held by both classes of gentleman and by many who did not claim any gentry status; the only exception found to this generalization was in the very small hundred of Ottery St Mary which was co-terminous with the parish boundaries and sometimes had an esquire as head constable.[24] This exception points to the situation among parish offices, where office-holders could be drawn from all levels of the gentry and from none. Recent research has revealed that parish officials, nationally, were often more substantial members of the community than used to be assumed and that the gentry did serve among their number. In Devon, five current or future JPs have been found among gentry serving as churchwardens or overseers of the poor.[25] This fact that the leaders of the county government might also be among those dealing with problems at the grass roots is a valuable indication of the breadth of their knowledge of county affairs at all levels.

Although this book is concerned with the gentry leaders of the county, no overall setting for the gentry government would be complete without mention of the rest of the inhabitants of the county. It is fortunate that this study follows so closely on the work of Mark Stoyle, *Loyalty and Locality*, which considers the Civil War allegiance of ordinary Devonians, those of Exeter and the corporate towns as well as the county; men who did not unthinkingly follow the opinions of their 'betters'.[26] This provides a counterpoise to this work on the gentry; together the two studies should provide a balanced account of the county in the early seventeenth century. Dr Stoyle's book emphasizes the importance of religion in determining the allegiance of many Devonians in the Civil War although its influence tends to stand out more clearly in such moments of crisis and decision than in times of peace. Some discussion of religious issues is an essential component of seventeenth century history but religion did not lie at the forefront of the affairs of the gentry government, rather it was an underlying feature of all life in the county. Three bishops were on the commission of the peace while they ruled the diocese of Exeter in the early seventeenth century: William Cotton (1598–1621), Valentine Carey (1621–1626) and Joseph Hall (1627–1641). Only Bishop Hall has been found taking any part in county government, nevertheless the nature of his and his predecessors' rule in their diocese is an essential part of this account of the gentry government.

There was no home-grown Protestant party in Devon at the time of the Reformation. Protestantism had to be imposed upon the county and the strongest local influences in this were the first and second earls of Bedford. The second earl's determination to have a diligent, preaching divine led to the appointment as bishop of John Woolton (1579–1594). He had been a canon of Exeter cathedral, lecturing there twice weekly as well as preaching twice on Sunday. He continued to preach regularly as bishop as well as writing a number of idealistic tracts. During his episcopate a solidly 'Anglican' Chapter began to emerge at the cathedral, holding the middle ground and providing a firm, broad, intellectual basis for the church in the south west.[27] Dr Vage, writing on the Exeter diocese, considered that Woolton should be viewed on his own terms and not committed to either the conformist or puritan party. He terms Woolton a Grindalian bishop, which has been defined as a Calvinist who overlooked divisive issues of non-conformity in favour of the common endeavour of bishop and puritan to spread the gospel and resist Roman Catholicism.[28] This was the kind of influence at work in Devon for fifteen years at the end of the sixteenth century; it may well be taken as the foundation for understanding the development of religious views in Devon in the early seventeenth century.

At this time all appointments of bishops were of Calvinists. Woolton was succeeded briefly by the ineffective Gervase Babington and then by William Cotton. The need to secure subscription to the

Canons of 1604 brought any opposition out into the open. After the Restoration Cotton gained the reputation of having been 'a strict and prudent prelate who plucked up puritanism from the roots before it grew to perfection'. Yet he should not be thought of as a puritan hater as his wife was of a 'godly disposition' and was used by puritans as an intermediary with him. He was conciliatory to ministers over the Canons and succeeded in persuading some, who privately dissented, to conform.[29] One of those ministers (Samuel Hieron) was threatened with suspension several times but could say in a sermon of 1615 that he rejoiced to be a son of 'our English Church ... and wherein, it shall be my glorie and my crowne in the day of Christ to have been employed as a minister'. Dissension may have existed beneath the surface, but this declaration of Hieron's allegiance suggests that the Exeter diocese under Cotton lay close to King James' ambition for a united church of moderate and conformist Calvinists.[30] The episcopate of Valentine Carey may have introduced more controversial elements into the diocese, but its five year span was too short and his absences at Court were too long for them to have an obvious effect. He felt that it was his mission to enhance the prestige of the clergy and he was called an Arminian at his death in 1626, but at that date this could have been a term of puritan abuse for the failure of a courtier bishop to support rigid predestination.[31]

The appointment of Joseph Hall to Exeter in 1627 was to prove to be the last appointment of a Calvinist bishop in England until 1641. There had been signs under Cotton that there were puritans in the diocese who needed to be conciliated, so this account of gentry government might well have been less harmonious if an anti-Calvinist, such as William Piers (appointed to the next diocese of Bath and Wells in 1632) had been sent to Exeter. Hall was a Calvinist with moderate beliefs on predestination, though able to respect the more extreme view; he was ready to appoint lecturers but expected them to be orthodox and peaceable; he valued equally catechizing and preaching on Sunday, regarding the whole week sanctified by the way Sunday was observed. This was a bishop who could steer a moderate course, encompassing the majority and

FIGURE 1 Joseph Hall, Bishop of Exeter 1627–1641 (Emmanuel College, Cambridge)

making it possible for all but the most extreme to remain within the church. His success is reflected in the 'Devonshire Petition' sent to the House of Lords early in 1642. Nearly 8,000 knights, esquires, gentlemen and others of ability within the diocese of Exeter professed that they had 'for these many years found the benefit and comfort of Episcopal Government, under which we have lived hitherto peaceably and happily, with great freedom and frequency of the Preaching of the Gospell, and incouragement of the conscienable and paineful Preachers therof . . .'. In a period of religious discord in the country, Hall managed to maintain a peaceful diocese by smoothing over differences and not enforcing new directives. This finding is not at odds with the different situation apparent in the changed political and religious climate of the 1640s when the differences which Hall had kept below the surface emerged. Joseph Hall's achievement in minimizing religious unrest in Devon is an essential part of this background to the government of the county.[32] It ensured that the bench could function without the disruptive effects of local religious conflicts.

Chapter 2

The Collegiality of the Devon Bench from 1625 to 1640

The strength of the Devon bench from 1625 to 1640 lay in the quality of its members, in its freedom from internal disputes and in its ability to work together. Such breadth and depth of strength was unusual among the county governments of this period. Circumstances had relieved Devon from one possible cause of disruption, for although peers were included on the commission they were either non-resident, such as the lord lieutenant, the earl of Bedford, or they took little part in county affairs, like the earl of Bath.[1] This was very different from the situation in Essex where the earl of Warwick, an extensive landowner, an aggressive Protestant and lord lieutenant, held sway.[2] The Devon bench was one of equals with no struggles for supremacy between ambitious rivals, like the rivalry of Lord Poulett and Sir Robert Phelips which plagued affairs in Somerset. Nor had divisive parties developed in support of rival politicians, such as those between the followers of the duke of Buckingham and the earl of Pembroke in Cornwall. Freedom from personal and political rivalries meant that Devon was also saved from the danger of religious labels being attached to such parties and so inflaming both religious and political differences. A recent study has suggested that this could be the cause of the development of factions in Cornwall.[3]

This freedom from internal disputes was essential for the effective government of Devon by its gentry but it also required able and dedicated leaders, capable of working together. Two contemporary quotations throw light on the way in which such public servants viewed their labours. Sir Richard Grosvenor, a Cheshire JP, wrote of 'the thirsting desire I have (upon all occasions) to doe my countrey service (for thereto are wee all borne)'. Bishop Hall described the good magistrate as one who was both 'the faithful Deputy of his Maker' and 'the father of his Country'.[4] In the twentieth century we are too apt to keep religion and government in separate compartments and to think, perhaps, that Hall's portrayal of a JP as both the servant of God and of his country was an episcopal aspiration. That would not have been the thinking of the gentry governors of Devon. They would have seen themselves as serving God, the King and their country, by which they might mean the nation, the county or their immediate neighbourhood. None of them have left their own view of a godly magistrate but there is little in the words of Sir Richard Grosvenor of Cheshire which conflicts with what is known of Devon's JPs. As it has been claimed that one can reconstruct the mentality of a local governor of this period from his writings, he will have to speak for the gentry leaders of Devon and so suggest the ideals which permeated their government of the county. His charge to the grand jury exhorted local governors to follow their consciences, fight sinfulness and fulfil their calling in the service of God and the commonwealth.[5] As most of this book is concerned with the practical aspects of county government, it is appropriate at the outset to emphasize that many of the gentry leaders would have shared this ideal concept of the godly magistrate.

A seat on the bench was a prized position which acknowledged a man's status within the county, so there must have been some anxiety among the JPs when it became clear that the new Lord Chancellor, Sir Thomas Coventry, was intent on some substantial pruning of the bench. There had been a considerable increase in the size of all benches during the later years of James I which may have been due to the king's high opinion of JPs. In 1616 he referred to them as 'the king's eyes and ears in the country ... I esteem the service done me by a good justice of peace .. as well as the service done me in my presence.'.[6] The Devon bench had averaged sixty members during the first half of James' reign, but then numbers increased so that on the accession of Charles I there were probably seventy-four JPs.[7] The hand of the Lord Chancellor now led to a marked reduction, with the bench falling to an average of only fifty-four for the first four years of the reign, rising to an average of sixty-four for the next four years and then falling back to a membership of about sixty for the remainder of the peace-time years. Stuart commissions of the peace have not survived for Devon before 1643 so details of the bench have had to be established from other sources.[8] These can be relied upon to identify the 112 JPs appointed during these years but they may not always reveal any very temporary breaks in service.[9] This means that one has to rely on evidence from attendance at quarter sessions or signing recognizances to note the very definite changes which were taking place in the winter of 1625–6. Ten active JPs suddenly disappear from these records, although they were reappointed between 1626 and 1628.[10] Eighteen more disappear from the lists at this time, but only two of them were eventually restored between 1629 and 1631. Thus over a third of those on the bench at the beginning of the reign were almost immediately, briefly or permanently, excluded from the commission. At the same time six new JPs were added to the bench between 1625 and 1628.[11] The bench may well have been startled by a reduction at a single stroke, such as that which reduced the Sussex bench from forty-eight to twenty-seven in December 1625.[12]

There are obvious reasons for the permanent exclusion of some JPs. The passage of time accounted for some changes; six JPs had died and three more may have been considered too old. Sir William Courtenay was omitted as a suspected recusant and Sir John Whidden may have been dropped because of his Catholic associations.[13] Five others were guilty of non-attendance at quarter sessions.[14] It is more difficult to find any shared reason for the very temporary exclusion of ten JPs and the slightly longer exclusion of two others. Age could have been the reason for the omission of the 65-year-old Robert Haydon, though age did not stop his restoration for the remaining ten months of his life. Sir Edward Seymour may have been dropped for non-attendance at quarter sessions and earnt his restoration by his active service as a deputy lieutenant. Three other JPs had only been on the commission for about a year before their omission so may not have had long enough to establish their position.[15] The remaining five all had a record of conscientious and regular service to their credit.[16] There is no evidence that any JP was removed for a political reason, in particular for refusal to pay the forced loan. Walter Yonge's comment in his diary in October 1628 that 'all the JPs who were put out of the Commission about the loan are forthwith to be put in again',[17] must refer to the national not the Devon situation. All Devon JPs who had had any break in their service had been dropped from the commission before the forced loan and, with the exception of Sir Richard Edgecumbe and Sir William Waller, had been restored to the bench before October 1628.

After these changes at the beginning of the reign only four JPs were omitted from the commission: Sir William Pole was replaced as a JP by his son Sir John in 1628 (when Sir William was sixty-seven years), Sir Richard Grenville fled abroad after imprisonment for debt, Sir William Waller left the county after the death of his wife, a Devon heiress, and Nicholas Luttrell ceased to be an active JP. Thirty-four JPs died in office and death was the reason for all the deletions from the 1634 *liber pacis* amended for 1638. No one was removed from the commission for refusal to take the oaths of supremacy and allegiance as ordered in the Lent assizes of 1636 nor for refusal to pay ship money.[18] Thus the Devon bench may claim to have been a particularly loyal one. Although no JP was dismissed, the smaller bench of the 1630s may suggest decreased enthusiasm for the position. This is particularly notable in the different behaviour of the heirs of deceased JPs. Sir Peter Prideaux, John Bampfield and Henry Walrond rapidly took their fathers' place on the bench in the late 1620s, but Sir Francis Drake, John Northcott and William Fry did not step into their fathers' shoes in the 1630s. As they did serve on the commission in the late 1640s (after the king's supporters had been removed), this suggests that they may

20

have been reluctant to serve in the 1630s.[19] The Caroline bench must have gained from stability in its membership, moreover it was also full of experienced county governors. Thirty-four of those on the bench on Charles' accession already had more than ten years service to their credit (twenty-one of them had twenty years) and thirteen had become JPs under Elizabeth.[20] Such permanence on the bench was not a feature of all counties; in Essex, the average length of service was about ten years.[21]

There is no clear evidence who acted as deputy *custos rotulorum* and so chairman of quarter-session proceedings. Some historians think that the first JP named in the minutes held the position; others consider that the legal knowledge essential for this position would have caused the senior barrister present to fulfil this duty.[22] The list of names of those present at quarter sessions was always strictly according to status, so if the first named was chairman, the position could have changed from session to session. If a barrister was deputy *custos*, Richard Reynell is the most likely candidate; he was assiduous in his attendance at quarter sessions and stored the records in his house in Exeter, thereby literally keeping the records.[23] Another detail of quarter-session membership which deserves a mention was being 'one of the quorum'. This was supposed to be an indication of legal training but this cannot be assumed. A very high proportion (at least five-sixths) are listed as 'of the quorum'. It seems more likely that it was a question of status rather than qualification. Some newcomers to the bench served a time before they became 'of the quorum' even if they were barristers, and long service ultimately led to the inclusion of those without legal education.[24] It is possible that other reasons caused omission from the quorum. For example, Sir Henry Rosewell may have been omitted because of his appearances before the Court of High Commission for refusing to attend his parish church and having a private chapel at his home, which was attended by more than his family.[25] He was the only knight on the bench not to be 'of the quorum' even though he had attended the Middle Temple.

So much for the composition of the bench and its weight of experience, what of its common bonds, its collegiality? Many of its features stand out in contrast to other counties and, collectively, underline the exceptional nature of this bench. The effective members were all drawn from the highest rank of the Devon gentry and so some of their characteristics have been described in the last chapter.[26] They were considerable landowners and the families of eighty-five of them had been in the county for at least a hundred years.[27] This gave a cohesion to the gentry body which was lacking in Warwickshire, where many of the gentry were comparative new-comers.[28] Any attempt to assess the value of their estates is open to various difficulties. For example, Sir Henry Rolle's estate was said to be worth at least £100,000 when the 1625 forced loan was under consideration. Yet his principal manor of Stevenstone was valued at only £18 in the *inquisition post-mortem* and at £120 14s 9d in the feodary survey; both very low if the £100,000 figure has any basis in reality.[29] The best method of valuation lies with the subsidy rates. As they only assessed the main source of a man's income (for all the Devon JPs this was landed wealth), they can provide a means of showing the comparative value of their estates. Legible assessments have been found for sixty-three of the gentry JPs in the rolls of 1621–28.[30] Sir Henry Rolle had the highest rate of £60, three more JPs were assessed between £40 and £50, another six between £25 and £36 and thirty-two between £20 and £24. The rates for the remaining eighteen JPs ranged from £6 to £18. These subsidy rates provide grounds for comparisons with other counties though they must be used with some caution. Standards of assessment could vary between counties, some JPs might ensure their own low assessment or alternatively, in Sussex, they might accept an increase on their appointment to the commission.[31] To compare the landed wealth of Devon's JP with those of other counties, the average was taken of the sixty-three rates cited above which proved to be £20. Devon JPs were clearly wealthier than their neighbours of Cornwall, where not more than eight were rated at £20 or over; a similar figure has been noted for Cheshire and a slightly lower one for Shropshire.[32] It appears that the Devon bench was as wealthy, if not wealthier than those of other counties. Perhaps the most tangible evidence left to us of a prosperous gentry body is the fine long gallery at Cadhay, built by the long-serving JP, Robert Haydon.

A feature common to all these gentry JPs was that their wealth was based on inherited estates. The cloth trade had provided the money for the forbears of some gentry JPs to invest in land. The manufacture of kersey had laid the foundation of the wealth of the Northcott and Davy families in Crediton, but their seventeenth-century descendants, John Northcott and John Davy, both JPs, had moved to country estates outside Crediton. In the South Hams another JP, Sir Edward Giles, with estates at Bowden, owed his prosperity to John Giles of Totnes, who had been the richest merchant in Devon in the sixteenth century.[33] Although no JPs have been found to be still involved in the cloth trade, the county's principal industry, they were very ready to act in furtherance of its welfare. The same was true of the other industries, but in these some gentry also had a personal interest. The Strode family were the biggest single owners of tinworks in the county.[34] There were also JPs on the eastern edges of Dartmoor, at Chagford and Ashburton, who may have gained profit from mining. Other JPs resident in the coastal regions looked towards another main aspect of the county's economic life – the sea. Sir Ferdinando Gorges, Sir James Bagg, Sir Edward Seymour and John Upton all had stakes in privateering enterprises. Another JP from this area, Arthur Champernowne, was engaged in shipping and suffered losses during the war with Spain.[35]

This chapter has shown that the effective bench were drawn together by their equality of status, their long residence in the county and their inherited wealth, but this was only the foundation of their collegiality. They were also drawn together by a common educational background; in this one must include the clerics as, unlike most of the peers, they were resident in the county and would have had their influence on quarter sessions. Forty-one JPs attended a university and as one would expect geographically, Oxford was the choice of all but six of them; twelve of them (five of them the clerics) gained degrees. The fact that twenty of them were at Exeter College may show more than the strength of the local connection as Exeter was acquiring the reputation of being a puritan stronghold. Sixty-six JPs had attended an Inn of Court (thirty-four of them in addition to a university) and sixteen of them became barristers. This time at an Inn may well have brought the future JP into contact with the politics of the day as the meetings of Commons Committees were often held at an Inn.[36] It is possible to add the numbers for Devon to a table compiled by J.H. Gleason for six other counties for 1636.[37] It shows that the Devon gentry was comparable to other counties in educational experience though fewer of those attending an Inn of Court were called to the Bar. Gleason also compared the number of members of parliament; so that feature is included in Table 2. Service in parliament must have raised the horizons of the JPs and shown them that the problems of their county were common to many. Over half those on the bench between 1625 and 1640 had been an MP, a higher proportion than in other counties. This was probably caused by three factors: the size of Devon, the rarity of any MPs from outside the county being elected (John Pym being the notable exception), and the large number of Cornish seats, some of which were filled by Devon gentlemen. The number of seats available to Devon gentry may have helped prevent electoral conflicts (common in some counties), and so saved the county from political and religious differences being fostered by electioneering.[38]

Table 2:
The education and parliamentary experience of the JPs of seven counties in 1636 (excluding office holders)

Number of:	JPs	Oxford Oxon.	Cambridge Cantab.	Inn	Bar	MPs	None of these
Kent	63	20	23	47	18	23	6
Norfolk	52	1	34	32	16	22	5
Northants.	39	13	15	21	7	11	6
Somerset	51	24	4	33	10	18	4
Worcestershire	22	11	0	9	2	9	4
North Riding	39	5	14	29	7	16	4
Devon	62	30	5	41	8	32	4

The JPs were drawn together by duties other than those of the bench. The commission of sewers for the whole county was made up entirely of JPs, and all the JPs also served on the commission for loans with some additional members who were thought likely to further the collection.[39] Forty-two JPs served on other commissions: some living in south-west Devon were involved in billeting soldiers embarking and disembarking at Plymouth on the various expeditions, some of these also had powers of martial law. Financial demands led to the creation of commissions assessing knighthood composition and for raising money for St Paul's.[40] The commissions for pirates, charitable uses and for innovative offices and exacted fees also included JPs.[41]

The two other county offices, deputy lieutenant and sheriff, were nearly always filled by JPs. No commissions for deputy lieutenant were issued after the accession of Charles I, but twenty-three of the JPs have been found holding this most prestigious of the gentry offices during the first fifteen years of the reign, though not more than ten at any one time. With three exceptions changes were due to death; Sir William Courtenay was removed after he had been accused of recusancy, Hugh Pollard replaced his father Sir Lewis, and Sir Alexander St John appears to have left the county. Sir William Strode tried to resign from both the deputy lieutenancy and the commission in 1632 (when he was in his seventies), but was restored.[42] This is a valuable indication that even the father of someone in prison for opposition to the Crown, and himself a critic in many parliaments, could yet be regarded as a valuable servant in the county. Eleven deputy lieutenants also held a militia command and fifteen other JPs were militia officers. Thus organizing and serving at musters was another area where the bench were drawn together. Only two of the holders of the other major gentry office, that of sheriff, were not JPs when they were appointed.[43] However, holding this office did not contribute to the collegiality of the bench, as the sheriff was rather detached from the gentry body during his year of office as the King's principal servant in the county.

Devon's JPs were appointed to a single commission, sitting on a single bench and always meeting in Exeter in normal times. These were crucial factors in making it possible to be a united county government. They were the largest county with this organization. The only two larger ones, Yorkshire and Lincolnshire, had three separate commissions for the different ridings or parts. In other counties divisions were almost as definite though without more than one commission. The separate benches for East and West Sussex only met together at midsummer, and in Kent quarter sessions alternated between Canterbury and Maidstone, with considerable rivalry existing between the two halves.[44] Other counties had less definite divisions but met in different towns for each session with the inevitable result of the session consisting chiefly of the nearest JPs and being concerned primarily with local rather than county interests; this happened in Somerset, Cheshire and Wiltshire.[45] Yet can one assume that the Devon quarter sessions were really gatherings of the whole county, or were they just meetings of those resident near Exeter? The list of those who attended each quarter sessions, usually included in the minutes, provides the evidence to answer this. These lists show that only five of the seventeen JPs, who were the most regular in their attendance, lived within ten miles of Exeter.[46] As for the rest, if distances are measured 'as the crow flies' and not as they would have had to ride across difficult country, three more lived under twenty miles, five between twenty and thirty miles, and the other four came from distant parts of the county, two from beyond Dartmoor, one from north of Barnstaple and one from the South Hams. Clearly this was a bench which represented the interests of the whole county.

The requirement for JPs to be present in Exeter extended beyond the three days of quarter sessions. They were also supposed to attend the assizes which probably lasted for two days, and there were also other meetings such as those of deputy lieutenants and loan commissioners which sometimes coincided with quarter sessions or assizes. It is not surprising to find that some JPs had their own houses in Exeter, especially those who came from distant parts of the county. Sir William Strode from Plympton St Mary had a house near the cathedral, Sir Edmund Prideaux and Walter Yonge from near Colyton, William Cary from Hartland on the far north-west coast, and Richard Reynell of Creedy and John Bampfield from closer areas are all known to have had residences in Exeter.[47] This would have increased the possibility that times of official meetings also became times of social gatherings. This would have been furthered by the close relationship of many members of the bench which must have had a considerable effect on the character of the Devon bench. There was a great deal of intermarrying among the families of JPs. Twenty-two of them were married to the daughter or sister of a fellow JP, the most notable example concerned the family of Sir William Strode. Four of his daughters married JPs and the other two a brother and a nephew of a JP. Relationships sometimes determined the joint activities of the JPs. Sir Francis Vincent and John Acland often acted together; Sir Francis was both the father-in-law and step-father of John Acland. Richard Reynell of Creedy and his son-in-law, Richard Reynell of Ogwell, though normally living some distance apart, signed

FIGURE 2 Part of the Memorial to Sir William Strode in the Church of Plympton St Mary. His ten children include the wives of four JPs - Sir George Chudleigh, Sir Francis Drake, Sir John Chichester and John Davy

recognizances together over the Christmas period, when they were apparently visiting each other. The brothers-in-law John Northcott and Sir Lewis Pollard also acted together at times, although they were from different divisions of the county. The last chapter showed that the gentry as a whole tended to marry within the county, these examples and the genealogical tables included in the individual studies show that the JPs tended to marry into the families of their fellows on the bench. Business relationships also drew JPs together. There are instances of sales of land between them and of them acting as trustees and executors for each other. This is not surprising but it does emphasize the widespread contact and trust which existed between some members of the bench. No examples have been found of litigation between different members of the bench, such as occurred in Gloucestershire.[48]

Clearly there were many common bonds which drew together the JPs of Devon, bonds developed by the practical needs of government and by the personal associations this tended to develop. Although the emphasis of this chapter has been on the bonds which linked the gentry governors within the county it would be a mistake to assume that this made them an inward-looking body. Some of the factors which linked them developed their interests beyond their county boundaries. Three-quarters of them had had some period of education outside the county and over half of them had served in a parliament. Devon's extensive seacoasts led to some being ship-owners, others promoters of colonial expansion and all of them were well aware of the profits and dangers of foreign trade.[49]

Chapter 3

Ancient and Modern Divisions
in the Localities

The last chapter commented on the unifying effect of the JPs throughout the county being drawn together on a single bench in Exeter. This chapter concentrates on the other side of the coin, the importance of the JP within his home area. The foundation of this was as a member of his own parish, where he was well aware of the parochial side of raising rates, dealing with vagrants, keeping the parish arms and paying the trained soldiers. The JP was not above serving as a churchwarden. The surviving churchwardens' accounts only cover a fraction of the home parishes of the JPs yet at least eight of those on the bench between 1625 and 1642 have been found serving as churchwarden or being active on the parish council.[1] The JPs not only sent out orders from quarter sessions but had practical experience of how those orders were dealt with at the parish level. The effective administration of the county depended upon the dual role of the JP acting at quarter sessions and in his locality. Many cases brought before quarter sessions or assizes had started before a JP in his home; many orders and referrals in the quarter session minutes were to 'the next JPs' or to named JPs. Quarter sessions was the centre of the web of local government but it depended upon the effective work of the JPs in their home area. As statutes increased the amount of work to be done by JPs locally, the need grew for administrative units which could utilize, effectively, the

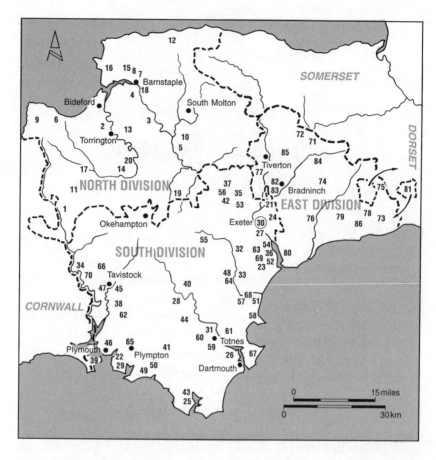

MAP 2 Residences of the JPs in the three major divisions

North Division

1. Edmund Arscott
2. John Arscott
3. Arthur Basset
4. Edward, earl of Bath
   Henry, earl of Bath
5. Humphrey Bury
6. William Cary
7. Sir John Chichester
8. Viscount Chichester
   Sir Robert Chichester
9. Nicholas Luttrell
10. Sir Lewis Pollard
11. Sir Nicholas Prideaux
12. William Richards
13. Sir Henry Rolle
14. Sir Samuel Rolle
15. Sir Ralph Sidenham
16. Sir Edward Southcott
17. Sir John Speccot
18. James Welsh
19. John Wood
20. Leonard Yeo

30

South Division

21. John Acland
22. Sir James Bagg
23. Peter Ball
24. Sir Amias Bampfield
    John Bampfield
25. William Bastard
26. Ambrose Bellot
27. Bartholomew Berry
28. Richard Cabell
29. Sir Shilston Calmady
    Sir Warwick Hele
30. Bishop Valentine Carey
    Bishop Joseph Hall
    Dean William Peterson
31. Arthur Champernowne
32. Sir George Chudleigh
33. Dr Thomas Clifford
34. John Cloberry
35. Archdeacon Edward Cotton
36. Sir William Courtenay
37. John Davy
38. Sir Francis Drake
39. Sir Richard Edgecumbe
40. Thomas Ford
41. Sir Edmund Fowell
42. Sir Francis Fulford
    Thomas Tuckfield
43. Nicholas Gilbert
44. Sir Edward Giles
45. Sir Francis Glanvill
    Alexander Maynard
46. Sir Ferdinando Gorges
47. Sir Richard Grenville
48. Elias Hele
49. Sampson Hele
50. Sir Thomas Hele
51. William Hockmore
52. Sir Nicholas Martin
53. John Northcott
54. John Peter
55. Humphrey Prouz

Sir Thomas Whidden
56. Periam Reynell
    Richard Reynell
57. Sir Richard Reynell
    Sir Thomas Reynell
58. Thomas Ridgeway
    earl of Londonderry
59. Thomas Risden
60. Robert Savery
61. Sir Edward Seymour
62. Sir Nicholas Slanning
63. Sir George Southcott
64. Sir Popham Southcott
65. Sir William Strode
66. Arthur Tremayne
67. John Upton
68. Sir William Waller
69. Richard Waltham
70. Sir Thomas Wise
    Thomas Wise

East Division

71. Henry Ashford
72. John Bluett
73. John Drake
74. Sir Thomas Drew
75. Nicholas Fry
76. Robert Haydon
77. Sir Simon Leach
78. Sir John Pole
    Sir William Pole
79. Sir Edmund Prideaux
    Edmund Prideaux
    Sir Peter Prideaux
80. Sir Thomas Prideaux
81. Sir Henry Rosewell
82. Peter Sainthill
83. Sir Francis Vincent
84. Henry Walrond
    William Walrond
85. Humphrey Weare
86. Walter Yonge

uneven spread of JPs throughout this large county. It is one of the main contentions of this chapter that the development of Devon's own particular variety of these administrative units owed as much to the initiatives of the bench as to any occasional orders of the Privy Council. Devon had four kinds of internal unit between quarter sessions and the parish: the ancient organization into hundreds and the newer ones of division and, most unusually, two forms of sub-division, one for financial and the other for administrative purposes. It was this second type of sub-division, created for administrative purposes, which shows that Devon's JPs were ready to organize their county on a pragmatic basis, without being dominated by the ancient historic hundred units like so many other counties.

There is no evidence of any JP being appointed because of a need for one in any particular area. The argument is that new administrative units grew in strength because they made better use of the existing spread of the JPs over the county. Map 2 marks the homes of nearly all the JPs of 1625 to 1640 whose principal residence was in Devon. Some of their homes can still be visited today, Sir Francis Drake's Buckland Abbey, Sir William and Sir John Pole's Shute and Robert Haydon's Cadhay; parts of others are now incorporated into later houses, such as the Bampfields' home at Poltimore or Sir Thomas Drew's near Broadhembury. The homes of most of the rest of the JPs have been learnt from their name on the subsidy roll or from the parish where they were buried. As one would expect the distribution of the estates of the JPs was affected by the varied quality of the soil of the county. No JPs were resident on the expanse of Exmoor on the county's north-eastern border or on the barren land mass of Dartmoor which divided much of north from south Devon. North Devon, except round Barnstaple, was largely a pastoral region and here the JPs were spread thinly, presumably because they also based their livelihood on this form of farming, with its need for extensive ownership of the poorer quality land. Sixteen market towns existed in these northern areas but it was only round Barnstaple that there were sufficient JPs resident to provide a centre for a sub-division. In the southern part of the county there were rich corn and fruit growing areas in the Exe

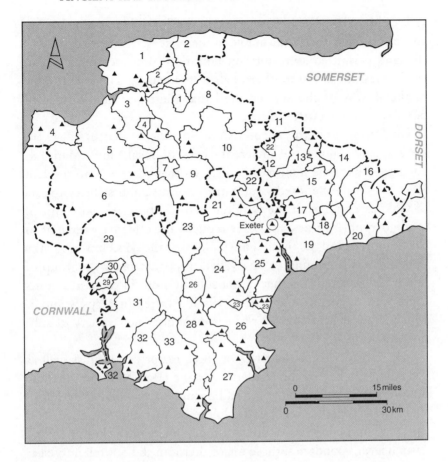

MAP 3 Residences of the JPs in the hundreds

NORTH DIVISION – (1) Braunton; (2) Sherwell; (3) Fremington; (4) Hartland; (5) Shebbear; (6) Black Torrington; (7) Winkleigh; (8) South Molton; (9) North Tawton; (10) Witheridge.
EAST DIVISION – (11) Bampton; (12) Tiverton; (13) Halberton; (14) Hemyock; (15) Hayridge; (16) Axminster; (17) Clyston; (18) Ottery; (19) East Budleigh; (20) Colyton.
SOUTH DIVISION – (21) Crediton; (22) West Budleigh; (23) Wonford; (24) Teignbridge; (25) Exminster; (26) Haytor; (27) Coleridge; (28) Stanborough; (29) Lifton; (30) Tavistock; (31) Roborough; (32) Plympton; (33) Ermington.

valley, along the edge of Torbay and in the South Hams. Pasture was also intermingled with the arable in these areas. The finer quality of the land permitted a greater concentration of estates and most of the JPs resided in the southern half of the county. The twenty-nine market towns of the area ensured that there was no shortage of possible administrative centres.[2]

The four maps in this chapter show how the residences of the JPs were spread among the different types of local units. Map 3 is concerned with the hundreds and shows that there was no resident JP in five of the hundreds at any time during the first fifteen years of Charles I's reign. If the hundred had still been the only unit of local government this could have reduced the effective oversight of the hundred and its head constables by the JPs, but now the hundred was beginning to be rivalled in importance by a group of hundreds gathered together into a sub-division. In these new units there was an adequate spread of JPs illustrated in Maps 4 and 5, which show at least four JP residences in both new variety of sub-division.

Map 2 marks the boundaries of three major divisions as well as providing the key to the residences of the JPs. The origin of these divisions is unknown but they had become 'accustomed' by 1574.[3] They drew together ten hundreds of the east and the north and thirteen hundreds in the south. Although many of the hundreds had natural river boundaries, these major divisions did not fall into clear geographical units; not even the Exe was a divisional boundary. These divisions were unchanged fifty years later. For the work of the JPs the divisions were far less important then the sub-divisions created later. They were, however, the basis for the sub-divisions, none of which straddled the boundaries of these three major divisions. There were a few occasions when the JPs acted in their divisions; these were all concerned with financial matters such as collecting the loans and over shipping in 1627.[4] Occasionally a division had to levy rates for specific purposes such as assisting a plague-stricken area or providing a bridewell, and the three divisions were the units for the treasurers of the hospitals and maimed soldiers, though the north and east combined with a single treasurer. The division was of significance in the work of the deputy lieutenants who assembled musters in divisions.

In contrast to divisions, it is possible to date the origin of administrative sub-divisions. The Council Orders of 23 June 1605 required the creation of sub-divisions in all counties. JPs were:

> To be assigned to have special charge and care of every such division [which was] to be so made as none be driven to travel above seven or eight miles. [The JPs of] every such division be assigned to assemble themselves together once between every general session of the peace, near about the midtime . . . at some convenient place within their several divisions to inquire and see the due execution of these things following.

These 'things' were their responsibilities under a number of statutes: those of labourers, those dealing with alehouses, tipplers, rogues and vagabonds, those setting the poor to work and those binding the children of the poor as apprentices. The JPs were all:

> To be informed of all manner of recusants as well Popish as Sectaries, murderers, felonies and outrages within that limit. And to execute the Statute of Artificers, matters of the peace and all other things within their several divisions as aforesaid.[5]

The sub-divisions were to be agreed at a meeting of the justices of assize and the JPs but, in Devon, this meeting in the Chapter House in Exeter on 19 July 1605 was so poorly attended that the decision was postponed to meetings in the three major divisions. The JPs of the south division were to meet at Ashburton on 8 August, those of the north at Torrington on 1 August and those of the east at Ottery on 13 August, all at 9a.m.[6] The results of these meetings were not included in the minute book.

In January 1615 eight sub-divisions were listed for the first time. They have been accepted as the administrative divisions of Devon.[7] However, there are strong grounds for not accepting these sub-divisions as those agreed in 1605 or as the later petty session sub-divisions. The most powerful argument against their acceptance is a minute in the midsummer quarter session of 1642. In referring to

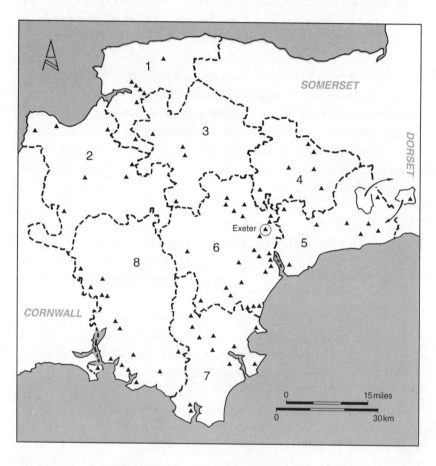

MAP 4 Residences of the JPs in the financial sub-divisions

Sub-divisions

1. Braunton, Shirwell, Fremington
2. Black Torrington, Hartland, Shebbear, Winkleigh
3. Witheridge, South Molton, North Tawton
4. Hayridge, Tiverton, Halberton, Bampton, Hemyock
5. Axminster, Colyton, Ottery, East Budleigh, Clyston
6. Wonford, Exminster, Crediton, Teignbridge, West Budleigh
7. Haytor, Coleridge, Stanborough
8. Ermington, Plympton, Roborough, Lifton, Tavistock

the levy of a rate it states that 'the sub-division intended being the same used for the subsidies and division of rates, not those for the petty session which in some places differ.'[8] The list of January 1615 and two later lists of sub-divisions in the minutes were all concerned with financial matters and so useless to define the administrative sub-divisions if they differed from the financial ones.[9] If all these lists are rejected, one must ask if any administrative sub-divisions resulted from the 1605 Orders or did they perhaps have to await a new stimulus from the Privy Council such as the certificates required over grain shortages in 1623?

There is evidence that sub-divisions were, in fact, created in 1605. The assize judges in 1606 reminded the JPs of the need for reports on their midterm assemblies so at the next quarter sessions it was agreed:

> JPs at their next private assembly of session take pains and send their certificate fair written and subscribed by them unto the clerk of the peace of this county before 23 October, he to file them all to be delivered to justices of Western circuit on feast of All Saints.[10]

This proves that there was an immediate response to the orders of 1605, but did it last? In my earlier study of the gentry government I tried to substantiate the existence of sub-divisions between the Council Orders of 1605 and the grain certificates of 1623 by examining the signatures on recognizances. There are gaps in the records but this material does show that meetings were held in seven distinct groups of hundreds for the licensing of alehouse-keepers within two months of the 1605 orders, and that the JPs from those groups occasionally met afterwards over their judicial work. These sub-divisions were not the same as those listed for financial purposes in the minutes in 1615; this shows that a divergence between financial and administrative areas had already occurred.[11] The evidence is not detailed enough to say that these sub-divisions had already taken exactly the form later shown in the certificates which followed the grain orders of 1623. The fact, however, that it was decided in 1623 to divide some hundreds does suggest that the JPs had sufficient experience of working in sub-divisions to recognize the advantages of compact groupings. As well as this evidence for the existence of seven sub-divisions between 1605 and 1623, recognizances reveal some identity in groups of JPs administering three more areas. Another sub-division becomes apparent in the grain certificates of 1623, so by this date eleven distinct or embryo sub-divisions existed in the county; they are illustrated in Map 5.

Reports survive from six sub-divisions over prices of grain in 1623. These certificates show that Devon's JPs had evidently decided that administrative units should be drawn up according to practical considerations and not adhere slavishly to hundred boundaries, as was the practice in other counties. This decision had been taken before 1623 in the case of at least one sub-division as a certificate refers to the sub-division of Haytor, Teignbridge and parts of Stanborough, Exminster and Wonford hundreds as 'anciently alloted' whereas another was 'alloted to the care of the justices dwelling within the same at our late general meeting for that behalf'.[12] The suggestion that eleven sub-divisions were established in the county by 1623 can be confirmed by the evidence of the next seven years as one no longer has to rely solely on the evidence of recognizances. The certificates of 1623 provide exact detail on six sub-divisions and the certificates which followed the Books of Order from 1631 are available to confirm the shape of all the sub-divisions. Churchwardens' accounts also provide evidence of some petty sessions. There were six administrative sub-divisions in the south division, two in the east and three in the north. Although eleven sub-divisions existed for administrative purposes by 1623, this is not to claim that Devon had yet got a system of petty sessions. There are, however, features which shows that Devon was moving towards holding petty sessions. The terms 'privy' or 'petty' session or 'midsession' had appeared on recognizances before 1623. Certain towns were becoming the customary meeting places in all the sub-divisions of the south division (Plympton, Tavistock, Exeter, Crediton Kingsbridge or Totnes and Newton Abbot or

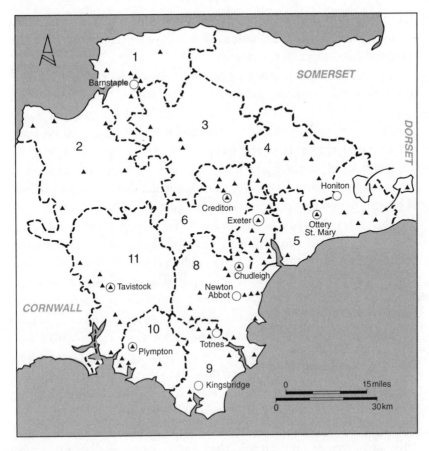

Map 5 Residences of the JPs in the administrative sub-divisions. The towns marked indicate where petty sessions were held.

Administrative sub-divisions

1. Braunton, Shirwell, Fremington
2. Black Torrington, Hartland, Shebbear, Winkleigh
3. Witheridge, South Molton, North Tawton
4. Hayridge, Tiverton, Halberton, Bampton, Hemyock
5. Axminster, Colyton, Ottery, Clyston, East Budleigh
6. Crediton, West Budleigh, West Wonford
7. Most of Exminster, East Wonford
8. Haytor, Teignbridge, 3 parishes Stanborough, 9 Exminster, 5 parishes South Wonford
9. Coleridge, rest of Stanborough
10. Plympton, Ermington
11. Roborough, Lifton, Tavistock

Chudleigh). In the east and north divisions only one sub-division in each area had an obvious centre (Honiton or Ottery St. Mary in the east and Barnstaple in the north).

T. G. Barnes, in his study of Somerset from 1625 to 1640, found no evidence of the term 'petty session' before 1631, and considered that referrals from quarter sessions to groups of JPs meeting in the localities cannot be endowed with any formal existence. In his view an essential element of any petty session system was a 'regular meeting, fixed in time and place, to transact regularly appointed business'. He wrote that petty sessions had a distinct function and were not dependant on referrals from quarter sessions, 'which were by their very nature extraordinary'.[13] In Devon there is evidence that at least two sub-divisions could claim to have had regular meetings, fixed in time and place, before 1631. This suggests that the concept of petty sessions was established in Devon before the Book of Orders, in contrast to the position in the neighbouring county of Somerset. The two sub-divisions which showed evidence of holding petty sessions were those meeting at Crediton and Exeter. Between 1625 and 1630 there are twenty-nine references in the quarter-session minutes to 'the JPs that meet at Crediton', suggesting that these meetings were established routine and not something to be arranged to deal with a particular matter. By checking the dates of recognizances signed by two or more JPs in this sub-division, it appears that there were regular meetings, sometimes weekly and most often on Wednesdays.[14] The other sub-division where there is a reference in the quarter-session minutes to a weekly meeting is that of certain parishes of Exminster hundred and the eastern part of Wonford hundred. This time the reference is to those 'that meet in Exeter any Friday'. Recognizances show that they did meet on Fridays, for example on 31 August, 7, 21 and 28 September 1627.[15]

Two other sub-divisions provide fairly convincing evidence of regular meetings, one is the sub-division of Haytor and Teignbridge with parts of Exminster, Wonford and Stanborough. A quarter-session minute in 1626 referred to the 'last petty session' at Newton Abbot and merits quotation as its shows a petty session initiating

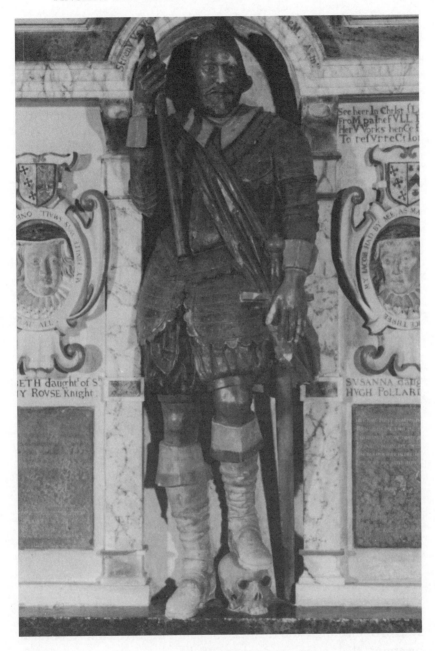

FIGURE 3 Memorial to John Northcott in the Church of Newton
St Cyres. He was one of the three JPs regularly meeting in Crediton

action which was later confirmed in quarter sessions, not just responding to an *ad hoc* requirement.

> It is ordered according to an order made by the justices at their last petty session at Newton Abbot (for part of the South division) that all persons that keep tippling without license . . . shall be committed to the Bridewell.

There are examples of two, three or four JPs resident in this sub-division signing together intermittently between 1625 and 1630. The frequency increased in 1629 when there was at least one instance of such signing in every month except November.[16] Evidence of a fourth sub-division holding privy sessions comes from the churchwardens' account for Dartington, which refer to privy sessions at Kingsbridge or Totnes between 1624 and 1628; this would have been the sub-division of Coleridge and Stanborough.[17] Three of these sub-divisions which provide the best evidence of sub-divisions in action were, significantly, in the adjoining sub-divisions which had some divided hundreds. This suggests that the JPs who were developing regular meetings were the ones most likely to create compact sub-divisions, less tied to the hundred boundaries, if this suited their convenience. One cannot say which came first, the practice of meeting as a sub-division or the realignment of boundaries on the most convenient geographical basis; it seems probable that the two developments went hand-in-hand.

The quarter-session records from 1592 to 1630 suggest that the evolution of sub-divisions in Devon was a gradual process, varying in its strength in the different parts of the county. There is, however, sufficient evidence to show that eleven sub-divisions did exist before the Books of Orders provided a new stimulus and that some of these were distinct from the sub-divisions used for rating; that the sub-divisions centred on Crediton and Exeter had a regular system of meetings, and that the one centred on Newton Abbot had meetings that were more than *ad hoc* responses to particular assignments; and that some already used the term petty session to describe their meeting. Petty sessions were clearly not as firmly established in Devon as in Essex, where there were regular meetings from 1605, nor Sussex, where petty sessions had evolved in two of the rapes, but the foundation of a petty session system had been laid.[18] The most significant outside stimulus to the development of sub-divisions before 1630 were the Council Orders of 1605 and the requirement to produce certificates of grain prices in 1623, but these orders, in themselves, might only have ensured a temporary response. The extent to which the sub-division had become a permanent part of the Devon county administration depended on its usefulness to the gentry government. The Devon bench had clearly seen its value for some areas and been prepared to ignore hundred boundaries to make it more effective. No other county has been found with administrative sub-divisions which differed from the financial ones, nor have other county leaders been prepared to break-away from the traditional hundred boundaries to mould the best administrative sub-divisions for their county.

If the development of Devon sub-divisions depended primarily on their value to the gentry government, what was the effect of the requirement in the Book of Orders to hold meetings in sub-divisions? The sub-divisions meeting at Crediton and Exeter were already fulfilling the order for regular meetings, but for the other sub-divisions the Book of Orders may only have been a temporary stimulus to extra action. The sub-division centred on Newton Abbot had a flurry of activity in 1632, meeting every month, but after 1632 the recognizances do not provide evidence of more than six meetings in any year. The Coleridge and Stanborough sub-division declared in their certificate of 7 January 1633 that they 'constantly between the Quarter Sessions do hold a Privy Session in the said two hundreds and sometimes we have other meetings touching the affairs of these hundreds'.[19] In the northern sub-division of South Molton, North Tawton and Witheridge there was a good response to the Book of Orders and they wrote at the end of 1633 that they 'have usually met once every month since receipt of His Majesty's book'. Evidence from churchwardens' accounts show that these monthly meetings were still being held in the late 1630s.[20]

The other two sub-divisions of the North were both active in 1631 and parish accounts reveal that there was an annual meeting at Barnstaple for parishes of the Braunton, Shirwell and Fremington hundreds to bring their accounts before the JPs.[21] In the southern half of the east division there are intermittent signs of weekly meetings at Colyton from 1631 to 1634, but this was nothing new as similar successive meetings had occurred in 1629 and 1630.[22] The other three sub-divisions provide little evidence of any change in their proceedings except that recognizances were being signed at a town rather than at the home of a JP, which suggests meetings were becoming more organized.[23] One concludes from this that the Book of Orders accelerated slightly a development towards meetings in sub-divisions which was already occurring but did not make any marked change. The gradual evolution of sub-divisions depended on their usefulness for conducting the business of the county. In this the daily experience of the JPs in ruling the county was a greater influence than the occasional orders of the Privy Council.

A desirable background to this chapter and the next two chapters is some detail on the population of the county and its distribution among the internal divisions of the county. Table 3 is drawn from an estimate of the population of Devon in 1660.[24] The population of the corporate towns have been excluded so that it only numbers those ruled by the county bench.

Table 3:
Population of the eleven sub-divisions (excluding corporate towns)

North division:

Braunton, Shirwell, Fremington	14,398
Black Torrington, Hartland, Shebbear, Winkleigh	22,030
Witheridge, South Molton, North Tawton	18,148
Total for North division	54,576

South division:

Roborough, Lifton, Tavistock	12,045
Plympton, Ermington	10,756
Coleridge, Stanborough (less 3 parishes)	16,019
Haytor, Teignbridge, 3 parishes of Stanborough, 9 of Exminster, 5 of Wonford South	25,000
Rest of Exminster, most of Wonford East and West	8,201
Crediton, West Budleigh, rest of Wonford West	14,471
Total for South division	86,492

East division:

Hayridge, Tiverton, Halberton, Bampton, Hemyock	25,865
Colyton, Clyston, Axminster, Ottery, East Budleigh	27,857
Total for East division	53,722
Overall total	194,790[25]

Chapter 4

The Devon Justice of the Peace at Work

The last two chapters of this section have outlined the organs of government within the county and the character and quality of the gentry leaders of Devon. Now, before this chapter turns to examine the JPs at work in the county, it is salutary to remind ourselves that the position of a JP should always be seen in its national setting. A justice of the peace was appointed in the King's name and his first duty was to maintain the peace against those who might hurt it and so injure the symbolic victim, the King. It was this need that had led to the institution of the office in the fourteenth century for some of 'the most worthy in the shire' and to the establishment of quarter sessions to provide the framework for the office.[1] The JPs had begun as the means of executing the King's justice in the shire and they gradually became the most important means of furthering the King's interests in the county. In addition to their judicial duties they were expected to carry out a mass of administrative duties largely imposed by Tudor legislation and increased by orders of the Stuart Privy Council. They were also required to act as one of the King's instruments in the collection of taxation but that side of their work will be left to the next chapter as they shared these duties with other gentry leaders. Although this chapter may seem at times to be deeply involved in the internal affairs of the county, the judicial and administrative tasks of the JPs must always be seen in their proper perspective as services to the King.

The Judicial Work of the JPs

Many of the JPs would have had some knowledge of their duties before their appointment to the bench from the experience of other members of their families. Two-thirds of them had had some legal education and may well have been familiar with the works of William Lambarde and Michael Dalton, even though it will be shown that they also liked to use their own initiative over their proceedings. Other studies have considered all aspects of the judicial process, particularly the recent work of Cynthia Harris in *The Common Peace*, but this book is concerned primarily with the part played by the JPs. They were required to attend the assizes and quarter sessions but their position was very different in the two courts; at the assizes a JP's function was to inform and listen, whereas at quarter sessions he judged and punished.[2] The material available to assess the individual activity of a Devon JP at the two courts also differs widely. No details survive of their attendance at the assizes nor of their part in the preliminary investigations of a case tried there. This restricts comparison of the Devon JPs at the assizes with those of other counties, yet they evidently realized the need to relate their work at the assizes to that at quarter sessions as they had the assize judgements copied into the quarter-sessions minute book where space permitted. This was a practice apparently unique to Devon's JPs.[3] These lists show that a total of 2,238 cases came before the twenty-seven assizes, which were included from 1625 to 1640, that is an average of eighty-three cases for the thirty-two assizes of these years. Most cases would have required the same detailed preparation by a JP which can be followed at quarter sessions.

'His nights, his meals are short and interrupted: all which he bears well, because he knows himself made for a public servant of peace and justice.' So Bishop Hall portrayed the good magistrate at work in his home, and he himself was one of Devon's JPs from 1629. For each case which was finally heard at assizes or quarter sessions there would have been many matters which never led to a trial but which would still have caused work for the JP for, 'his doors, his ears are ever open to suitors'.[4] This initial approach would sometimes have been to a meeting of JPs in their sub-division, often in the home of one of them but sometimes at a conveniently placed inn, possibly on market day. The JPs' line of action can be traced most clearly over felonies, that is with deliberately malicious acts. A case began when the victim, or his spokesman, went to the JP, usually in his home, and often accompanied by the suspect, the witnesses and the constable. The JP himself or his clerk noted the details of the examination of all concerned with the case. If the JP then decided that the offence was a felony, the suspect was committed to prison or, if suitable, a recognizance was taken for the accused to appear at the next assizes or quarter sessions. Recognizances were also taken for the witnesses to appear at the trial. The decision whether to grant bail or not rested on the JP's judgement of the offender and the case as well as on his sureties. Recognizances do not survive for cases sent to the assizes, but they were granted for about 50 per cent of the offenders sent to quarter sessions; about 80 per cent of those bailed were later acquitted which suggests that the JPs showed good judgement of the likely outcome of a case and did not enforce a period in an unhealthy gaol unnecessarily.[5] The largest number of cases were heard at the Epiphany session which implies that JPs also saved offenders a long period in gaol by sending them to quarter sessions, even if the seriousness of their case might have justified sending them to the assizes.[6]

The next stage of the judicial process was the concern of the grand jury rather than the bench, although the JP's original examination would be among the material considered. The Devon grand jury was drawn from all parts of the county and normally consisted of fifteen or seventeen jurors, who were usually termed 'gent'. If they thought that the charge was unreliable it was declared *ignoramus* and the accusation was supposed to be destroyed and the suspect released. It is estimated that about 40 per cent of the cases which came before the Devon grand jury during the early years of Charles were declared to be *ignoramus*; the reaction of the bench to most of these decisions will be described later.[7] When the grand jury decided that the case was substantial, the indictment was marked *billa vera* and the accused was sent for trial before a petty jury, twelve men with no claim to any gentry status and so much nearer to the social level of most of the accused. At this stage there was scope for both the JPs and the petty jury to use their discretion. The JPs could allow benefit of clergy to any man provided the charge did not involve certain crimes (such as treason, murder, piracy, rape, horse theft and burglary), and a statute of 1624 allowed similar relief to women accused of larcenies worth less than 10s. These benefits were only allowed after confession or conviction and the accused was branded on the thumb, so that such relief could only be claimed once.[9] The number (about 35 per cent) who profited from this concession in Devon was considerably less than the 54 per cent said to have benefited in Sussex.[10] The reason for this was not that the Devon bench was stricter than the Sussex one, on the contrary they were more merciful because they followed their own judgement in assessing what was grand larceny. They considered that thefts of goods valued at the lower end of grand larceny, that is between 12d and about 5s, could be punished by flogging instead of the correct sentence of hanging (though many might have been entitled to benefit of clergy). As they sidestepped the dividing line of 12d between grand and petty larceny in this way, they also did not follow the practice of many counties and undervalue stolen goods to make the crime petty larceny. This avoided inconsistencies found in other counties, for instance in Essex where wide variation was put on the value of sheep at the same session.[11] There is also evidence that the Devon bench allowed women to benefit from the statute of 1624 even when the value of the goods stolen exceeded the 10s limit.[12]

The sentences tabulated in Table 4 do not cover all those decided by Devon's JPs after the petty jury had found a prisoner guilty; some incorrigible rogues were branded with the letter R, an occasional criminal convicted of grand larceny was sent to a house of correction, and some guilty of petty larceny were set in the stocks rather than suffer a flogging. It can be claimed that, whenever possible, the JPs adjusted the punishment to what they judged was suitable for the crime and the criminal. They did not punish a guilty person who was *non compos mentis*, nor did they

Table 4:
A summary of the principal decisions reached on billa vera *presented to quarter sessions between 1625 and 1640.*

Hung	44	(10 reprieved)
Benefit of clergy	213	
Women receiving benefit according to statute of 1624	79	
Whipped	397	
Acquitted	475	
Total	1,208	

enforce a flogging on someone who was infirm. The flexibility of the bench suggests that this was a group of gentry leaders who gave serious thought to their responsibilities and did not simply enforce the accepted punishment for each crime. They had the power to modify the punishment and could decide on a reprieve or to sponsor a pardon.[13] There is one particularly significant example of the Devon JPs being merciful. This was at the midsummer session of 1630 which was held during a period of particularly severe economic distress. The grand jury returned *billa vera* on fifty-three offenders, the petty jury acquitted eighteen, but apart from ten incorrigible rogues, none of the rest were punished by the bench. Fourteen guilty of grand larceny and granted benefit of clergy were remanded to the autumn assizes instead of being branded, there they were ordered to be bailed to appear at the next assizes. Some of them continued to be bailed, 'to expect grace of the king', in the next three assize calendars. The midsummer calendar of 1630 also referred nine petty larceny cases to the King's mercy rather than enforcing the legal penalty of flogging and they remanded two guilty of extortion.[14] It is of particular interest to see that the bench were providing their own response to the suffering in the county before the Privy Council produced their answer to the same problem nationwide with the Book of Orders.

It has been estimated that the grand jury considered about 40 per cent of the cases brought before them to be unreliable, yet these were all matters which the JP, in his home area, had judged worthy of trial. The *ignoramus* indictment should have been destroyed immediately but in Devon, like Sussex, many survived, yet there the similarity ends for Devon's JPs had their own particular method of dealing with cases declared *ignoramus*.[15] They referred the majority of these cases to the assizes.[16] The names appear in the quarter-session calendars, 404 of them from 1625 to 1640 of which 244 have been found repeated in the twenty-seven assize calendars included in the minute books for those years.[17] There they were said to have been delivered by proclamation. In this procedure the assize judges could try indictments found elsewhere, 'most significantly before justices of the peace in sessions and deliver by proclamation all prisoners who had not been indicted by the end of the assize sitting'.[18] Yet the Devon cases had already been declared *ignoramus* and therefore had not been brought before the JPs in sessions. They should have been discharged and no longer be prisoners. These cases are so numerous that one cannot explain them as requiring a re-examination of some offenders of whom a JP had special knowledge, for example, the theft of a ram in 1626 from the JP, John Davy. The JPs possibly considered a second court appearance was a valuable lesson to the offender, even if he was then delivered by proclamation. Delivery by proclamation would not have involved an appearance before an assize grand jury but it would have involved the expense and strain of attendance at assizes. This particular stratagem has not been noted in other county studies; it suggests an unusual determination to try to enforce judgement upon offenders, even when the quarter-session grand jury had not found a case to answer. Those who were transferred to the assizes but have not been found among those 'delivered by proclamation' have not been found anywhere in the assize gaol deliveries. One can only assume that they were brought before the assize grand jury and found *ignoramus* again; in this event their names would not have appeared in the assize calendar.

The JPs' role in dealing with suspected felons is the best documented aspect of their judicial work. This discussion of it can draw on four sources, the decisions listed in the minute books and the surviving examinations, indictments and recognizances. Yet suspected felons were only a very small percentage of the number of the matters brought to the JP's door which required him to take some judicial action. For most of the rest there is only one source, a recognizance, though this can be supplemented after 1631 by some of the certificates produced at petty sessions in accordance with the Book of Orders.[19] If a case was brought before a JP and he decided it was not a felony, he could require the accused to attend the next quarter session and grant a recognizance for that. About 85 per cent of the recognizances strung together with those for suspected felons and labelled, collectively, as 'for suspected felon', are in fact this type of recognizance.[20] They all required an appearance at the next quarter sessions and most of them gave no indication of their cause. A few of them were for theft or assault and led to an appearance before a grand jury, though not termed felonies. Some did have comments added which showed that they were concerned with matters such as selling ale without a licence, or for abuse of officials or for some offence connected with bastardy. In some cases the quarter-session minutes record what action was taken; three days gaol and a fine imposed for selling ale without a licence or gaol until the next session for abusing a constable. In many cases the order to appear at quarter sessions seems to have been enough, tempers may have cooled and the original dispute been settled; an injured person might have recovered or the father of a bastard married the mother.[21] Some of these recognizances without any clue to their cause may have been drawn up in response to petitions of complaint or grand jury presentments, but these two major sources of information are missing from Devon's records. In Cheshire, petitions survive against disturbers of the peace, for example, from neighbours afraid to sign a petition as 'he is such a pestiferous and turbulent minded man that they are afeared to do so, he does so threaten'. Grand jury presentments reflected similar concerns and may well have been more reliable as they were less likely to be affected by malice. The principal means for the JPs to control such situations was the use of recognizances to bind over to good behaviour or to keep the peace. The nature of the petitions and grand jury presentments and the number of recognizances in Cheshire suggested to Steve Hindle that the use of recognizances could just contain the 'manifest tensions of this highly contentious, conflict-ridden society'.[22] Without the petitions and presentments in Devon one has not the grounds to compare the state of Devon society to that of Cheshire. Yet the very large number of recognizances for good behaviour or to keep the peace drawn up by Devon's JPs' is evidence that many suitors must have come to their doors and that their home life was often disturbed by potential troublesmakers. Over four thousand such recognizances survive for 1625 to 1640 (an average of eighty-two a session); they are proof that Devon JPs frequently used this means of preventing possible breaches of the peace. These bundles of recognizances reflect the widespread presence of JPs ready to diffuse inflammatory situations and are a potent reminder of the labour of the JPs in maintaining the peace in their neighbourhood.

The Devon JPs have been shown to be, to some extent, a law unto themselves in their conduct of judicial business. Studies in three other counties (Sussex, Cheshire and Essex), which have even more extensive records have not shown the JPs using their initiative in similar ways. This suggests that the Devon bench was one at ease with itself, able to carry out their judicial duties without disagreements among themselves. They showed their practical good sense in raising the dividing line for the punishment of grand and petty larceny rather than undervaluing goods. They showed their initiative in sending most of those declared *ignoramus* to the assizes; this in itself displaying their confidence in their own judgement that a case they had sent before the grand jury merited trial. They showed also their concern for those who might have been driven to theft by economic distress in their readiness to remand cases to the mercy of the King as such a time. Such a bench may well have gained a reputation in the county as a strict one but also as a fair one. In Cheshire at least fifteen instances of 'scandalous abuse of magistrates' have been noted but the position is very different in Devon where no recognizances or session orders suggest such verbal attacks on the JPs of Devon.[23]

The Administrative Duties of the JPs

It makes for clarity to describe the work of the JPs under separate hearings, judicial and administrative, but this must not be allowed to obscure the amount that these two aspects overlapped. JPs were required to enforce the poor laws and this might require them to punish an incorrigible rogue; they licensed ale houses and also had to punish the selling of ale without licence. Quarter sessions was as much the linchpin for the administrative work of the JPs as for the judicial. They decided some matters at quarter sessions but delegated many others to be dealt with by JPs in their home area. The orders from the bench for investigation, action or a report were sometimes directed to a sub-division, at other times to named JPs or to the nearest JP. The weight of administrative duties had greatly increased under the Tudors and the bench had been reminded of their obligations under various statutes in the Council Orders of 1605.[24] The Caroline bench were to find themselves repeatedly subjected to orders to carry out these statutes by proclamations or Council orders, sometimes accompanied by criticism of their slackness or with new orders to enforce greater efficiency. They probably also had to listen to stirring addresses from the judges of assize in the same vein but none of the Devon ones survive. An account of the administration of the county is also an account of the JPs' relations with the royal government. Devon's JPs responded to all the orders they received but these orders seldom gave more than a temporary minor boost to their activities; not because they were negligent but because they were already acting efficiently.

The range of orders emanating from quarter sessions from 1625 to 1640 are summarized in Table 5. This reflects all the major administrative responsibilities of the JPs: their supervision of the work of the lesser officials of the county; their duty to maintain communications; their administrative commitments under various laws, particularly the poor law; their response to Privy Council orders; and finally, their residual responsibility to act on all the problems which had not been successfully dealt with at any other level of the county. It has been suggested by some historians that the 1631 Book of Orders had a dramatic effect on the administrative

Table 5:
Analysis of Orders in the Minute Books for the regnal years 1–15 Charles I

Regnal year	1 1625	2 1626	3 1627	4 1628	5 1629	6 1630	7 1631	8 1632	9 1633	10 1634	11 1635	12 1636	13 1637	14 1638	15 1639	Total
Appointments	12	16	2	6	3	3	8	13	12	10	6	8	7	6	7	119
Supervision of Officials	11	7	8	6	1	5	3	6	3	3	3	4	7	4	5	76
Bridges and Highways	14	15	10	12	11	12	9	12	19	13	19	14	16	11	11	198
Poor relief	16	10	15	6	6	5	6	3	1	3	7	10	14	9	9	120
Bastardy	10	8	6	4	9	7	4	4	7	8	9	12	17	4	8	117
Apprentices	4	9	6	4	2	8	9	9	12	9	19	18	25	12	17	163
Rogues	4	1	2	2	3	1	1	1	–	5	–	1	1	–	–	22
General orders on rogues	–	–	1	–	2	–	3	1	–	1	–	–	1	–	–	9
Arbitration by JPs in localities	6	2	7	6	3	11	4	3	2	7	12	6	10	11	4	94
Alehouses	7	4	4	–	2	1	2	4	2	–	3	1	6	4	3	43
General orders on grain shortages	1	–	2	–	3	3	4	–	3	2	1	2	–	–	–	21
Abuse of officials (including JPs)	6	8	3	6	–	1	–	2	3	2	5	8	–	5	4	53
Pensions & grants for fire, etc.	4	4	3	7	3	7	2	3	10	7	–	4	7	7	2	70
Organizing of bridewells	2	3	2	–	–	2	1	2	2	–	2	3	2	2	2	25
Payment to maimed soldiers	3	2	2	4	4	6	2	5	8	11	2	8	6	5	3	71
Total	100	89	73	63	52	72	58	68	84	81	88	99	119	80	75	1,201

56

work of the JPs.[25] Table 5 not only suggests that, in Devon, it had little effect, except over the use of apprenticeship, but also why it had so little effect. Clearly the Devon bench were already doing most of the things they were commanded to do in the Book of Orders.

The heading 'supervision of officials' does not just imply routine oversight, the Caroline JPs were prepared to act if they considered it necessary. The JPs were responsible for the appointment of all the principal officials of the county. They made yearly appointments of the treasurer for hospitals and maimed soldiers and named two or more JPs to examine their accounts each year. In 1635 they became aware of the incompetence of some treasurers and were flexible enough to change the routine, giving the efficient treasurer of the gaol (Edward Jones) responsibility for all these offices.[26] When it was necessary to appoint and swear in new head constables, the nearest JPs were ordered to do so. The head constables were the essential local executants of many quarter-session orders and the bench took steps to ensure that they performed their duties efficiently. Any head constable who failed to pay their rates to the treasurer was threatened with being bound over and from Easter 1632 no head constable was allowed to leave office until he had made all the payments required.[27] If the head constables were to provide the link between their hundred and the bench it was essential for them to attend every quarter session and bring presentments from their hundreds. Quarter sessions ordered this in 1627 and in 1629 enforced it by fining those who did not attend. This was, apparently, in conflict with an assize order which only required the head constables to be present at the assizes, so the assize judges remitted the fines. Nevertheless, the JPs were not prepared to accept this diminution of their authority over the head constables; they ignored the assize order and in April 1632 again required the head constables 'to appear at every general session and make their presentments there'.[28] Other appointments, such as the keepers of the bridewells and county marshals, where also made in quarter sessions and the conduct of all these officials and others such as parish constables and bailiffs was overlooked by the JPs.

Some of the additional duties laid upon the JPs in Tudor statutes concerned maintaining efficient lines of communication by river and highway. Hardly any quarter session passed without some reference of the need to report on the state of a bridge or organize its repair. At least four JPs had to be appointed to decide who was responsible for the decayed bridge and they had the power to organize the collection of local rates to pay for any repair.[29] Decisions over bridges were not an easy task as some rivers were the boundaries between different hundreds or landowners and they were often the vital means of communication for a wide area; this led, for example, to the cost of repairing Teignbridge being shared among all the hundreds of the south division. JPs were sometimes slow to act and some orders had to be repeated in quarter sessions and the matter might eventually be referred to the assizes, where the judges could impose fines on JPs still failing to act.[30] After the bench had appointed Mr Jones as county treasurer in 1635, they began to require money collected for bridges to be paid to him and then spent on the bridges as the bench thought fit.[31] This enabled them to use any surplus from one bridge to repair another; once again the bench was showing its ability to make administration more efficient. The need to improve highways concerned quarter sessions far less than bridges, only six orders have been found referring to their condition but then highways were, in the first instance, the concern of the surveyors of highways, chosen by each parish.

So far this chapter has dealt with administrative tasks which occurred regularly in quarter sessions; there were others which arose under particular circumstances. Special demands were made upon the bench during outbreaks of plague and in periods of economic distress. The early Caroline bench had to face both types of emergency in Devon. In these conditions they were given special directives by the central government. They received three different types of Books of Orders; they had received the first, concerned with directions for dealing with an outbreak of plague by Michaelmas, 1625.[32] The second was the Book concerned with grain shortage issued in September 1630, and the third, the more general and best known Book of Orders was issued in January 1631. The orders dealing with scarcity of grain are part of a long line of such orders stretching back to 1527. The plague directions were part of another sequence of orders starting in 1578. The 1631 Book was different in that it collected together matters previously dealt with in various statutes, though it did also propose the use of the same machinery suggested in the plague and dearth orders such as regular meetings of JPs out of sessions and reports to the Council.[33]

Plague reached Exeter in the summer of 1625 and led to the Michaelmas session being moved to Crediton. When the bench met they were ready to act in accordance with the Plague Act of 1604 and the book of plague orders which revived those of 1578, with minor alterations. They made a general order for the constables to shut up the houses, for one month, of those who risked infecting themselves or others by going into Exeter or any other infected places. They also made a specific order for the relief of Moretonhampstead, ordering two nearby JPs to raise a weekly rate from people living within five miles of the town.[34] At the Epiphany session it became clear that rating the area within five miles of Chulmleigh would not relieve the plague victims in that town so six adjoining hundreds of the north division were required to pay rates. They did so for three months and then at the Easter session three other hundreds of the north division took over the relief. The bench were concerned that relief should be effective but also that it should be raised fairly from areas free of plague. By the summer of 1626 the worst of the outbreak was in the Plymouth area, probably spread by the movement of troops arriving back from the Cadiz expedition. As the south division was affected by the presence of soldiers as well as plague, the bench decided to require rates from the most distant hundred of the south division (West Budleigh) and the ten hundreds of east Devon, as well as from the two hundreds surrounding Plymouth. They organized the means of collecting these funds to relieve Plymouth, appointing the head constable of East Budleigh as treasurer for the five south-eastern hundreds and the head constable of Halberton as treasurer for the five north-eastern hundreds. These treasurers and the head constables of West

Budleigh were then to pay their weekly collections from the parishes to the mayor of Exeter, who presumably arranged for its transfer to the mayor of Plymouth. These orders were reinforced at the Michaelmas session and anyone who refused to pay the rates were to be bound over to appear at the next session. The outbreak of plague in Plymouth had eased by the Easter session of 1627, and then three JPs were required to examine all the steps taken to relieve Plymouth and see that all arrears of the rates were paid to the mayor of Plymouth.[35] It says much for the quality and ability of the bench that they were not distracted by the dangers of plague or their problems in billeting soldiers from weighing up carefully the best means of relieving the suffering in their county.

Sickness was only one of the causes of suffering and death that required action from the bench, another was scarcity. The same areas did not suffer equally from these two hazards. The south with its greater number of towns, many ports, and warmer climate was more likely to be affected by plague. Yet this was the more prosperous region and the main area for arable farming and so it was less affected by dearth of grain. The isolated pastoral areas of the north tended to be free of plague but had not the corn production to survive bad harvests.[36] Few of the Devon bench of 1625 would have had experience of dealing with a major outbreak of plague but they were nearly all accustomed to following orders over shortage of grain. The most recent ones were those of 1623 whose effect upon the development of sub-divisions has already been discussed.[37] The certificates produced in 1623 show some JPs carrying out the orders most conscientiously. They were visiting the markets regularly to ensure that grain was sold at reasonable prices and in the sub-division of Stanborough and Coleridge their careful report gave details of the grain production of each household with the number of inhabitants, sometimes stating how much they could spare to bring to market. The households of the two JPs signing the certificate were included in this survey.[38] The bench did not relax after the shortages of 1623 had passed but made their own orders to conserve supplies. In 1625 they suppressed seven unlicensed ale-houses and eight recognizances were issued for this offence before the proclamation of December 1625 demanded similar action.[39] The bench's appreciation of the local situation also led them to take the initiative in October 1629 to prevent a dearth of barley needed for bread and they required all JPs to reduce the number of maltsters in their divisions.[40] Thus they had already acted before the proclamation of 13 June 1630 required JPs to take all possible action to husband grain; though they did underline this order at their next session by instructing JPs 'to take especial care' to act in accordance with the laws and this proclamation[41] They were clearly alert to the dangerous shortages and acting upon them before they received the September Book of Orders in time for the Michaelmas session.[42] They included full details, in their minutes, of the actions to be taken by the JPs, except for the order to compile certificates, apparently a matter of secondary importance in their eyes. Although they noted these orders, they probably felt that they were already enforcing the statutes reiterated in the Book. A recognizance against the conversion of malt, dated days before the Book of Orders was enforced by proclamation, had the comment that the two named were 'not to buy or suffer to be bought for them or use barley to be converted to malt during this time of restraint according to the law'.[43] The JP making this comment clearly did not need any extra pressure from the Book.

Before the Book of Orders of January 1631 drew together many aspects of the poor law, the Caroline bench were pressed to act on these laws by various orders of the Privy Council and by proclamations. The Devon JPs acted on these orders though they would have been justified if they resented being blamed for the increase in the number of dissolute, vagrant persons in the orders of 31 March 1627. They were ordered to search out all deserting soldiers and sailors and commit them to prison or to a house of correction.[44] They probably did not receive this in time to act at the Easter session, beginning on 3 April, but at the midsummer one they ordered that as there were so many 'rogues both sturdy and vagrant' there should be a watch set 'one day and one night weekly till the next session' and a diligent search made for the 'apprehending of the evil members aforesaid'.[45] In February 1628 a proclamation demanded that each JP should send a monthly certificate to his lord lieutenant on his execution of the laws against rogues and vagabonds but no evidence has been found of any such certificates being sent to Devon's lord lieutenant to forward to the Council.[46] When they became aware of a problem in Devon the JPs acted. At the Easter session of 1629 they ordered that 'the Irish rogues with which the country swarms', should be sent back to their place of birth or, if this was not known, to their place of landing. This order was accompanied by a general warrant to all the Devon head constables to arrest all rogues and vagabonds.[47] The Devon bench thus anticipated by a month the proclamation ordering the speedy sending away of Irish beggars and the enforcement of the laws on English rogues and vagabonds. That proclamation required the JPs to meet monthly and report to their next general session.[48] This order may have been the stimulus for the more frequent meetings which have been noticed in the sub-divisions in 1629.[49]

It is possible to make some assessment of the number of vagrants dealt with after the Book of Orders. The eight sub-divisions which produced certificates in 1633 listed 301 vagrants, including at least fifteen Irish but, apart from the production of certificates, there is no evidence that the actions of quarter sessions over vagrants had been changed by the Book. They continued to order the occasional special watch to be made for vagrants, and they continued to instruct head constables to see that their petty constables appre-hended 'all rogues and wanderers' and dealt with them 'according to the law'.[50] They did, however, reward a hard-working county marshal with an increased salary in 1633 and again in 1634 for 'his extraordinary charges and travel in apprehending sturdy and vagrant rogues and beggars'.[51] This suggests that increased work was being required of this marshal, Rawlings Jago, who obviously travelled widely, as references have been found, in examinations, to him arresting vagrants in areas as far apart as Hartland in the north, Marychurch in the south and Combe Raleigh in the east division. In addition to his wages a marshal received 4d. for each rogue committed, probably as powerful an incentive as any pressure for action from the JPs.

One requirement of the Book of Orders which did cause considerable discussion at quarter sessions was the order that a house of correction should adjoin the prison so that the gaoler as governor could employ prisoners committed for small causes:

> So they may learn honestly by labour and not live idly and miserably long in prison whereby they are made worse when they come out than when they went in and when many houses of correction in one county one at least near the gaol.[52]

Devon was well supplied with bridewells (or houses of correction), four had been initiated by an order of Easter 1598, and ones at Great Torrington, Honiton, Newton Abbot, Tiverton, Newton Bushell, Tavistock and Crediton are mentioned in the minutes before 1630.[53] In spite of these seven bridewells, the JPs now had to establish one in Exeter. It was not until the Easter session of 1639 that a sub-committee of ten was appointed to meet every Friday at Mr Bampfield's house in Exeter until the business of the new bridewell was finally settled.[54] The JPs also approved requests for the erection of bridewells at Totnes in 1632 and one for Hemyock hundred in 1639.[55]

Unlike the problems caused by grain shortages and vagrants, apprenticeship was the one feature of the Book of Orders which had not been the subject of recent national or quarter session orders. This accounts for the fact that it is the one area where the Book had an appreciable effect. The Orders reiterated the principle of the poor laws of 1598 and 1601 that poor children should be apprenticed to husbandry. The immediate effect of this is shown in the nine certificates produced between November 1633 and April 1634 (those for the north and north-west sub-divisions are missing). These certificates reported the binding of 589 apprentices.[56] This was not just a reporting exercise for the JPs, two of them had to confirm each indenture of apprenticeship after it was agreed between the overseers and the prospective master. More cases concerning apprenticeship now came before quarter sessions, some concerned with a master refusing to take an apprentice, others for parents refusing to allow their child to be apprenticed, and others with ill-treatment of an apprentice; all suggesting the increased use of this form of poor relief.[57]

So far this chapter has concentrated on the way the JPs fulfilled their administrative role as the servants of the King, carrying out commands in accordance with laws, Privy Council orders and proclamations. James I had referred to them as 'his eyes and ears' but what of the other side of the coin, how far had the JP his eyes and ears on the needs of his countrymen? Did the ordinary Devonian seen the JP in quarter sessions or in his home area just as a figure of authority or did he also see him as someone to whom he could appeal in distress? Calls for help usually reached quarter sessions as petitions, sometimes supported by well-wishers. The commonest request was for aid for a maimed or injured soldier. In this case there were the funds collected for this purpose and pensions of about £3 *per annum* were usually assigned. Other petitions concerned those who were impoverished by having losses from fire, flood and shipwreck or from people who sought help to ransom a relative held by pirates. If the JPs were 'credibly informed' by a certificate of the truth of the claim, they made a small grant but their resources were very limited and these grants were usually made from the funds intended for the hospitals. JPs also occasionally accepted a petition for a cottage to be erected for a needy family, provided the request was supported by the inhabitants of the parish concerned.[58]

Presentments were the other means of bringing matters before quarter sessions. These could be brought by a JP himself, by head or petty constables and by members of the grand jury. No presentments have survived for this period and the minutes only occasionally state that an order is the result of a presentment, but it is safe to assume that this was often the case. It may well have been true of the numerous orders for the relief of a number of plague-stricken towns between 1625 and 1628. Once their need was made known to the bench, steps were taken to provide relief from the areas still clear of infection. Presumably it was a presentment which led to the bench being 'credibly informed' of a different kind of problem, of great abuses over apprenticing in Buckerell which led them to order two JPs to investigate it.[59] When the worsted-combers felt that their livelihood was being endangered by a patent granted to Exeter citizens, quarter sessions found themselves being 'daily pressed by ... the petitions of a multitude necessaire poor people', and their case 'likewise presented to us by the Grand Jury'. Assailed by both means of approach the bench referred the matter to the Privy Council.[60] Clearly, when an individual, a parish or an economic group was faced with particular difficulties they regarded quarter sessions as the body to which they might appeal in hope of some action being taken on their behalf.

Some of the problems brought before quarter sessions were decided there by the orders of the bench but others were referred back to the JPs in their sub-divisions or individually for settlement, report or arbitration. Some of these matters were of public concern, such as disputes between parishes or hundreds over rating or poor relief, and some were disputes between individuals. It is probable that JPs, in fact, arbitrated on far more disputes than actually came to the notice of quarter sessions. The disputants often agreed in advance to accept the decision of the JP named and such confidence could well have led to his decision sometimes being accepted without a preliminary reference to quarter sessions. The matters delegated by quarter sessions to the JP in his locality were only a minor part of the work expected of him in his home area. The certificates produced in response to the Book of Orders give some idea on the range of tasks which came before petty sessions; supervizing local officers, reforming alehouse abuses, caring for the poor, keeping highways repaired and ordering regular watch and ward.[61] This was, of course, in addition to their judicial work of dealing with many minor offences, taking examinations and drawing up recognizances for those they referred to quarter sessions.

The King might value the justice of the peace as the executor of many tasks, the Devonian might fear him as the upholder of the law but also respect him as a possible help in time of trouble but what of the JP himself? Is there any evidence of his attitude to all these administrative duties? It was only over the requirement to produce

FIGURE 4 Sir William Strode's manor of Newnham near Plympton St Mary

certificates following the Book of Orders that any Devon JPs have been found showing any resentment. When one sub-division acknowledged the receipt of the Books from the sheriff, Henry Ashford, they expressed their view 'that the diligence which we have formerly used in His Majesty's service cannot be much improved by the survey of any eyes besides those of our consciences'.[62] This opinion of Devon JPs lends some support to the suggestion of J.S. Morrill that resistance to the Book by JPs was because it interfered with their established methods of meeting local needs.[63] Yet the Book fitted into the existing pattern of the government of Devon and made no marked change in the way the gentry ruled the county. It was only the oversight enforced by the certificates which was unnecessary in the eyes of Devon's JPs but that did not lead them to produce reports which were stylized, curt or merely recording 'omnia bene' like some other counties.[64] The certificates do reveal to us their 'diligence' and a reference in one of them may epitomize their conscientious service:

Mr Sheriff you may not expect Sir William Strode's hand to this certificate for his extreme sickness could not be present at our assemblies nor join in this, albeit to our knowledge he hath been very careful and forward in reforming the abuses above mentioned.[65]

Chapter 5

The Gentry As Royal Tax Collectors

This chapter on the response of the leading gentry to the King's demands is more than an account of efficient tax collection. It also provides some answers to three questions about the nature of the county government. The first concerns the relationship of the royal government and the gentry leaders of the county. They recognized that it was their duty to serve the King by organizing tax collection but the way in which they responded gives us some insight into their view of the justice of the King's financial demands. The second question concerns how far the gentry leaders were able to reconcile the needs of the King with the interests of their countrymen's pockets, not to mention their own. The third question raises the view of some historians that a common economic interest might lead to a sense of county community.[1] Does this chapter provide any evidence to support that concept or does it not rather reveal the collective strength of the gentry government in the face of the royal tax demands?

The members of parliament who voted subsidies were usually also JPs so their attitude towards the grants of subsidy are equally revealing of the opinion of the leading gentry of the counties. It was not until the parliament of 1606 that it was accepted that subsidies could be raised in peacetime. This suggests that members of parliament were only slowly accepting the death of the medieval concept that the King should 'live of his own'. They seem to have believed that subsidy grants were substantial, that a grant of subsidy could be bargained as the price for James I giving up impositions, when, in fact, impositions brought in more annually than a single subsidy grant. The subsidy acts of 1606 and 1624 both claimed that they were granting more than had ever been granted before in so short a time; this was true as regard the number of subsidies granted but not of the amount of money raised because of increasing under-assessment.[2] Evidently the members of parliament and, under their other hats, the JPs, magnified the real value of the taxation granted and so would be little inclined to increase the subsidy rates in the counties, especially when they saw how James dissipated the resources he had.

James I had succeeded to an almost solvent crown with the potential to increase its revenue by increasing the rates for customs and managing the crown lands more effectively. Yet in spite of various measures to improve these resources, James' extravagance and his gifts to friends soaked up the gains. The King was not able to provide his officials and servants with adequate incomes, so he supplemented them with pensions or with grants such as ones on the farms of customs. In these ways he committed future revenue and reduced the possibility of increasing its yield. In spite of his treasurer, Cranfield's, success in reducing some expenses, the last year of his accounting (1624) showed a deficit of £160,000.[3] As resources had been found insufficient to meet the expenses of government in peacetime, they became even more so when Charles and Buckingham prepared for an adventurous foreign policy against Spain in 1624, after the collapse of the Spanish match. The three subsidies granted in 1624 and the two subsidies of 1625 could not meet these expenses and so extra-parliamentary expedients were initiated from the first year of Charles' reign. In 1626 the need for such alternatives became even greater when Charles dissolved parliament to prevent the impeachment of Buckingham before the four subsidies expected that session could be voted. The offensive foreign policy, however, first against Spain and then against France continued until all hope of further parliamentary grants ended with the dissolution of the third parliament in 1629. Meanwhile the country had suffered a series of financial experiments, some moderately successful and others abortive. All of them bore particularly heavily on a county, such as Devon, which also had to billet soldiers without adequate payment. When peace was made with France in 1629 and with Spain in 1630 the situation eased, but there remained the need to defend the coasts and in particular to strengthen the navy against Turkish pirates. The eleven years without parliament involved further financial experiments, the most successful of which was ship money. This chapter will deal with the subsidies and with all the expedients which were the responsibility of a body of gentry governors (JPs, deputy lieutenants or commissioners), leaving the collection of ship money to the later chapter on the ship money sheriffs.

Subsidy

Thirty-four Devon commissioners for the subsidy have been identified from their signatures on folios of the subsidy rolls between 1624 and 1629. All of them were also JPs but as this number is only about half the total number of JPs for those years, not all JPs served. When the commissioners had to raise a subsidy, they required the head constables to appoint between two and eight 'discreet and substantial men' in each parish as assessors to draw up an assessment of their parish. These men, often termed rators, then appeared before the commissioners who adjudicated on their assessments; a procedure sometimes involving as many as four meetings. This right of the commissioners to adjudicate gave them the power to control the taxation of their county and so they occupied a sought after position.[4] Clearly Sir Edward Giles was more effective in restricting payments by his countrymen when he approved the assessments for Coleridge and Haytor hundreds than when he spoke to the same end at Westminster.[5] The use of the leading gentry as commissioners ensured that taxation did not arouse the same opposition in England that it did in France, but this was at the cost of a low yield; in 1625 only 3.5 per cent of the total revenue of the Crown came from the subsidy.[6]

The Privy Council's instructions for the collection of subsidies were sent to the commissioners. In February 1626 JPs were associated in the order not to keep to the low valuations of recent subsidies and in particular they were to assess themselves at the £20 required by law.[7] Soon after they had received these orders, the commissioners met during the Lent assizes and appointed Sir Simon Leach as collector; he had just completed his term of office as sheriff but did not become a JP until 1628.[8] There is little evidence that Devon's commissioners then followed the Council's instructions to raise the assessments. Only eighty-eight examples have been found to compare the rates of gentry in the roll of 1624 with those in any roll of 1625–8. Fifty-two of these rates remained the same, only eleven were increased, but twenty-five were decreased. The commissioners did not even ensure that all JPs were rated at £20 or more as ten were rated below this figure. Someone rated at £20 was only required to pay £4 for each subsidy granted, even though they might well have been worth £1,000 a year.[9] At the other end of the Devon subsidy range a man with an income between £20 and £30 might be rated at £1.[10] Clearly there was no scope for tax increase at the bottom end of the scale and the commissioners did not wish to burden the lowest incomes; indeed, Sir George Chudleigh proposed in 1624 that all rated below £5 should be relieved of payment.[11] Assessments of commissioners in Sussex and Norfolk suggest that the Devon commissioners may well have been ready to assess themselves more highly than those of other counties, but even so their passive opposition to any realistic assessment of their wealthier countrymen undermined the subsidy as a tax raising measure and made inevitable extra-parliamentary expedients.[12]

Although the Devon commissioners did not make any significant changes in the subsidy rates in 1626, they did secure collection of the amount assessed. This is shown by a comparison of the total for the second subsidy of 1626, £5,802 19s 10d,[13] with that of the subsidy roll of 1624, summarised in Table 6, and the only complete one for Devon at this time. The receipts found for the five subsidies of 1628 suggest a declining yield, the first three subsidies averaged £5,442 but the fourth raised only £4,673, and the fifth £3,217.[15] The commissions for the last subsidy were only sent out on 31 March

Table 6:
Amount due on the Devon subsidy return of 1624.[14]

South Division	£2,685 18s 8d
North Division	£1,185 10s 8d
East Division	£1,886 5s 8d
Total	£5,757 15s 0d

1629 and by then parliament had been dissolved 'in great discontent'. A proclamation was out to apprehend William Strode, the son of one Devon JP and brother-in-law to four more, for his part in passing the three resolutions while the Speaker was held in his chair.[16] In these circumstances it is not surprising if Devon's subsidy commissioners made little effort to collect the subsidy.

The Forced Loan of 1625

Subsidies had been granted in 1624 in anticipation of war but as no war was in progress when parliament met in June 1625, there was great reluctance to make any new grants. A grant of two subsidies was agreed but Sir John Coke, as Secretary of State, produced detailed figures to show that this grant would be quite inadequate to pay for the planned expedition. Coke suggested that 'some new way' would have to be found if no more was granted by parliament. In August parliament was adjourned to Oxford because of plague, the issue of supply was renewed and the King made a personal appeal for a further grant but all to no avail. Parliament was dissolved on 12 August, leaving the King and Council faced with the urgent need to find an immediate source of additional supply. The other alternative, that the idea of war against Spain should be abandoned, does not appear to have been considered.[17]

Devon were already billeting about 8,000 soldiers without adequate funds when machinery was set in motion for loans to be raised under letters of the privy seal, which would be, in theory, the warrants for repayment. Lords lieutenant, with the advice of their deputies, were to make a list of those able to lend and send it to the

Privy Council.[18] The orders for the loan went out from a Council held at Plymouth while Charles was inspecting the invasion fleet but apparently ignoring the hard-pressed gentry struggling to billet his forces.[19] In these circumstances the competent, though reluctant, response of the Devon deputy lieutenants was a tribute to their diligence. They wrote to their lord lieutenant enclosing a certificate of those who could 'with least inconvenience lend His Majesty the sums against their names'.[20] Unlike many counties who selected less than fifty contributors, Devon's list contained 277 names and the sum to be collected was £4,526 13s 4d. One of the deputy lieutenants, John Drake, was appointed collector but no deputy lieutenants were included on the list; they probably considered that they should be relieved because of 'their expensive employments in the commonwealth'. Only eight serving JPs were named, none of them concerned in billeting commitments. The deputy lieutenants paid attention to the 'late losses' suffered by some, as almost as many were chosen from the less populous north division (99), as from the south (106), which had been much more affected by billeting.[21] They were very well aware of these expenses as the JPs were drawing up 'a general list or bill of all payable' to the county for billeting troops.[22]

The deputy lieutenants were outspoken in their letter to their lord lieutenant (known as Lord Russell of Thornhaugh until he succeeded his cousin as earl of Bedford in 1627). They felt like those of Cheshire who had expressed their 'distaste for the motion'.[23] They showed their personal dislike for their task, which was 'against the stream of one's nature (unapt to this kind of information) and against those storms of envy which we may chance to suffer for it'. Then they widened their objections to 'how irksome we believe it will be to the country as well as it hath been unpleasant to us', and, finally, they opposed it on principle.

Lastly for ourselves we humbly desire that our diligence in this service grounded upon His Majesty's necessities and our own observant duties may not be a means to invite His Majesty to an often recourse to this kind of supply, but rather to those which for their antiquity and indifference are and ever will be more pleasing to his subjects. This far hath our faithfulness carried us both in the performance and in the tender of our poor opinion of this service.[24]

This letter is the first expression of the themes reiterated in other responses of the leading gentry to the King's fiscal demands. They recognized the King's 'necessities' but they feared for the effect of the demand upon their countrymen and they objected to any departure from the established forms of taxation. In this letter the deputy lieutenants also wanted to make sure that Lord Russell realized how much they disliked being used in such an un-accustomed duty for deputy lieutenants. In spite of their objections to the loan, Devon's deputy lieutenants decided on contributors more quickly than those of other counties. They must have done so before 28 December when the Council wrote to many lords lieutenant, but not to Lord Russell, complaining that certificates had not been received from them.[25] The fact that the Council decided to use the money for the benefit of soldiers returning from Cadiz and billeted in the West Country may have stimulated contributors in Devon to pay up but even so money came in slowly. On 20 January 1626 the billeting commissioners reported that they had received £4,280 of the £11,000 allotted to them from the loan collections of Devon, Cornwall, Somerset and Dorset and 'the rest hath been earnestly written for'. Three of the deputy lieutenants who had selected payers for the forced loan were now among the billeting commissioners waiting to spend it. An account of their trials due to its slow collection belongs to the next chapter.[26]

A Succession of Failures to Aid the King's Finances, 1626–1627

Charles' need for further grants of supply led to him summoning his second parliament to meet on 6 February 1626. On 27 March the Commons decided to vote three subsidies and three fifteenths but they also decided to delay embodying the grant in a bill until their grievances were redressed, that is until, in effect, the duke of Buckingham was removed from office.[27] Although the Commons

75

resolved on 26 April to increase the number of subsidies to four, this was still dependant on action being taken against the duke. The King's last hope that subsidies would be granted on the strength of promises rather than action faded on 12 June and so dissolution followed on 15 June 1626.[28] In the debates on the subsidies, Sir William Strode (a Devon JP) had been particularly outspoken; he exhorted his colleagues to sit morning and afternoon to prepare their grievances so that they could be submitted to the King with a financial measure.[29] Devon members were understandably most reluctant to sanction fresh subsidies as those of 1625 were still being collected in the county.[30] Moreover, many Devonians were out of pocket from having to billet, without payment, soldiers involved in the unsuccessful autumn campaign, and the county's prosperity had been affected by the break in trade with Spain.

The dissolution of June 1626 was followed, in rapid succession, by three attempts to counter the loss of the parliamentary grant. Two of them were financial, a plea for a benevolence followed by an attempt to reactivate the machinery of the first forced loan. The third was an order for a grant in kind, for the supply of manned ships. On 7 July the King requested a benevolence, this was to be the people's opportunity to show their loyalty in contrast to the 'malicious practices of wicked spirits' opposing him in parliament.[31] Such loyalty was assumed, as it was ordered that the roll to be sent to the exchequer should list those who had contributed and those who refused, 'if any such be'. The JPs were expected to exhort the people to make a gift in place of the grant parliament would have made if it had not been dissolved, and they were to assure the people that the king would 'use the money for the defence of the realm and for no other purpose whatsoever'.[32] The loyalty of the Devon JPs was never put to the test as they were overwhelmed with other affairs which stopped them acting on these orders. They could not even hold their midsummer session in Exeter because of plague, instead they met in Crediton where they organized relief for the plague-stricken in Plymouth. At the same time the deputy lieutenants had to interrupt their meeting, called to plan the summer musters, because of a rumour that an enemy fleet of 400 had been sighted off Lands End. In addition to these emergencies, there was the constant difficulty of billeting soldiers without adequate funds.[33] All these tasks were obvious means of giving service to the King whereas they may well have doubted the legality of the benevolence, especially as the parliamentary grant had been uncertain as it was 'not agreed on, but upon conditions'. News of general opposition to the benevolence had reached Devon, they heard that many were imprisoned in London and 'many refused to pay and others gave very little'.[34]

While the benevolence was failing to meet the urgent need for money, a second scheme was launched, a proposal to revive the machinery of the forced loan of 1625. This time the only Devon figure involved was John Drake, who was again named as the collector for the county. On 14 August the King instructed the Council to draw up lists of those suitable to lend, relying on the lords lieutenant's certificates of 1625.[35] In contrast to the 1625 loan very few lenders were selected but they were highly assessed. The only name found for Devon was Arthur Champernowne, who was to be charged £100.[36] It has been suggested that names were selected for opposition to Buckingham, but no evidence has been found in support of this in the case of Champernowne.[37] This attempt to revive the loan was suspended on 22 September 1626. Five days later the benevolence was remitted by proclamation.[38] The only evidence of any payment from Devon for either of these demands was a payment of £340 into the exchequer by John Drake in the summer of 1627 for a forced loan.[39]

While these two projects drew little or no response from Devon, a different kind of demand was addressed to the county on 30 June 1626. Five of the port towns were ordered to supply ships to guard the seas. Barnstaple, Plymouth and Exeter were expected to provide two ships each and Dartmouth and Totnes three each. The ships were to be of 200 tons, manned with 133 men and victualled for three months. This request primarily concerned these corporate towns but the county JPs were also involved, as those living near the ports were ordered to assist them with supplies and in recruiting up to a third of the crews from the county.[40] Five county JPs resident near Exeter tried to persuade the mayor and magistrates of the city to act on the Council's orders but they had to report their failure to their Lordships on 28 July 1626. They had been given various excuses. Some concerned with 'the embargo in Spain and the stay of their goods in France', others with the need to ransom their children and friends 'in captivity under the Turks' and others with the troubles within the county of plague and of having soldiers billeted among them.[41] A series of letters followed with the Council expressing their surprise at the inaction of the ports and the towns continuing to make their excuses.[42] This pressure from the Council eased in January 1627, perhaps to ensure a satisfactory launch for the second forced loan, but the demand for ships was revived once the loan was organized.[43]

The Partial Success of the Forced Loan of 1626–1628

When the Council decided on a new forced loan in the autumn of 1626, they showed they had learnt from their failure over the benevolence and the attempt to revive the first forced loan and prepared the ground more carefully. The loan was launched by proclamation on 7 October 1626.[44] Privy Councillors first put the case for the loan to taxpayers in Westminster and after a good response there, went on to London and the five home counties. These early meetings seem to have aimed at achieving compliance by coercion but as opposition grew the policy changed and, before any meeting was held over the loan in Devon, the Council had become willing to negotiate rather than coerce.[45] The Devon commissioners, who were 'summoned and greatly assisted by our noble lord lieutenant', met at Tiverton on 24 January 1627.[46] This is one of the very few occasions when Lord Russell is known to have been in Devon, he never attended quarter sessions. The loan commissioners were supposed to be chosen from those who, 'in Parliament or otherwise have made demonstration of their good affection to His Majesty's service', but this did not prevent the inclusion of Sir William Strode who had been active in opposition in parliament a few months earlier.[47] All the Devon JPs on the *liber pacis* of October 1626 were named and also a few former JPs who were briefly off the bench between 1625 and 1628; the only person included who was never a JP was Francis Courtenay.[48]

The situation in Devon had improved since the failure of the benevolence the previous summer. The fit troops had been marched into other counties in September, and though the billeters remained unpaid, at least they were not still having to house the soldiers.[49] It is not known which Councillors were present at the meeting at Tiverton with the Devon commissioners when they accepted the argument of the King's commission for 'a speedy supply of money at this time by way of loan'. They considered it their duty to 'advance the operation of this Commission, both by our examples and best diligence; in performance whereof we directly pursued the instructions sent us'. Yet they also noted the King's intention (in his proclamation) not to make this a 'precedent . . . to the prejudice of the ancient and approved way of parliament'. They then dispersed into their divisions to start organizing the collection. They agreed to meet again on 13 February 1627 at Exeter, when they had hoped they would be able to give the Council 'the fruits of all our labours' but the north and east divisions were not ready so they decided to give their 'lordships only a brief relation of the success of our proceedings in the South part of this county'. In reality their report was not of success but was an explanation that 'many have had a necessity upon them to make conditionary offers of lending'. In other words they wanted to strike a bargain that if they were paid the cost for billeting the royal army they would be willing to lend the sum proposed. Otherwise the commissioners feared that this service would not 'be done without difficulty and confusion'. This was a bold approach but, as they added, they were aware that other counties had secured this privilege who had not been owed so much for so long. Moreover they pointed out the administrative convenience of paying the billeters directly from the payments collected. Such an action 'would establish His Majesty's honour and your own justice in the hearts of a people to whom your lordships not long since vouchsafed the title of well deserving.[50] They were not satisfied with just writing to the Council, they also said they were sending Sir George Chudleigh 'to solicit your lordships in this business' and begged them to order the collectors of the loan in Devon to pay their receipts direct to Sir George, who was already the treasurer and paymaster of the army in the county. This letter was signed by seventeen loan commissioners, all resident in the south division, fifteen of whom were JPs.[51]

The Devon commissioners achieved their objective and the Council allowed them to use the loan payments to defray the billeting costs. They were commended for their diligence and assured that 'if the loan pay not the billeting' and other expenses 'then some other source will be found'.[52] The Council also agreed that Sir George Chudleigh should receive all the loan payments for Devon and Cornwall.[53] His trials fulfilling these duties are examined in more detail in his biographical study,[54] here the concern is primarily with the work of the commissioners for the collection in Devon. They could now organize the loan in Devon with the knowledge that this would also ease the distress of the billeters. The detailed return made by four commissioners for Coleridge hundred shows that, in most cases, the King's indebtedness to his subjects for billeting was greater than their liability for the loan. The most outstanding example of this was one man, probably an innkeeper, who was due to pay £3 for the loan and to receive £160 for 'billet of soldiers and entertainment of officers'. A co-ordination of this loan book with the subsidy roll of 1624 shows that most subsidymen were expected to pay five times their subsidy assessment. It also shows that some commissioners let themselves off lightly; John Upton assessed for subsidy at £12 only paid £3 in loan, and his entry is marked 'commissioner'.[55] Probably commissioners, like the deputy lieutenants assessing the forced loan of 1625, felt that their labours for the loan justified favourable treatment.[56]

The gentry leaders had just given their full support to this second forced loan when they received a letter from the Council reviving the demand for them to aid the port towns in supplying ships, though this demand was now reduced to two ships from each town.[57] The letter arrived during the Easter sessions and the JPs decided to confer again with the towns and then meet a fortnight later to answer the Council's letter.[58] This special meeting brought back to Exeter eleven JPs living near all the ports affected (except Barnstaple). Their reply to the Council supported the statements from the towns that they could not meet the charge. Moreover the JPs expressed their own view that:

> If we had been forced at this time to put them to a new charge while the loans (which lie not everywhere easy) are yet in collection, we should have hazarded His Majesty's honour upon a repulse of this service. For as we believe the towns have answered your lordships the truth of their estates . . . so we assure your lordships the country people are much weakened in their abilities and would have been hardly drawn to the late loans but in hope this would have fully supplied His Majesty's occasions.[59]

Exeter, Barnstaple, Dartmouth and Totnes made separate answers in a similar vein.[60] Unlike some counties Devon's JPs did not base their objection to this charge of ship money on doubt of its legality[61] but on the practical consideration that it could not be met because of the forced loan. Actually they were doing more than this, they were showing that they could only collect the forced loan if the county was relieved of the order to supply ships. They were striking another bargain with the Council, like the one they had just made over billeting payments.

The loan was supposed to be collected within three months. It was hoped everyone would pay in twenty-four days, otherwise they were to pay half in fourteen days and the rest in three months.[62] The Devon collection did not achieve this schedule but at least it was more successful than other counties who were written to by the Council with demands for speedier action.[63] The loan commissioners (meeting during the midsummer quarter sessions of 1627) tried to stimulate the collection. They found that those who had refused to pay the first instalment, 'have discouraged many others in their second payment', so they ordered Sir George Chudleigh to select some refusers and report them to the Privy Council.[64] He sent the names of fifteen refractory persons to the earl of

Marlborough on 28 July 1627.[65] One of them, John Delbridge, may have had considerable influence in deterring others from paying the loan; he had been mayor of Barnstaple, its MP in 1626 and was a prominent puritan; he had also gone to the Council, earlier in the year, to explain Barnstaple's inability to supply ships.[66] Chudleigh asked for a pursuivant to aid him and the commissioners in the collection, and a Mr Ralph Robinson had arrived by the Michaelmas quarter sessions. The 'fear apprehended by the presence of the Pursuivant' was to prove of powerful assistance in enforcing payment.[67] No examples have been found of Devonians being imprisoned for opposition to the loan but Walter Yonge had news that elsewhere 'many are daily imprisoned for refusing to lend the King so that the prisons in London are full'.[68]

So far as Devon's loan commissioners were concerned the collection was a remarkable success. Devon was expected to pay far more than any other county, loan payments were to be the equivalent of five subsidies, based on the assessments of 1625. This meant that Devon was expected to contribute £30,015, while Yorkshire, the next highest county, was only charged £19,070.[69] This suggests that, in spite of the under-assessment noted earlier, Devon's subsidy commissioners were making better returns than other counties and so the loan commissioners were faced with raising a greater total. A letter of 1628 claims that they exceeded this amount and collected about £41,000. Devon had done as much and even more than expected yet their collection had not even cleared the King's debts in Devon. The bargain of the commissioners with the Council to use the loan in Devon meant that it had no effect on the King's future needs. Moreover the commissioners had also made a bargain with the people of Devon, apparently based on the King's instructions to them. They had engaged their:

Faithful promise to our countrymen that if they willingly yielded to His Majesty's necessities at this time, we would never more be instruments in the levy of aid of that kind: His Majesty's intentions so clearly manifested not to make that a precedent was the cause of that engagement.[70]

The loan in Devon may have succeeded in raising the money expected and thus far it can be called successful, but as a means of alleviating the King's wider financial difficulties it was of little use. Moreover, the future had been mortgaged and the King's promise that it would not become a precedent meant that Devon's leaders would be justified in refusing the next demand.

Request For Ship Money in 1628

The forced loan brought in the equivalent of five subsidies but this did not prevent Charles' government from being in dire financial straits by the end of 1627.[71] Discussions on methods of raising revenue became the almost daily agenda of the Council. Some Councillors advocated summoning parliament but others thought this might be seen as surrendering to the opponents of the forced loan. It was therefore decided to request ship money before the summons of parliament and present it as a means of the subjects proving their loyalty.[72] Letters were sent to both the sheriff and the JPs for a levy for a fleet to support the King of Denmark. Once again the demand from Devon was higher than that from anywhere else. The county was expected to produce £17,475 and Exeter an additional £642; the next highest demands were from London for £12,135 and Yorkshire for £10,602.[73] Walter Yonge was the sheriff who received this demand and he commented that it was, 'to set a fleet at sea, which was appointed to be at sea the first of March, we having but 6 or 7 days to raise the money and return it to London; but our county refused to meddle therein'.[74] This impossibly short period for collection suggests that this may have been part of the Council manoeuvring to invite refusal and so strengthen the case for summoning parliament.[75]

Devon's reply to the Council survives in three undated and unsigned copies, which suggests that it was well publicized. It was, 'the vote and opinion of us all which was this day almost in the same words delivered by every one of us.' This unanimous opinion of the gentry governors was not only a refusal to this demand but also a commentary on the burdens placed on the county during the first three years of the reign. Part of their refusal has already been quoted in the account of the forced loan.[76] Their experiences in that task led them now to, 'have much more cause to wish than hope that these parts so lately and so many ways impoverished can yield it'. After the forced loan had been organized and used to meet past billeting charges Devon had been subjected to a fresh spell of billeting which meant that many new costs were due to them. The county was also disturbed by the number of sick soldiers they had to house, 'whose mortal infection hath more discouraged the people than the charge'. Incomes had been hit 'for the want of trade' and so 'how then can there be any quantity of money to disburse'. They asserted the loyalty of the county for 'their bodies and goods are left which (we are assured) will be ever ready for His Majesty's defence, and to be employed in His Majesty's service as far forth as ever our forefathers have yielded them to His Majesty's Royal progenitors'. Finally, they asserted that although they could have provided proof of 'the peoples disability to have satisfied His Majesty's demands, they preferred to 'adventure ourselves and this humble advertisement' rather than 'expose His Majesty's honour to a public denial'. This they felt would have wasted 'his precious time which applied to more certain courses may attain his Princely and Religious end'.[77] The writs which had already gone out for parliament, would have been the way that these gentry leaders would have considered to be the more certain way of achieving the King's purposes. Four days after the letters had been dispatched to the counties, the levy was abandoned by proclamation and when parliament assembled on 17 March the King declared that 'supply at this time' was 'the chief end of it'.[78] The price he had to pay for a grant of five subsidies was to be the Petition of Right.

A comment on Devon's response to this succession of financial demands is provided in the words of a newcomer to the county. Joseph Hall, consecrated bishop of Exeter on 23 December 1627 and carrying out his first visitation of the diocese in August 1628.

And how willingly of late the more populous and more knowing and religious parts of my Diocese have yielded to all charges of the state, above other parts of the kingdom, I leave to the testimony of those noble commissioners which have been employed in these services. Only this I say that I doubt not but it will be made good to any gainsayer that His Majesty hath not more true hearted and open handed subjects in all the compass of his Dominions than those within my verge.[79]

The fact that he singles out the 'more populous and more knowing and religious parts of my Diocese' as the willing contributors to the royal demands may be intended to show that in Devon there could be no suggestion of a popular/puritan opposition to royal policies. As a preacher at Court in the spring of 1628 he would have been aware of the conflicting views circulating there, including those fearing such a combination.[80]

Knighthood Composition

The first steps towards this charge were taken after the dissolution of Charles' first parliament, when it was obvious that the subsidies granted would not meet the cost of the war against Spain.[81] As the expedition failed at Cadiz, Nicholas Fry, sheriff of Devon, received a warrant summoning all freeholders of land worth £40 to attend in London at the time of the coronation; in theory to receive knighthood, in practice to be fined for not receiving it.[82] No fines appear to have been imposed, perhaps because parliament was due to meet at the same time and might seem to be a better prospect for supply. Names of those liable, however, must have been sent as the sheriffs were ordered to supplement the original numbers in November 1627. Writs were issued by May 1628 to enforce attendance at the exchequer of all named but then the tempo for action dropped.[83] The Petition of Right was consented to on 7 June and the first payment of the five subsidies granted was to be paid on 16 July 1628,[84] so it would be insensitive to require knighthood composition, even though the exchequer did continue to demand more names from the sheriffs. Walter Yonge, as sheriff in 1628, would have received these demands, but he does not mention the charge until after the dissolution of parliament in March 1629 when he noted that, 'commissions are to be sent for the summoning of such as are capable of knighthood by the old statute, that they come in and take oath upon them or compound for it'.[85] So, although no one was actually fined until 1630, plans for this charge weave in and out of the other taxes described in this chapter.

The method of dealing with this charge was changed and the King decided to send commissions into the counties instead of ordering people to compound in a plague infected capital.[86] These commissions of 6 July 1630 were intended as a brief concession and anyone who did not take advantage of them would have to compound at the Council.[87] However, doubts about the legality of the charge led to a very poor response in many counties (but not in Devon) and a fresh commission was instituted on 12 February 1631 after a case in the Court of the Exchequer had tested its legality.[88] Sir Francis Fulford and Sir James Bagg were the collectors for the composition in Devon and the seven JPs named on the second commission may well have served on both.[89] The county was divided between the two collectors, Fulford being responsible for the whole of the east division and for the five adjoining hundreds of the south; Bagg collected from the rest of the south division and all the north. The commissioners had to draw up their lists after seeking information from all the county officials, from undersheriff to petty constable and after consulting the subsidy roll, the book of the freeholders of the county, the muster roll and the book for the collection for the poor in the parishes. Anyone rated for the subsidy at £3 or less was to pay £10, wealthier subjects were to pay three and a half times their subsidy rate. (This was an increase from the rate of two and a half times under the first commission.) JPs were to pay at least £25, regardless of their subsidy rate, as it was 'presumed that they are all of good estates'.[90] With all this information at the commissioners' disposal, assessments should have been based on established rates but the collection in Devon suggests that a good deal depended on the commissioners' judgement or perhaps their partiality.

Under the first commission 219 paid the composition in Devon for a total of £3,477.[91] The assessments of the two groups of commissioners can be compared and show that Fulford's area was treated more generously than Bagg's.[92] This is not surprising as Sir James Bagg was primarily a vice-admiral rather than a JP, he never attended quarter sessions or showed any particular concern for the interests of his countrymen. The comparison between the two assessments cannot be continued over the later commissions as no detail survives of individual payments in the hundreds administered by Fulford. Sir James may have lined his own pocket under the commissions as there is a difference of £1,245 6s 8d between the amount assessed for 461 persons in his area and the amount paid into the exchequer.[93] This discrepancy may represent the amount assessed but not collected or it may be the amount which had disappeared into the hands of the notoriously corrupt Sir James, nicknamed 'bottomless Bagg'.

All but one (Alexander Maynard) of the JPs resident in Bagg's part of the county are listed for the charge, but the absence of names under the second commission for Fulford's area leaves doubt of the policy there. The JPs, however, do seem to have made their fair contribution to the charge as all named were assessed for £25 or more. Thirty-three Devonians compounded at the exchequer, some may have been required to do so by a schedule, which survives with the second commission in some counties; this instructed commissioners not to compound with any of those named, who were 'to compound here'.[94] This might have applied to Nicholas Fry and Walter Yonge who possibly were penalized for not returning suitable names for composition, while they were sheriffs; both were charged more than three and a half times their subsidy rate. Ten others probably compounded at the exchequer because of their slowness in responding, some of them were also charged more than three and a half times their subsidy rates. The most severely treated was the wealthy JP, Sampson Hele, who paid £150 (more than seven times his subsidy rate of £20) in 1633.[95] Delay in payment to the exchequer may suggest some opposition to the charge in Devon, yet the work of the Devon collectors compares very favourably with those of other counties. Sussex raised about £1,600 and Essex only just over £2,000 and there no JP was charged.[96] The total amount paid into the exchequer by Devonians was £13,915 10s, that is equivalent to two subsidies (the size of the parliamentary grant of 1625).

Conclusion

As this account has examined the labours of the leading gentry in response to a succession of tax demands, it has also revealed something of their relationship with the King. Taxation was, inevitably, a test of this relationship. The problems which had to be faced were due to two sets of circumstances. The one of long-standing was the crucial situation reached after many years of a steadily declining subsidy yield, coupled with massive inflation and the increasing cost of warfare. The other was the specific situation arising from mismanagement and misconceptions during the first four years of the reign. The decline in the subsidy yield undermined the value of parliamentary taxation, but even so the forced loans might not have been required if the Commons had granted the subsidies requested in the King's name in 1625 and 1626. However, members (who were also JPs, such as Sir Edward Giles and Sir William Strode) either could not accept that such grants were necessary or had no confidence in the way they would be used by a government dominated by Buckingham; moreover they would have been reluctant to face their county if they imposed heavy subsidies. This was an understandable attitude in Devon members whose county was having to billet a royal army whose very purpose was, at times, undecided.[97]

When the desired number of subsidies were not granted, the gentry leaders found themselves having to organize forced loans to supply the need. They did this efficiently but they objected to this method of raising money, instead of parliamentary grant, and pleaded that it should not be taken as a precedent. None of the other extra-parliamentary demands of 1626–8 received more than a verbal response from Devon's leaders. The rejection of the order for ship money in 1628 emphasized not only the state of the county, weakened by billeting, plague and loss of trade, but the promise made by the King that if the loan was collected no more similar demands would be made. Their concern for the King's honour in this can be, to some extent, linked to their own, for he was the source of all their authority. Their work as royal tax collectors also reveals something of the gentry leaders concern for their countrymen. In spite of royal requests to raise the rates for subsidy they continued the practice of severely under-assessing them. With regard to all the requests for extra-parliamentary grants, their letters to the Privy Council show them acknowledging the needs of the King and expressing their readiness to serve him but, in fact, in collecting them they gave priority to the needs of their county. They tried to get permission to use the subsidy (of 1625), when it was being collected in April 1626 in order to clothe soldiers on the verge of mutiny.[98] They did successfully bargain to use the second forced loan to relieve the billeters and dealt fairly with billeters and loan payers. This chapter is not just an account of the activity of the gentry leaders as royal tax collectors, it also reveals the strength and cohesion of that body as it presented a united front to the royal demands.

PART II

THE GENTRY GOVERNORS
OF DEVON IN THE EARLY
SEVENTEENTH CENTURY

Chapter 6

Sir George Chudleigh:
His Rise to Prominence in the County

Sir George Chudleigh is one of those little-known local figures whose career, once highlighted, can illuminate our view of early Stuart England. He held a central place in the county government yet he was not a dominant leader, no one held such a position in Devon. He often acted with a group of his fellow governors, yet even then his personality and influence stands out, and one can see his hand in the decision-making. With such a man at the centre of affairs, a man steeped in the collegiality of the bench and ready to take on additional responsibilities without trying to further his own interests, Devon was administered with efficiency and apparent harmony. Chudleigh was the most active of the gentry governors and his work is the best documented but he was never more than *primus inter pares.* This means that a biographical study of Sir George Chudleigh is not just a medium for describing county government from a personal angle but is also a means of revealing much of the quality and nature of that government. The fact that the bench remained united, until the outbreak of war forced division upon them, suggests that many of its members shared the same principles and ideals as Chudleigh, and that in describing him one is also throwing light on the character of the bench as a whole.

George Chudleigh came from a family long established in Devon with a tradition of service reaching back to the reign of Richard II,

FAMILY OF SIR GEORGE CHUDLEIGH

Christopher Chudleigh

Christiana Stretchleigh = (2) ? Cary
|
William Cary

Strechley d. 1570

John = Elizabeth = (2) Sir John Clifton of Soms. d. 1591
Speake of = (3) Sir Hugh Pollard
Whitelackington Somerset
d. of Sir George

(1) Dorothy Sir John Sir Robert Chichester
Chichester Chichester

Viscount Chichester

Sir Lewis Pollard

Susan = John Northcott

Bridget = Sir Richard Carew of Cornwall

Dorothy = Sir Reginald Mohun Cornish JP

Sir William Strode [six of ten children]

William   Julia,   Jane,   Ursula,   Elizabeth,   Mary = Sir George   Sir John = Margaret d. of Sir William Courtenay widow of Sir Warwick Hele
          =   =   =
          John   Sir   John Yonge, son of
          Davy   Francis John   Walter Yonge
                    Drake   Chichester

William b. 1610   James b. 1617 killed at Dartmouth 1643   Richard b. 1619   Christopher b, 1620   Thomas   Anne

Mary = Henry son of Dr Clifford

Elizabeth = Arthur son of Henry Ashford

George b. 1608

John 1606–1630

when Sir James Chudleigh had been a JP, sheriff and a knight of the shire in nine parliaments. Their family estates were within ten miles of Exeter, centred on Broadclyst to the east and Ashton, their principal residence, to the south. Their wealth increased when Sir Richard Chudleigh was appointed commissioner for church goods under the first earl of Bedford, and so evidently was one of the early supporters of the reformation in the county. This relationship between the earls of Bedford and the Chudleigh family was to recur when Sir George Chudleigh served as a deputy lieutenant to the fourth and fifth earls. Sir Richard's son, Christopher, married an heiress, Christiana Stretchleigh, and so extended the family estates and influence into the far south-west, near Plymouth. This wealth was partly dissipated by the adventurous schemes of their son John who, after serving with his distant relative, Sir Walter Raleigh, as knight of the shire in 1586, fought against the Armada and then in 1589 lost his life leading an expedition which had hoped to circumnavigate the world.[1] As Prince commented: 'he did not live long enough to accomplish his generous designs, dying young he lived long enough to exhaust a vast estate'.[2] His eldest son George had been born on 14 November 1582 and may have been taken to Somerset on the death of his father as that county was the home of both his guardians, his mother Elizabeth, daughter of Sir George Speake of Whitelackington and her brother-in-law, Sir Edward Gorges. His mother married again in that county but was soon widowed and returned to Devon as the wife of Sir Hugh Pollard, whose family were strong upholders of the 1559 church settlement.[3] These varied influences on his childhood may account for the fact that George Chudleigh did not follow the usual pattern of education of most Devon JPs; he went to New College, Oxford in 1596,[4] rather than to Exeter, the college with the Devon connection and one gaining a reputation for puritanism. He did not go on to an Inn of Court, but completed his education abroad, acquiring 'the most exquisite breeding that age could yield', and returned home 'well improved'. One of his future colleagues, Sir William Pole, wrote of him as having 'a grave understanding' and to be a hopeful gentleman to continue the worth of his ancient family.[5]

Chudleigh was drawn into a different circle with his marriage in 1605 to Mary, eldest daughter of Sir William Strode. Sir William was already a long-standing member of the bench and regularly elected to parliament. He was also the wholehearted supporter of Samuel Hieron, rector of Modbury, who led the clerical opposition to subscription in the diocese and was suspended five times by Bishop Cotton, but each time he was reprieved through Strode's influence.[6] Chudleigh's marriage clearly brought him into contact with a more vigorous puritanism than he may have met in his earlier years. Sir William inaugurated a series of lectures at Modbury and had Chudleigh's support in this measure, both of them attending Hieron's opening lecture in 1615. In his dedication to them of the first lecture, Hieron expressed his thanks to God who had put it into their hearts to establish a weekly lecture, though he hoped that they had 'not drawn preaching hither for a form, or out of glory; but that in sincerity of heart you have sought your own furtherance in the ways of piety.'[7] Soon after the Modbury lectures Chudleigh showed his continuing support for lecturers by using his powers of patronage to appoint clerics at Jacobstowe in 1617 and 1621 who were later Saturday lecturers at nearby Okehampton. He also supported the appointment of a vicar at Plymouth in 1620 who undertook to preach, or cause deputies to preach, four times a week.[8]

These signs of puritan sympathies all belong to the early period of Chudleigh's life when he was usually resident at his manor of Stretchleigh in south-west Devon, and only about three miles from Newnham, the home of the Strodes. The Chudleigh household may well have been influenced not only by Sir William but also by Lady Strode who spent four hours a day at her devotions. She left her daughter, Mary Chudleigh, a Bible in which she wrote, 'the word of the Lord shall endure for ever; And blessed shall you be if you constantly, unto the end, delight to seek and follow that, with faithful and true hearts.'[9] Lady Strode died in 1619 and Sir William remarried in 1624, factors which may have weakened the impact of Strode's puritanism on the Chudleigh family. Another change of these years was Chudleigh's increased use of Ashton, near Exeter, as

FIGURE 5 Sir George Chudleigh's house at Ashton

his principal home, which meant that after 1628 he was seldom at his Stretchleigh manor and so in close contact with Strode. At Ashton he would have worshipped in a church with a particularly fine rood screen, covered in paintings of saints, several in their papal tiaras; an uneasy setting for him if he had been strongly anti-papist. He became friendly with the new bishop of Exeter, Valentine Carey, and entertained him for some weeks at Ashton in 1626 while there was plague in Exeter. Carey has been termed an Arminian but this was principally due to him being seen as a courtier rather than a diocesan bishop. He was really a clericalist who saw his mission as enhancing the prestige of the clergy.[10] It is perhaps significant of Chudleigh's standpoint that he was not deterred by the bishop's opinion that the surplice was 'the armour of light', from inviting the bishop's wife to be godmother to one of his children.[11]

Chudleigh has never been found referred to as a puritan and he certainly would not have been called one by Joseph Hall, who became his diocesan bishop in 1627. Hall had decided to accept the bishopric after he had reassessed the religious situation in the

97

country and decided that such a position would be his best means of working to restore harmony to the church.[12] This task laid him open to charges of both encouraging puritanism and opposing it. In an undated letter, he denied that there were puritans in his diocese, though he defined puritanism narrowly as being, 'refractory opposition to the Government, Rites and Customs of the Church'. However, he also recognized that modern puritanism may have become 'more subtle than in former times and that under colour of a full outward conformity there may be nourished some unquiet and pestilent humours which may closely work danger to the Churches peace'. But he asked how he could 'take hold of that indisposition if it vent not itself into words or actions', as he had 'no door nor window into men's hearts'. In the Exeter diocese it was his policy to prevent religious differences becoming the subjects of widespread controversy by smoothing them over and avoiding innovations, thus he was able to maintain a peaceable diocese with no major disputes to align conflicting parties. He rejoiced that 'the knowledge and Love of the Gospel hath dilated itself and gathered strength' since he arrived and 'that faction hath abated'. In this the preachers and lecturers had played their part, for 'there may be as soon too many Angels in heaven, as too many conscionable, discreet, Orthodox teachers in God's church'.[13] There is every reason to think that Chudleigh, a supporter of lecturers but not an opponent of ceremonial, would have been content with such a bishop. Hall's moderation would have encouraged the varied shades of religious opinion to work together on the bench; his words would have impressed upon them that it was the duty of a magistrate to be 'the faithful Deputy of his Maker'.[14]

Chudleigh's career unfolds against the constant background of his duties as a JP which began in 1614. For the first ten years his service was fairly conscientious but not outstanding, with him attending quarter sessions, on average, twice a year. When new responsibilities were thrust upon him, between 1625 and 1628, and he became a central figure in the county, his importance at quarter sessions also increased. He then attended on almost every occasion, and became the obvious choice for any special sub-committees such as for a rating dispute or a petition of cloth workers.[15] He was also ready to carry out the orders of quarter sessions to take on routine tasks in his sub-division, appointing head constables, examining bridges and arranging for their repair; and he was available in his home to take examinations and issue recognizances.[16] Whatever other responsibilities he might take on, his duties as a magistrate provide the framework to his career.

As George Chudleigh approached his fortieth year there were signs that his standing in the county was growing. It was an indication of his substance (as well as his relationship with Sir Ferdinando Gorges) when Gorges included him among the members of the New England Council which he promoted in 1620.[17] Two years later Chudleigh had enough resources to purchase a baronetage.[18] This was also the time when he began to spend less time in the south-west of the county and was more often near Exeter, the centre of county affairs. Although he had sat in several parliaments for Cornish constituencies, it was not until the parliament of 1621 that he made an impression on that national stage.[19] He spoke in the debate on the privilege of freedom of speech and showed his ability to put a considered opinion on a matter generating much feeling. It was significant of his outlook that he was prepared to take part in debates on wider issues than those concerning the West Country though he also spoke on a matter of local interest, the expansion of the 1610 law on seasand.[20] He had to raise this matter before the petition of the inhabitants of Devon and Cornwall (dated 6 June) could be received because of the early adjournment of parliament.[21] Although it was too late to achieve anything that session, Chudleigh would have been able to report that he had pointed out the need.

He was only once elected for a Devon seat, when he was returned for Tiverton in 1624. This may have owed something to his brother-in-law, Sir Reginald Mohun's landed influence in Tiverton but it is unlikely that he could have been imposed upon a reluctant borough. He made a considerable mark in this parliament with his speech on the breakdown of the Spanish policy being widely reported by the diarists Nicholas, Spring, Rich, Holland and Pym. His most significant point was that 'Spain intended not the match but to make rebellion here'.[22] As he suspected this danger he was probably ready to accept the need for war. In this he can be associated with Buckingham and his immediate followers who desired the war likely to follow from ending the treaties.[23] The prospect of war raised the need for subsidies and the King stated that he would require a grant of six subsidies and twelve fifteenths before he would be willing to enter the war.[24] Chudleigh was among the forty members who spoke in the subsidy debate, many of them Privy Councillors, but he struck an independent line. He was not prepared to express a view on the foreign policy issue but concentrated on the financial one. He proposed that they should agree 'a fit sum between two or three hundred thousand' (this was very far short of the King's requirements estimated at £900,000 by Sir Edward Coke). Chudleigh then added the original view that 'the Way' should be 'somewhat a New Way', which did not include any subsidyman with land valued at less than £5.[25] He was thus proposing taxation which he thought should meet the King's need without injuring the weaker of his countrymen.[26] His views evidently carried some weight as he was later appointed to the committee to prepare the preamble to the subsidy bill.[27]

After the Easter recess the Commons began to consider a petition against Catholic recusants, which showed their strong anti-Catholic and anti-Spanish prejudice. Chudleigh was one of forty-eight members of the Commons who were involved in discussion with the Lords on this petition. The Lords caused it to be modified so that it was acceptable to the King.[28] Chudleigh's contributions to debates on two other matters also merit notice. On 29 April it was proposed that a bill should be drawn up to continue all bills next session *in statu quo* which would save much time. Chudleigh supported this, so far as petitions were concerned, though he commented that they should 'have some look, whether any such Precedent or no'.[29] This was an unprecedented motion which was strongly supported by 'great parliament men'.[30] Chudleigh may have valued it for the effect it could have had on the petition over seasand in the previous parliament. According to Dr Stone,

Chudleigh attacked the earl of Middlesex in the debate on his impeachment but this view is not reflected in the tone of the reports found of Chudleigh's speech.[31] He considered that care should 'be had of the honour of so great a person', and he moved that witnesses should be called speedily 'lest practice be, for everyone that doth ill knows to whom to repair to prevent testimony'.[32] Chudleigh also served on a number of committees during this parliament. Some were of national interest, such as the one to continue some statutes and repeal others, and the one to view several patents and provisions tendered for monopolies. Other committees were of more local concern, such as the one for freer fishing and fishing voyages and for making void a monopoly for packing and drying fish.[33] He may have chaired the committee on the private bill affecting the inheritance of John Mohun (his sister's step-son) as he reported on the measure twice.[34]

Chudleigh's part in the parliament of 1624, his contributions to debates and his inclusion on important committees suggest that his reputation was rising nationally as well as locally. Was there any particular reason for this? R.E. Ruigh in his account of this parliament calls Chudleigh a partisan of Buckingham, yet the duke was at the height of his popularity at this time and in support-ing Buckingham's policies Chudleigh was following the almost unanimous view of the House.[35] It is important to establish the strength of Ruigh's grounds for naming Chudleigh one of Buckingham's partisans in case this, rather than his own standing, was the reason for him being called to speak in several crucial debates and for his membership of delegations to the Lords and of Commons' committees. If Chudleigh was really a client of Buckingham this could, later, have been the reason for his increasing importance in the county. It might also have been the cause of his fellow JPs choosing him as their spokesman in the belief that he had access to that powerful influence. Yet the only grounds Ruigh gives for terming Chudleigh a partisan of Buckingham is a letter (dated July 1626, two years after the debates) from the commissioners of the duke's estates to the secretary of the admiralty which refers to him, among others, as a gentleman of 'worthy spirit and integrity in the Country and well affected to my lord'. This letter proposed him for a commission to investigate the vice-admiralty of Sir John Eliot.[36] This is not strong evidence to suggest that Chudleigh was a client of Buckingham. He may have gained the reputation of being 'well-affected' from his associations with some of the duke's party. His brother-in-law, Sir Reginald Mohun, was among the duke's supporters in Cornwall.[37] His correspondent, Sir John Coke, was a spokesman for Buckingham in the Commons as well as Secretary of State; in 1625 when Chudleigh heard that Sir John was doubtful of his parliamentary seat, he offered him 'a blank burgesship', which he had received from Sir Reginald Mohun.[38] Chudleigh was returning a favour Coke had done him in remembering him 'to His Majesty when I was in danger of the Sheriffwick'.[39] If Chudleigh had really been a partisan of the duke, one would expect to find some evidence of it during the crucial years 1625 to 1628, but there were very few contacts and no evidence that Chudleigh entertained Buckingham when he visited Devon. The duke stayed with John Drake or Sir James Bagg on these occasions, although Chudleigh's manor of Stretchleigh was conveniently placed near Plymouth.[40] Chudleigh did not owe his advancement to the duke's influence, instead the account of his service will show that he owed it to the trust of his fellow governors and the patient competence of his response to the royal commands.

When Sir George became a deputy lieutenant in 1625 he had achieved a position regarded as 'the pinnacle in the hierarchy of county offices'.[41] From this year he became an almost automatic choice for *ad hoc* commissions within the county and for several demanding individual appointments. The greatest concentration of these tasks were in the years 1625 to 1628, when Devon became the launch pad for some aggressive foreign expeditions and the gentry governors learnt, from personal experience, of the vagaries of their country's foreign policy, involved in war first with Spain and then also with France. Devon was first drawn into these national affairs in May 1625, when a force of 10,000 was ordered to Plymouth although no firm decision had been made concerning its purpose. It delayed there until October and then sailed to Cadiz in the hope of emulating Elizabethan successes, but achieved nothing and returned in December. The Council had no plan of what to do with the distressed soldiers landing in Devon (and nearby areas of Cornwall), except to order that they should not be discharged. It was not until August 1626 that it was decided to spread these forces among other counties, so the Devon gentry had fifteen months, in all, to provide for their billeting, frequently without payment. A year later they had to accommodate 4,000 soldiers intended as reinforcements for the Ile de Rhé. Two thousand of them embarked in November but as they were too late to be effective, they returned with troops who had seen service on the Ile de Rhé. This time steps were taken more quickly to remove the fit men, but the sick remained to be dealt with within Devon. However, this was only a brief respite as an abortive expedition to France, planned in the spring of 1628, brought some of this force back to Plymouth.[42]

Chudleigh was the most active of the gentry governors dealing with all these manifold demands upon Devon. His first task was as a commissioner for mariners, pressing sailors for royal service. On 1 April 1625 he had about 600 sailors assembled in Exeter, only to find it impossible to keep them together when news of James' death led to doubt about the validity of the commission. Chudleigh wrote from Ashton to Sir James Bagg, at midnight, in considerable anxiety over this situation and then later played his part in reorganizing the press.[43] This first experience as an *ad hoc* commissioner was to be straightforward compared with the duties entailed in his next appointment to a commission. On 16 May 1625 Chudleigh was one of the billeting commissioners ordered to receive and provide for 10,000 soldiers in the Plymouth area, this was, indeed, a formidable task as this figure was nearly equal to the population of Exeter at this period; the population of Plymouth was between 8,000 and 9,000. In addition to the sheer problem of numbers to billet, 8,000 of this force were recently impressed men, and these soldiers were usually the least valued members of a parish. On 23 May Chudleigh and the other principal commissioners were given powers of martial law to aid them in their task.[44] Chudleigh did not move immediately from Ashton to his manor of Stretchleigh and so missed some of the first meetings of the commissioners as they tried to deal with numerous complaints of the billeters and soldiers. He reached Plymouth at the beginning of June, about the same time as the commander of the troops, Sir John Ogle, who had very reluctantly accepted the position.[45] Almost immediately Sir John and the commissioners were disturbed by the rumour of a hostile fleet near Teignmouth, which caused the firing of some beacons. Chudleigh rode across south Devon to investigate and on 12 June was able to report from Powderham, on the Exe estuary, that no fighting had ensued when four English ships had been chased by twenty-five Flemish ones.[46]

Chudleigh may have delayed his return to the Plymouth area, as it was Sir John Ogle and John Bere, paymaster of the forces, who were the ones most often reporting on affairs during June and early July. The situation had eased somewhat as John Bere had brought an exchequer grant of £9,312 with him, so it had been possible to give the billeters their back pay. Also the troops were arriving more slowly than expected so the money for billeting could be diverted to meet some of the essential cost of fitting out the soldiers, some of whom were desperately in need of hose, shoes, shirts and even breeches. About £1,000 was being spent each week, a rate which meant that the money would last until the end of July.[47] At this time Sir John Ogle could report that there was, 'for the most part a good corresponding and friendliness hitherto between the country in-habitants and the soldiers' and that the commissioners had declared that they had never known 'the soldiers in better order and when there hath been so little occasion given for justice to use the sword'.[48] This rosy picture of affairs was not to last much longer and faded as the money ran out.

As Chudleigh did not attend the quarter sessions on 13 July, he may have returned to the Plymouth area before that date. He then found that a new problem had arisen for the commissioners, the fear of infection among the troops. There had been signs that spotted fever or even plague was present among the citizens of Plymouth in early May. Now ships coming into the harbour were bringing sickness, 'though we cannot say of great mortality . . . but some have died'; so it was evidently not yet diagnosed as plague. Chudleigh was closely concerned in this as his younger brother, John, was captain of one of the ships affected. He must have learnt from him that some captains 'in their care and charity' were lodging their sick men on shore under tents made of sails as the towns-people, understandably, were unwilling to house them. On 26 July Chudleigh and some other commissioners wrote to the Council accepting that it was 'approvable' for the sick sailors to be camped on shore while their ships were in harbour but 'must of necessity be altered if they shall be put to sea' and 'the sick men must be commanded to some other care and provision'. They required the Council's orders over this, especially as the numbers of sick were likely to increase as more ships arrived. They reminded the Council of 'the state of this town and country adjoining here, it is already filled with the land army – what detriment it may be to the whole service intended if any great infection (which God forbid) shall fall amongst them'. John Chudleigh soon wrote to Sir John Coke refer-ring to this recent letter written to the Council by some 'of the chief of the country' and hoping for a speedy order to deal with the sick.[49] His plea had no more success than his brother's. Sir George was to be faced with the personal risk of infection by the plague through-out the next two years as he worked as a commissioner and JP.

The Council had required the commissioners to report on the state of the army on 23 June, but they had been so occupied by 'the variety of business daily occurring to us' that they did not reply until 15 August. By then the money to pay the billeters had run out and so the commissioners' anxiety was growing. At this time there began to be a more outspoken tone in their letters to the Council; this development coincided with Chudleigh's regular attendance at their meetings so it may have been due to his influence. In one letter seven commissioners expressed their sense of injustice that the subsidy was to be collected even though the billeters had not been paid for three weeks:

When these complaints from soldiers and countrymen come unto us, we ease them the best we can by condoling with them, by promising them with all speed to advertise your honours of their conditions, by propounding the honour of His Majesty to see all those things reformed and by assuring them of His Majesty's royal nature and bounteous disposition to relieve the necessities of his most loving and loyal subjects and by these means we have hitherto kept them in good order and obedience. But where there are such powerful causes to produce extraordinary effects of ill consequences we appeal unto your honours most mature judgements whether our verbal promises so lately always to be accepted by them instead of real payment and satisfaction and whether we can with any conscience by martial commission punish such as out of necessities and want shall fall into misdeamours.[50]

They were clearly reluctant to use their powers under martial law to punish the billeters, though in no doubt that they had this power. This was to be one of the problems later voiced in the debates over the Petition of Right, that the presence of soldiers in the homes of civilians could make them subject to martial law.[51] The commissioners were prepared to use martial law to punish soldiers; they suppressed the one mutiny that occurred at this time by executing one of the ringleaders, chosen by lot according to martial law.

At the beginning of September Chudleigh with four other commissioners renewed their pleas to the Council:

The case stands thus, the poor Countryman is no longer able to entertain the soldier having already half starved his family to help the greedy appetite of the hunger bitten soldier: so the miserable billeter hath already in some places ... thrust the soldier out of doors. ... The soldier hath already broken out hereby to the taking away of the countryman's goods, robbing upon the highway and carrying away his sheep before his face and dressing this in the open view of the world ... the event we fear must follow ... that without some exceeding speedy course be taken both Army and Country will undoubtedly be consumed.

They went on to, 'humbly and importunately beseech your honours for the love of God, the good of our country, the saving of blood likely to be shed and the cure of our credit', to send them some considerable funds.[52]

This was the last letter directed to the Council at this time as the King with the duke of Buckingham and other members of the Council were shortly expected in Plymouth where they arrived on 15 September. The King went aboard many of the ships and took a review of the troops on Roborough Down. He knighted a number of army and naval officers, including John Chudleigh, but no evidence has been found of him having any contact with the hard-pressed commissioners.[53] Charles would have felt no responsibility for their financial difficulties; parliament had encouraged him to engage in war but then not granted sufficient funds, so the blame lay with them. He had to find an alternative supply and used his Council, held at Plymouth, to order a forced loan, and Sir George found himself, as a deputy lieutenant, required to select payers for this first forced loan. He had been the only deputy lieutenant among the signatories to the two outspoken letters quoted above. In view of the strength of the feeling demonstrated in them, Chudleigh may well have influenced the expressions of resentment in the letter of the deputy lieutenants which accepted the order to raise the loan. They were careful to select many of the donors from areas not affected by billeting.[54]

The problems of the commissioners were eased when the fleet sailed to Cadiz on 6 October, but nothing was achieved and only two months later ships began to arrive back at Plymouth with many sick soldiers aboard.[55] Chudleigh had left the Plymouth area before the expedition returned. The fact that there was now a definite outbreak of plague there may well have led him to go to Ashton, especially as his wife was imminently expecting another child. It was also during this period that he entertained Bishop Carey and his wife at Ashton.[56] Chudleigh may well have been thankful that he did not have to cope with the immediate problems of the commissioners which were even greater than those they had faced in the summer and autumn. This time they began with no money, no idea of how many troops to expect or how long they would remain, and now there was also this full-scale epidemic of plague.

Yet if Chudleigh put his family concerns before his responsibility as a commissioner in December and in January 1626, he made up for it once he returned to the Plymouth area. In his absence the commissioners had been through a confusing time. They acted on orders sent by the Council only to find these orders changed as the situation developed, with events in the West Country often running ahead of information available to the Council, with letters crossing, and military commanders and commissioners presenting differing views to the Council because of their different standpoints. The Council was indecisive about the movement of the troops and about the means of paying the billeters. At first they promised that payment would be sent to them, but they soon changed this to orders to use the forced loan, collected locally. This was to mean that the commissioners had to billet troops for six weeks before they had any of the loan in hand.[57]

On his return to Plymouth Chudleigh found that the commissioners were now to be in sole control of the billeting as all officers above the rank of captain had been gradually withdrawn. This change may well have been welcomed as the commissioners were now free to organize the billeting without having to cooperate with a military commander who did not share their local concerns.[58] After two months of confusion they could now see their task more clearly. They knew they were in sole charge of billeting approximately 4,000 men in Devon and nearby parts of Cornwall and for this they had received adequate power under martial law. Although their number included Cornish commissioners there is no evidence of any Cornishman attending meetings of the commissioners in 1626; Chudleigh's active colleagues were Devon JPs of the areas affected by billeting and some Plymouth JPs. One senior official remained to aid the commissioners, John Bere the paymaster of the soldiers. He drew up an account of the weekly payments (at the newly authorized rate of 3s a week) and on 16 March 1626 reported that two months' pay was now due. He had paid out all the money received, so far, from the first forced loan but it was 'very uncertain' when the rest would be paid. He kept expecting money from the Lord Treasurer but found 'no supply to come and our wants growing daily more and more'. As John Bere made no more reports from Devon, he probably left soon after the date of this letter. The Devon gentry leaders now had to deal alone with the serious problems caused by the failure of the Council to produce any more money for the billeting.[59]

One step that they took was to appoint Chudleigh as treasurer and paymaster for all the King's debts for clothing and billeting the soldiers. It was the deputy lieutenants, not the commissioners, who took this initiative. The first forced loan was the only immediate hope for supply for the commissioners and as this was organized by the deputy lieutenants, they were justified in making the appointment and choosing the only one of their number who was also a commissioner (apart from Sir William Strode who was about to attend parliament). The date of his appointment is not known but it may have coincided with Bere's departure.[60] That was also the time when Chudleigh became the most assiduous commissioner in attending meetings and signing letters to the Council.[61] The colourful language of the letters soon became reminiscent of that used during the previous summer when Chudleigh was also active, which underlines his influence. On 23 March they met at Plympton to avoid plague-infested Plymouth and wrote to the Council on the potential danger of the situation:

> And now it is come . . . that many of those on whom the soldiers are billeted seem plainly to protest that either they must thrust their wives and children out of doors or the soldiers for they cannot shift long for means to sustain them and we are daily informed of the increase of the sickness. . . . The clothiers that undertook the furnishing of the army with apparel, having finished their contracts . . . hold now the whole dead upon their hands not knowing what to do, in that they cannot have the return of the monies made good unto them . . . neither can the soldiers be exercised as was intended there being not sufficient means to repair their arms . . . the men being made rather worse than better being kept hitherto in a manner idle which breed soldiers misdemeanours.[62]

The fear that unrest among the troops might follow from inaction soon gained substance. On 4 April 1626 Chudleigh went to Plymouth to meet four of the commissioners resident there to discuss a rumour that some soldiers were determined to march on Easter Monday (10 April) to show the King their nakedness, if they were not clothed by then. The commissioners forwarded this report to the Council with their own comment, 'whereby it may be seen how the coals are akindling the which we are now assembled to quench'. They made the constructive suggestion that the subsidy being collected in Devon and Cornwall should be used to meet the needs.[63] They were getting used to the direct use of taxation with the first forced loan and were to press for the same principle to apply with the second forced loan the following year. The Council's reply concentrated on orders to prevent mutinous assemblies, but made no mention of a direct use of the subsidy, which might have removed the cause of the danger of mutiny but could have set a dangerous precedent. The commissioners acted on their orders and arranged watches to prevent troops gathering out of their quarters. When they reported their actions they also reiterated the need for money.[64]

Alone of the commissioners, Chudleigh rode from Plymouth to attend the Easter quarter sessions held at Crediton from 18 to 21 April. The minutes give no impression of the disturbed state of the county around Plymouth but it is hard to believe that Chudleigh would not have discussed the situation with other members of the bench. When he returned to the Plymouth area he found that no reply had been received to the commissioners' request for funds, so on 26 April they met at Plympton Maurice and wrote in stronger terms of their difficulties with the billeters:

> Whose clamour begin to be as vehement as that of the soldiers that are lodged with them. And although we have not quitted any course possible to take to hold them all contented; yet both the one and the other finding nothing else but words to follow, do begin to murmur and despair of anything and to continue to despise all that is spoken in that kind.

Six weeks passed and still no relief had arrived, so they wrote again but yet again received no reply.[65] There was a hint of desperation in their next letter which they addressed to Viscount Conway, the Secretary of State, on 29 June 1626:

> We had well hoped that the extreme necessities which we have at several times advertised your lordship with concerning the soldiers, billeters, clothiers, officers and plague should ere this have received redress or at least comfortable answers but hitherto we have failed of both which makes us to imagine that either our letters come not unto your hand or that you conceive it to be untruths and so not to regard them. We are constrained once again to protest that we have thus far done our best to satisfy all by our speeches, travels, purses and hazard of our lives further than this we cannot go and this we are no longer able to continue, the plague being already so far spread as we know not where to meet with safety. And we call heaven and earth to witness that we neither do nor have at any time written to your lordship any feigned fears but the very truth out of the sincerities of our hearts to His Majesty's service.[66]

This appeal to Conway fared no better than their earlier letters to the Council.

The danger of plague in Plymouth was an undercurrent to their letters, and on 8 July they were so 'frighted from all public meeting' that they met at Chudleigh's manor of Stretchleigh. They now resorted to some veiled sarcasm over what they supposed might be the Council's reaction to their letters:

> We doubt you continue to complain in regard of the fevers of the commissioners that subscribe them... But not to trouble your lordships too much with that which we have oft advertised, the officer is so discontented, the soldier so desperate, the clothier and billeter so impoverished as we instantly suspect by our next you shall hear of all to be in an uproar. Your lordships may at last think of it at your leisure which we desire the almighty to hasten you unto. In the meantime we will not fail on our part to continue as

111

heretofore our duties, though with the loss of our reputations and lives, as those that desire to approve ourselves true subjects to our king, lovers of our country and your honours.[67]

This profession of loyalty was really defeating the objectives of the commissioners. So long as the Council believed that they could rely on such service, they were not going to send the money, which they knew was needed but which they had not got. Parliament had just been dissolved without enacting the proposed grant of subsidies. The county was just about to receive a demand for a benevolence, equal to the proposed subsidies, to show their love and loyalty to the King. It is not surprising that Devon ignored that demand; the county was already showing their love and loyalty by their housing, unpaid, of the royal forces.[68]

It must have been some relief for Chudleigh and his father-in-law, Sir William Strode, to leave the struggles of the commissioners in the Plymouth area and go to a meeting of deputy lieutenants held on 12 July during the quarter sessions at Crediton.[69] They probably also attended the sessions (although the minutes do not list the JPs present) and were the source of the minute that some of the south division was greatly burdened with soldiers and 'divers places infected with the plague'. The contacts which Chudleigh and Strode maintained with the bench may well have been the genesis of the important meeting to be held on 29 July. Meanwhile, the meeting of the deputy lieutenants, called to deal with the routine organization of the militia, were faced with a rumour of an enemy fleet of 400 sail off Lands End. The meeting broke up to enable Chudleigh and Strode to ride back towards Plymouth to cope with the situation. When they discovered that the rumour was false, they were joined by Sir Francis Drake at Strode's house at Meavy to report to the Council. They used the reluctance of two discontented companies to obey orders to underline the danger which might have ensued if the attack had been genuine. They could now put a more effective kind of pressure on the Council than their recent pleas. They recommended the withdrawal of the troops from the West Country, considering it would be better to send the forces to areas which were not infected by the plague, 'and have not at all been charged with this most grievous lending to His Majesty of billeting his army without money'. A pertinent reminder that this was, in effect, yet another forced loan. They reminded the Council of the value of the West Country for overseas expeditions and considered, 'that after a breathing it may recover its wonted strength and willingness to do His Majesty service'. Ready money would be essential to move the army but the billeters might be willing to wait for payment, 'if they might find a present ease of their insupportable burden by the remove of the army'.[70]

The three commissioners sent their carefully argued case for the removal of the troops to the Council under the cover of a letter to Sir John Coke, the other Secretary of State. As he was a friend of Chudleigh, they evidently felt more able to express the depth of their feelings of abandonment:

> Much and often we have written to the body of the Council representing our desperate case to them as to our appointed physicians, but cannot receive from them so much as a cordial answer. By these enclosed we do expire our last gasps of hope, whereby you may expect the certain ruin of this country to approach, being possest at one time with the cold fear of foreign enemies, the burning heat of the devouring pestilenece and the strong convulsions of poverty and the unsatisfied soldier, and to these your own great judgement will easily add (as the worst of evil signs) an apparent distraction in the head by our rude and passionate letters.[71]

The county's leaders clearly felt that their task had become impossible and that the worst danger for the county would be if they lost control of the situation. They may well have hoped that this threat would achieve a response but the silence continued, their competence in managing for so long telling against this danger being believed. It was now that a different body of gentry governors took up the cause of the county, possibly impressed by reports they had received from Chudleigh at the Easter and midsummer quarter sessions. On 29 July, thirteen JPs, who may have been in Exeter for the assizes, decided to send Sir George to the Council. They wrote to the Council, claiming to have been critical of the commissioners as they could not believe that they had fully informed the Council 'of the miserable state of the Country', but having learnt that they had received no answer to their letters they decided to send:

> Sir George Chudleigh ... to acquaint you more particularly with our fearful and perishing condition, than can be done by letters. We most humbly and earnestly beseech your Lordships to vouchsafe yet at this last your most honourable and compassionate assistance in the speedy taking away of the intolerable fears and burdens from us.[72]

This manoeuvre worked. Chudleigh carried out his mission in a determined and outspoken fashion, his 'rude and intractable behaviour at the council board' evidently convincing the Council of the reality of the situation described in the commissioners' letters and the extent of their own disillusion with the task. At last, on 24 August, orders were sent to the deputy lieutenants as well as the commissioners to move the troops out of the county.[73]

When Chudleigh returned to Plymouth on 31 August he found that the Council's letter giving the commissioners detailed orders had arrived only two hours before him, so it was for him to initiate action. He wrote to Sir John Coke, recording how he and the rest of the commissioners had, 'set the business of the troops removing in so good a way as I cannot see how any let or hindrance can well fall'. They had a great deal to do: they had to collect the muster lists with the accounts for billeting, make fresh contracts with clothiers to replace those that had fallen through due to discontent at slow payment, and deal with officers offended at the order for constables to draw up their accounts with their creditors. This last matter seemed to be particularly troublesome as many of the officers felt it 'a great indignity unto them and some of them did not stick publicly to tell us so much'. This episode revealed an undercurrent of discontent in the relations of the junior officers with the commissioners: 'And in this dispute we were told . . . that in the present business of the removing the regiments we had respect only to the ease of our country and not at all to the captains. . . . They were at last pacified so as I hope you shall shortly hear of their quiet passage . . . to their new quarters.'[74] The departure of the troops reduced but did not end Chudleigh's service as a commissioner. He continued as the treasurer and paymaster for billeting and, later, as treasurer of the forced loan had the means to meet most of these costs.[75]

Chudleigh had spent six months engaged in exacting and frustrating work as a commissioner, often risking his life by remaining in a plague-stricken area. He had spent three days in the saddle to reach London and achieve a satisfactory response from the Council and then ridden back to cope with all the problems of moving the troops out of the county. After giving so much service to King and county, one might have expected him to lapse thankfully, into a quieter life. However, we now see a different side to the man. The adventurous spirit of his father lived on, and he had evidently impressed Coke, probably while he was in London, with his desire for active service. This led, in September 1626, to Coke securing from Buckingham an appointment for Chudleigh to the Council of War for a naval expedition to attack transports in Biscayan harbours. With hardly time to recover from one long journey, Chudleigh set out again from Plymouth and had reached Portsmouth by 14 September, where he found himself made welcome by the general of the expedition, Lord Willoughby. He embarked on his brother's ship and found John Chudleigh suffering from 'his wonted heaviness but I thank God upon my coming and my prevailing with him to take a little physic he is very cheerful and recovered.' He sailed from Portsmouth on 22 September but off the coast of Torbay he was persuaded by his brother to give up because of seasickness and 'a distemper I had taken with hard riding'. Although this was the public excuse given for him going ashore in Torbay, the obstruction he had met with in receiving and sending his mail suggests a stronger reason for his decision. He told Coke that:

[this] Confirms me in a conceit I had that some of the sea captains held me as a spy among them. .... I am satisfied that I had more reason to relinquish than to prosecute my intention for this voyage, yet I cannot choose but blush to think that I should not answer all points of your expectation but your honour knows that man's purposes are in God's hands.

Suspicion of his motives in taking part in this expedition evidently followed him after he landed at Torbay as:

Upon my coming on shore I found the noble Duke's honour and my own poor reputation much in question by my going. For some would have it that for my rude and untractable behaviour at the council board I was forced with this action by my Lord Duke and others gave it out that I had so much discontented the captains by that negotiation as I had withdrawn myself for fear of them. This last is ridiculous. But to the first wherein the Duke's honour is interested I shall give full satisfaction the next week at our general session.[76]

The suggestion that Chudleigh's adventure was a punishment rather than a reward shows that his countrymen did not regard him as one of the duke's partisans. Evidently, he satisfied quarter sessions of his probity as the meeting on 3 October ordered that he should receive £100 for his expenses on his mission to London.[77] This attempt to go on a naval expedition is an interesting reflection on Chudleigh's character. He was ready for 'the opportunity of my own experience', to leave all his commitments in Devon, both as a gentry governor and as a family man (he had eighteen children in all). The more adventurous spirit of his father had not been submerged by the routine of the administrator.

Chudleigh returned to the tedious duties which remained for the commissioners, even after the troops had departed. These centred on the problems of those who had contracted to supply clothes for the soldiers. The commissioners had tried to content the contractors but in October found they were faced with a new difficulty; the unpaid contractors were now being pressed by their creditors and one of the best contractors was even in prison because of his debts. The commissioners gave 'public and private warnings' that it would be 'ill taken' by the Lord Treasurer and the rest of the Council if contractors were molested by creditors when their debt was due to the King's service. Chudleigh wrote to the Lord Treasurer, the earl of Marlborough, on behalf of Mr Ball (the contractor in prison). It is, perhaps, significant of Chudleigh's new understanding of the national financial position, that he did not plead for money to pay the contractors but rather pointed out that the case against Mr Ball would be a 'leading case to the rest of the creditors of the contractors if your lordship and the rest of the lords do not resent it as a contempt and injury to His Majesty's service'.[78]

In spite of the problems with the contractors, Chudleigh enjoyed a partial lull in his public activities until February 1627. He did, however, keep his finger on the pulse of the county and was forming his own view of the current political situation. In December he expressed his view to Coke:

The stay of our goods in France on merchants here bears un-pleasantly and so much more hardly because the counter of French goods here carries no equality with their own in France. From our neighbour shires (possest with the soldiers from whom by your honourable favour and great pains we were happily freed) we understand of divers riots, murders and robberies committed by them, and our own people are not yet altogether out of the fear of the great subsidy, which, if it reach to them, being already so much exhausted, will certainly not be entertained without much dis-content. If the affairs of the state (as by the effects they seem) were not in a distraction beyond the apprehension of so weak a mind as mine, the faith and duty which I owe you would lead me to the boldness to offer you my poor thoughts towards a reestablishment, but I profess to God the courses taken are so far beyond my reach as I know not what to think will become of us if we fall not again and quickly to our old ways. God of his mercy grant it and put it into the hands of those that have power to do it.[79]

Chudleigh may have been implying a hope for another parliament in his reference to 'the old ways', this was sometimes code for a parliament.[80]

Chudleigh would have been well aware that the ground was being prepared for the collection of another forced loan, this may have been the levy he was referring to as 'the great subsidy'. He was among the loan commissioners appointed for the county in September 1626 who met the Council commissioners on 24 January at Tiverton.[81] Although details do not survive of those present, it seems almost certain that Chudleigh was one of them as the commissioners decided to send him as their ambassador to the Council, probably influenced by his success with the Council in getting the troops removed the year before. This time he had to argue the case for the loan being used to pay for the outstanding billeting costs in the county.[82] He succeeded in his mission and found himself appointed to receive the loan payments of both Devon and Cornwall. His warrant was dated on or before 3 March 1627 when the Council 'bad him heartily farewell'.[83] As the Council had accepted the direct use of the forced loan for the billeting costs it was logical to combine the duties of collector of the forced loan with those of treasurer and paymaster for billeting. As early as 21 April, Sir George was finding his duties arduous and sought the assistance of Sir John Coke, desiring his help, 'to free me of a part of those troubles ... a business not only laborious but very intricate'. In particular he found that the Cornish resented having a Devon treasurer and in this letter and one of the same date to the earl of Marlborough, the Lord Treasurer, Chudleigh asked for a Cornishman to replace him for the collection in that county. This was agreed and Sir Francis Godolphin took his place as Cornish collector on 2 May 1627.[84] Although Chudleigh was relieved of his duties for Cornwall, he continued as the collector for the city of Exeter as well as for Devon.

Chudleigh's account for the loan is dated from 19 January 1626 until 31 May 1628. This means that it covers the period of his employment as treasurer and paymaster for the billeting costs, which began over a year before his appointment as collector for the second forced loan. This account gives details of the amounts paid to the different hundreds for billeting; it shows that the whole of the south coastal region as far east as the Exe estuary was affected. It looks, therefore, as though the commissioners billeted troops where they would be most useful in case of any threat of invasion. The coordination of the two tasks of collection of the loan and payment of the King's debts avoided unnecessary discontent. Chudleigh reported to Marlborough that he had only attempted to collect from the areas which were free of soldiers, 'for with the billeters I have not thought fit to meddle till I had elsewhere gotten a sufficient sum fully to discharge them'.[85] He spent a considerable period in Exeter during the summer of 1627, possibly making use of the county's administrative facilities. His presence there would also have enabled him to receive the money from the city of Exeter, which had its own loan commissioners.[86]

When Chudleigh wrote to Marlborough on 23 July 1627 he hoped that he would soon be able to complete his account. However, new problems were about to descend upon the county, which would involve him in new orders and delay the collection. Continental war was once more to affect life in Devon. Relations with France had broken down and an expedition under Buckingham had landed on the Ile de Rhé on 12 July to relieve the French blockade of the Huguenots of La Rochelle. News of this reached Devon on 27 July when Buckingham's agent, Sir William Beecher, landed at Plymouth on his way to seek reinforcements from the Privy Council who, four days later, sent out orders to the lords lieutenant to raise 2,000 men.[87] Yet it was not until 3 September that the deputy lieutenants and JPs resident near Plymouth were told to expect these men by 10 September and ordered to billet them until they were embarked for the Ile de Rhé. These orders were passed on to them by Sir James Bagg, who, evidently, had grounds for thinking Chudleigh would not be prepared to serve but, in fact, he did join Bagg and three other JPs on 6 September to make the necessary preparations. These JPs wrote to the Council, from their meeting, showing their distaste for the task they had been given. This was a letter from men who had learnt from their earlier trials in billeting.

They did not hesitate to express their opinion, humbly but clearly, of the problems they faced. Some were created by the short time available to arrange the billeting; others by putting the whole burden on Devon and not following the usual precedent of involving Cornwall, for that 'we cannot but grieve exceedingly' and they 'entreated' the Council to send speedy orders to Cornwall to take their share of the billeting. They showed their doubt of the promise made to them that the costs would be paid by the Lord Treasurer and decided that, as they had 'full authority', they should take 'course for the raising of the full pay of these soldiers out of the whole body of this county, after the rate of 4s 8d a week'. Their letter showed the influence of Chudleigh in their request for the letter, promised by the Lord Treasurer that he would pay these billeting charges: 'otherwise we fear we shall find more difficulty in this business than ever we found the like', as the county had not yet been paid their earlier charges for billeting because of 'the backwardness of many to pay His Majesty's loans.[88] On the same day that he signed this letter to the Council, Chudleigh wrote to Coke reiterating some of these justified complaints but also mentioning his difficulties over the forced loan, knowing the disastrous effect these would have on the billeting as there was no 'hope that these parts about Plymouth will give cheerful entertainment to so many, they being yet unpaid of their former scores'. He begged Coke to get a pursuivant sent and so 'ease me your poor friend and servant of my intolerable treasurership which my fellows very gratefully left upon me as a reward of my service for them at the council board'. A pursuivant, Ralph Robinson, was sent and thus took some of the weight of the loan collection off Chudleigh's shoulders so that he could give more attention to the demands of the billeting.[89]

Chudleigh and his fellow billeting commissioners only waited until 26 September before they wrote to the Council again. The money was coming in 'so slowly and uncertainly' from the rate they had imposed, that they appealed for money to be sent to them. They also had a new anxiety lest Devon might be expected to make up the shortfall of 300 in the number of the troops who had arrived.

The long silence of the previous year was probably fresh in the JPs' minds when they asked for 'these and our former letters a perusal and such speedy and effectual answer as may be comfort'.[90] On 29 September they did receive a reply to an earlier letter which had been delayed a week in the post and this caused them (in their reply of 10 October) to, 'humbly beg your lordships pardon' for the 'great earnestness' in their last letter. They reported that they had been in touch with the deputy lieutenants of Cornwall, according to the new orders of the Council, and the Cornish had agreed to undertake some part of the task of billeting: 'But we most humbly intreat your lordships for the future that you will be pleased to allot to either county their duties apart.' This letter, inevitably, had a reference to the difficulty of 'billeting soldiers upon credit ... it is such as cannot be continual without great discontent to His Majesty's subjects and no less prejudice to his service it being the occasion of all disorders'. This letter added a postscript intended to make clear 'in the modestest manner some way that the charge of the country amounts to more than £400 by the week'.[91]

Chudleigh was probably present at the Michaelmas quarter session as two matters were raised which closely concerned him. One was an order for the forced loan commissioners to summon the non-payers who were referred to them by the pursuivant; the other was to approve the rate of 4s 8d for billeting the soldiers currently at Plymouth. The decision of the deputy lieutenants and JPs involved in billeting was supported by the rest of the bench. It was laid down that all in the county were to pay the rate and any who refused might have soldiers billeted on them and would be bound to appear at the next session. The JPs concerned in billeting were instructed to bring a true account of the expenses and return the overplus to the Christmas quarter session. Five of them, including Chudleigh, were present at that session on 10 January 1628.[92] This confirmation by the bench of the decision by deputy lieutenants and JPs to raise a rate on 6 September 1627 is important. The power to raise such a rate was claimed by deputy lieutenants but not by JPs (who could only have raised such a rate on the instructions of quarter sessions). With the exception of Sir James

Bagg, the others present on 6 September were all deputy lieutenants. In some counties the raising of rates by deputy lieutenants was strongly opposed and was condemned in the Petition of Right. There is no evidence of such opposition to the deputy lieutenants in Devon, possibly because they were ready to seek the agreement of the whole bench in such matters.

The fear, expressed in the letter of 26 September, that Devon might be expected to impress men as well as billet them was well founded. On 30 September the lord lieutenant forwarded the Council's order for 200 men to be pressed and sent to Plymouth by 1 November.[93] Yet those in charge of billeting at Plymouth had only received an order on 20 October to billet 150 soldiers from London who were also to be expected at Plymouth on 1 November; did these two orders presage further large-scale billeting in Plymouth? The JPs were obviously alarmed as they saw troops from other counties making their way to Plymouth, which was obviously to be the rendezvous for greater numbers than they had heard about. Their concern led to a meeting of eighteen JPs on 26 October. This is remarkable as it is the only known occasion when so many Devon JPs met outside the times of quarter sessions or assizes. The sheriff, John Northcott, was not present so the meeting may have been convened by the signatories most actively concerned in the billeting: Sir George Chudleigh, Sir Ferdinando Gorges and Sir William Strode. The JPs felt compelled:

> To make known the dangerous state we are like to fall into if these troops be not attended with a good sum of ready money both for satisfaction of late charge of 2,000 men now shipped which comes to about £2,500 and also for the weekly billet on these to come. We trust your lordships have not found such backwardness in our former service as shall draw us now into a suspicion of making feigned excuses. . . . We have done our utmost in the raising means to billet the foresaid 2,000 and so far failed as we are some of us deeply engaged both in our own purses and credits for the discharge thereof. And we are continually so molested with the cry of the poor billeters for present pay as our business is disturbed, our credit

lost with our countrymen and ourselves utterly wearied in the performance of this impossible service.[94]

In 1625–6 the commissioners struggled, isolated, for over a year before they were joined by the JPs in a protest to the Council. In 1627 they were united with the bench in speaking out after less than two months of this new experience of billeting without payment.

An undated, unsigned and undirected 'complaint of the intolerable burden laid on Devon and Cornwall by billeting soldiers upon them and not paying money' belongs to this same period. It can be dated fairly closely by its reference to the 200 men being levied in the county, these men were due at Plymouth on 1 November. In spite of Cornwall being included in this complaint, this was no united petition of the West Country. It bears all the marks of having been written by Devon's leaders, possibly at their meeting on 26 October. Most of its detail refers to affairs in Devon, but the strongest evidence that it was written in Devon is the grievance that Cornwall had not been required, at first, to billet any of the latest force, and when they were required to do so, 'their governors excused themselves by the smallness of their country and the poverty of their people'. This anonymous complaint was even more forthright in its opinions than the letters of the JPs. It held that:

> His Majesty's honour doth likewise suffer much in these penurious ways of billeting soldiers without money. What say the people 'will His Majesty make war without provision of treasure or must our country bear the charge of all England. It is not enough that we undergo the trouble of the insolent soldiers in our houses, their robbery and other misdemeanours but that we must maintain them at our own cost.' That sayeth the people. And the Lords have been at sundry times advertised of these things but it seemeth they are not believed or not remembered.[95]

The military commander, the earl of Holland, was now having to plead with Chudleigh and the other commissioners to billet the new levies arriving in Plymouth as the Council did not send any orders about these men until 4 November. When the orders did arrive, they also promised to send within ten days the £2,500 mentioned in the JPs' letter of 26 October, and they offered pacifying words to the gentry that His Majesty had been told of their efforts 'who take that service very graciously at your hands'.[96] Such soothing words were not likely to efface the impression of the King making 'war without provision of treasure'. Money was short not only for billeting but also for transports, provisions and payment of the soldiers; this meant there was a fatal delay in the despatch of the reinforcements which in turn led to the failure of the French campaign, as well as arousing resentment in the West Country. Buckingham could only hold the Ile de Rhé if he secured his position by capturing the citadel of St Martin which he had been besieging since mid-July. As his army became weaker, a French relieving force gained a bridgehead on the island and led to Buckingham making a desperate attempt to storm the citadel on 27 October. When this failed he had no alternative but to withdraw and, off the English coast, met the fleet commanded by Holland which had ultimately sailed from Plymouth on 6 November with the vital supplies and reinforcements. Buckingham ordered this fleet back to Plymouth and with it went some of the ships bearing the men who had fought through the summer campaign.[97] The duke showed his concern for his men by sailing to Plymouth and arranging to relieve the sick and wounded out of his own resources. Chudleigh and the other Devon commissioners made it clear to the Council in a letter of 20 November, that this aid was the only thing making it possible for them to deal with the returning troops. They had moved some of the most recently impressed men into more distant parts of the county so that they could accommodate the sick and weak near their landing point.[98] Relief, however, was at hand for the Devon billeters as the earl of Bedford pleaded their case at the Council of 21 November and it was agreed that the army should be moved out of the county.[99] This time army officers took a large hand in organizing the departure of the troops though Chudleigh was present at Tavistock between 17 and 20 December as one of those authorizing their movements. The result was that all fit soldiers, except for a force of 500 retained for a projected move to the Isles of Scilly, should have marched out towards Somerset, Wiltshire, Dorset, Surrey and Kent by 28 December.[100]

The county had a brief interval free of billeting when the major body of troops left, but even then they were still suffering from the aftermath of their presence. When the Epiphany quarter sessions received 'many earnest suits' from constables because of sick soldiers in their parishes, Chudleigh and five other JPs asked Bagg to send them confirmation, by return, that the duke would meet these charges. He did so and this enabled the bench to reassure the constables before they returned home from the sessions.[101] Nor was it only the soldiers who were sick, there was 'infectious sickness, which is no better than the plague, sweeping away many the prime of the people in all the places where the soldiers were billeted'. For Chudleigh himself there was still the problem of paying the billeters who were 'yet unsatisfied'. In the face of so many of the 'extra-ordinary burdens which heretofore and still these people groan under by reason of the soldiers', the gentry leaders must have been disheartened when new orders were sent, on 16 February 1628, to billet forces intended to relieve La Rochelle under the command of the earl of Denbigh, Buckingham's brother-in-law.[102] The organization of this expedition led to Buckingham being in Plymouth on several occasions early in 1628 and on at least one occasion Chudleigh raised with him some of the 'difficult and dangerous' tasks he and his colleagues were having to meet.[103]

Chudleigh was concerned in the billeting, but the main point of interest, so far as he is concerned, lies in the part he played during the aftermath of a mutiny by sailors at Plymouth. These men had been unpaid for nine months and were infuriated when they saw their 'best vituals being sold away'.[104] When the mutiny occurred Chudleigh was probably at Ashton, where his mother was on her deathbed, so presumably it was only the news of the mutiny which drew him to Plymouth to serve as a martial law commissioner. Before Chudleigh's arrival, one of the ringleaders, Robert Kerby, had been convicted on 20 March and condemned to be hung the next day. However, pressure of events led Denbigh to grant a stay of execution. There had been opposition at the court martial from one of the commissioners, Sir Ferdinando Gorges, thirteen captains had petitioned on behalf of Kerby and, most dramatically, when the gallows were erected for his execution, some sailors broke it down and threw it into the sea. They then tried to release the prisoners in the town jail but were driven off by soldiers on guard, and in the ensuing scuffle two mutineers were killed and several others wounded.

As soon as Chudleigh arrived, on 23 March, he met Sir Ferinando Gorges and Sir William Strode and together they drew up a statement against the execution of Kerby.[105] The statement questioned the commissioners' authority to exercise martial law over a sailor as their commission only referred to soldiers; they denied that Kerby's original offence had been mutiny and they considered that his breakout of prison was 'natural'. They argued that if the King's justice required punishment for the offence, then the mutineers who had been slain in the suppression of the mutiny should be seen as sufficient punishment. They considered it improbable that an execution now would serve as 'a profitable example'. All was quiet and there would need to be some 'new stir' by the sailors to make the execution 'politic' as it would be a 'great indiscretion in us now to provoke them to discontent by the execution of this man, of whose life they have hope by the delay'. These arguments were countered in an unsigned document, also dated 23 March. Denbigh was obviously confused by the contra-dictory advice he was receiving at Plymouth as he again postponed the execution. Chudleigh had returned to Ashton by 29 March in time to witness a codicil to his mother's will, and attend her funeral on 1 April.[106] He was back in Plymouth by 8 April and took action over billeting soldiers and, with the other commissioners, ignored an order to execute Kerby which had arrived in his absence. On 1 May the commissioners reported to the Council that Kerby had been reprieved by Denbigh because it was considered that his execution in the presence of the fleet would not advance the King's service.[107] One might interpret Chudleigh's involvement in the case of Kerby as showing his humanity and his perception of the feeling among the mariners; but one must not ignore the fact that the issue of martial law was currently under discussion in parliament where his brother-in-law, William Strode, expressed the fear of county governors that martial law might undermine their authority.[108]

The spring months of 1628 were a period of hectic activity for Chudleigh. The last week of March had seen him involved with the Kerby mutiny and attending at his mother's deathbed. When he returned to Plymouth at the beginning of April it was to deal with an order of 31 March to billet troops, recently billeted in Somerset and Dorset, but possibly the same men who had marched out of Devon in December 1627. Chudleigh may well have felt that nothing had changed when he and his colleagues were informed that the soldiers from Somerset and Dorset were in great want of clothes. They were also to receive 600 newly pressed men who should reach Plymouth by 12 April. This placed the commissioners in an unenviable position as a postscript to the orders required them to deal with the troops if Denbigh had already left, exactly what had happened. Chudleigh and Gorges were the commissioners who took the initiative and tried to prevent the advance of these new troops by writing to Buckingham. They pointed out that there were enough soldiers in the Plymouth area and the ones, in transit, would either 'devour the king's provisions which could be reserved for better use or else being discharged without money must needs spoil the country as they return'.[109] When Chudleigh broke off from these responsibilities in Plymouth to attend quarter sessions in Exeter, he found himself involved in more trouble over pressing, this time of sailors, which was really the duty of the vice-admiral or commander of an expedition, not the gentry. Bagg had complained at the lack of cooperation from the JPs in this task and Chudleigh was deputed to assure Bagg that all JPs were ready to assist in pressing mariners but, in view of the situation in Plymouth, it is not surprising that he added the pertinent proviso that someone be appointed to take charge of them.[110]

While Chudleigh had been dealing with billeting, he had also been completing his collection of the forced loan and was, at last, ready to discharge his account in London. The final meeting of the loan commissioners was held in Exeter at the end of the Easter quarter sessions, which Chudleigh had attended. This meeting completed 'the long and tedious business about the loan'. Sixteen loan commissioners signed a letter to the Council saying that Sir George, 'hath taken such pains as we hope will deserve His Majesty's and your lordships' approbation'. They asked for his speedy return, 'for we do assure your lordships in these troublesome times, there will be great need of him in this country there being so many of our principal gentlemen upon attending the Parliament'.[111] Chudleigh first returned to Plymouth and on 1 May reported, with other commissioners on their efforts to track down the sailors who had run away after the mutiny.[112] He then rode to London and discharged his account on 15 May and was paid £666 13s 4d by the Lord Treasurer in May 1629 'for his great pains and charges'.[113] Chudleigh's visit to London was at the height of the debate on the Petition of Right with its condemnation of the two matters which had governed his public life for the last three years, the forced loan and the billeting of soldiers. It is of interest to speculate that his presence in London, at such a time, would have made him fully aware, if he was not so already, of the extent of the opposition, nationwide, to those policies.

While Chudleigh was in London the earl of Bedford, 'one of the earnest ones for defence of the liberties', was ordered to Devon although he was 'not to know his commission till he gets there at which his family much perplexed'. Chudleigh would have learnt the reason for Bedford's departure to Devon when he was named on 19 May as one of the deputy lieutenants required to aid Bedford in billeting a force which was returning from La Rochelle, 'without doing anything'. Chudleigh probably returned to Devon promptly to aid his lord lieutenant, who had reached Devon by 23 May but, mercifully, the wind carried the fleet beyond Plymouth and so, this time, Devon was saved from more billeting.[114] Although some sick soldiers remained in the county, the summer of 1628 was to see the end of the labours of the leading gentry in billeting foreign expeditions. The testimonial provided by so many of Chudleigh's colleagues to the Council shows the esteem in which he was held, he

FIGURE 6 Francis Russell, 4th earl of Bedford, Lord Lieutenant of Devon
(Engraved portrait of Francis Russell from Clarendon's *History of the Rebellion*,
Volume 1, 1717, shelfmark 22856e. 80, opposite page 182. Bodleian Library,
University of Oxford).

was clearly now one of Devon's leaders even though they did not consider anyone was pre-eminent. Yet these years have also shown him to be the King's servant, accepting the lion's share of the trying and taxing tasks laid upon the gentry leaders in Devon. His criticism and even exasperation at the lack of support they received from the Council was confined to the practical aspects of fulfilling their orders, not to the policies behind them. This was in keeping with his opinion in the debate on foreign policy in 1624 that it was, 'improper for us to enter into all the Stratagems of a War: Unfit for this Place'. In his letter of December 1626 he had expressed the opinion that the affairs of the state were, 'in a distraction beyond the apprehension of so weak a mind as mine', so he may well have preferred to be the member of the gentry government who took most responsibility for dealing with the problems within the county while he left to some of his colleagues the task of opposing forced loans, billeting and martial law on the parliamentary stage.[115]

Chapter 7

Sir George Chudleigh:
Gentry Governor and Reluctant Rebel

The most significant parts of Chudleigh's career were spent in an environment of war. The last chapter detailed his work billeting the expeditionary forces leaving Plymouth but it only gave an occasional glimpse at the other side of Devon at war; the danger to its long, exposed coasts of possible foreign attack. Even after peace was made with France in 1629 and with Spain in 1630, the continuing continental war maintained a sense of emergency and kept the pressure on the deputy lieutenants to organize an effective militia. When war broke out against Scotland it became the deputy lieutenants' duty to detail some of the militia to leave for the north. Finally, some of them, including Chudleigh, accepted the orders of parliament to take the militia into action against the King. It was as a deputy of the King's lord lieutenant for Devon that Chudleigh responded to the orders of the Privy Council for the defence of the county until 1642, then his title remained the same but he became a deputy to the lord lieutenant, appointed by parliament and obeyed the militia ordinance of parliament.

Lords lieutenant were appointed by commission and their deputies were also named in them until the accession of Charles I when the lords lieutenant were given authority to appoint their own deputies. After the commission appointing Lord Russell in 1623, the only means of identifying Devon's deputy lieutenants lies in their names on muster reports or their signatures on letters.[1] Ten were named in Russell's commission and this probably remained the average number in office at any one time; thirteen more have been identified before 1642, replacing those who had died or become very old.[2] Chudleigh was not among the ten deputies named in Lord Russell's commission but he had joined the group of deputy lieutenants by June 1625.[3] There is no core body of material on the deputy lieutenants in Devon; no lieutenancy books survive nor extensive private papers such as those of Sir Thomas Jervoise in Hampshire. An account of their activities has to rely on the general orders sent from the Privy Council to the lords lieutenant, which were then passed on to the deputies in their counties. These orders often led to an immediate meeting of the Devon deputy lieutenants and a letter to their lord lieutenant or the Privy Council in response. These letters are usually the only evidence of their meetings and it is the signatures on these letters which underline Chudleigh's constant attention to these duties; he alone of the deputy lieutenants has been found signing all the sixteen surviving letters (John Bampfield, who signed thirteen, has the only comparable record of service). The letters reveal some evidence of regular meetings on the Thursday of the quarter sessions week, often at the Bear Inn in Exeter, in addition to meetings needed because of orders from the Privy Council. The only other major source of information on the deputy lieutenants are the orders sent by the deputy lieutenant, Henry Ashford, to his militia officers and to head constables, which will be examined in detail in the chapter on John Willoughby.

The office of deputy lieutenant had none of the ancient tradition attached to that of sheriff, nor the statutory authority given to the justice of the peace. It had only developed in response to the danger of invasion during the latter years of Elizabeth when many lords lieutenant were not resident in their counties and so deputies were needed to organize the militia. On the accession of the peace-loving James, the statute giving the legal authority for taking musters was repealed and for nine years little was expected of the deputy lieutenants. From 1613 the renewed threat from Spain led to the Council ordering steps to be taken to improve the state of the militia.[4] This was clearly very necessary in Devon as the lord lieutenant, the earl of Bath, reported that over half the militia of 5,000 men did not know how to use their weapons.[5] The Council continued to order musters to be held but it was not until 1621 that the deputy lieutenants were also required to organize training and to check the supply of arms. By then the outbreak of the Thirty Years War in 1618, even though England was not actively involved, had increased the awareness of the need for a militia for both 'inward rebellion and outward invasions'.[6] The Council took a constructive step to improve the trained bands in 1623 by sending out a manual, *Instructions for Musters and Arms and Use Thereof*, coupled with orders to hold at least yearly views and musters. This policy to improve the militia, started during the final years of James, had had the support of Prince Charles and Buckingham and was the beginning of the 'perfect militia' of Charles I.[7] In this task Chudleigh, as a newly appointed deputy lieutenant, would be closely involved.

The Council orders sent to the lords lieutenant in the early months of the new reign were pursuing two objectives. The first orders, of 10 May, aimed at increasing the efficiency of the militia, it criticised the deputy lieutenants for past slackness and required 'particular accounts' of their proceedings. The second letter, of 28 August, was influenced by the outbreak of war and contained detailed instructions for putting the county into a fit state to meet possible invasion.[8] T.G. Barnes thought that these orders were intended to create an atmosphere of imminent peril to assist the King's demand for a loan but, in Devon, the presence of the expeditionary force and alarms off-shore had already brought home the reality of war and of the need to secure the coasts.[9] Chudleigh and five other deputy lieutenants met at Plymouth Fort on 19 September to respond to the orders of 28 August. They produced detailed orders which were then considered at a further meeting, attended by three more deputy lieutenants, at Okehampton on 20 October. Some provisions in the first draft were dropped at this second meeting; in particular the one to make a roll of untrained bands and appoint captains to them; presumably, imminent invasion looked less likely by late October. The Okehampton meeting provided for the maintenance of the beacons and appointed two sub-committees to inspect the security of the north and south coasts. These were to organize the construction or repair of defences and select commanders of such bulwarks. Chudleigh was on the committee for the south coast, most of the nineteen named on the sub-committees were JPs or were later appointed to the bench. It is an indication of the authority the deputy lieutenants that they could assign duties to their fellow gentry, including JPs. They also dealt with other administrative matters, laying down the rates of pay for attendance at muster, ordering the recruitment of 100 pioneers for every regiment, and requiring 20 carriages to be available for each regiment with a carriage master, who was always to be aware of the location of these carts. The Okehampton meeting assigned a rendezvous to all the eight trained band regiments of the county in case of an attack, which they anticipated would be on the south coast between Plymouth and Exeter. In the event of any fleet approaching the coast, a pinnace was to be provided and two or three named billeting commissioners, including Chudleigh, were to use it to investigate the fleet.[10] The commissioners may have been assigned this task as none of them held a militia command at this time. Lord Russell forwarded the report of this Okehampton meeting to the Council, with the books of the muster master, which confirmed that the deputy lieutenants had managed to hold a muster that summer, in spite of the distractions caused by an expeditionary force in the county.[11] These muster books must have been the authority for the statement of 21 January 1626 that the strength of the Devon trained bands was 7,482 foot.[12]

The Council pursued their drive towards 'a perfect militia' by sending experienced sergeants into each county to assist the deputy lieutenants. These sergeants were on leave from the Low Countries and would have provided a more professional dimension to the training than was likely from the muster master.[13] When the customary orders were sent out to all the lords lieutenant on 21 May, they repeated their criticisms of the previous year about the slackness of deputy lieutenants in carrying out musters. This must have been galling to the Devon deputy lieutenants who would have been justified in thinking it was a considerable achievement to have held musters at all in 1625, in view of the disturbed state of the county. They now met, on 12 July, to try to organize musters with about 4,000 troops still billeted in the county. They also found themselves faced with orders, which must have seemed unreasonable, to report the colour of horses and to arrange to hold their musters on the same days as those in adjacent counties; an obvious attempt to prevent horses being shared by counties.[14] As Chudleigh and his colleagues met to act on the orders of 21 May they were distracted by news of a fleet of 400 sail near Land's End. Their reaction indicates the problems that would have occurred if the alarm had been genuine. Although they would 'labour to defend this country to the utmost of our powers', they needed to know who was in command of the billeted force in the county. They would have to use these men as well as the trained bands in the event of an invasion, but all their senior officers had been withdrawn. They also needed money to pay these forces, otherwise how could they be expected to maintain discipline among them?[15] The fleet off Land's End proved to be a false alarm, but fresh orders sent to all lords lieutenant on 10 July showed that the Council were anticipating imminent invasion. Members of the trained bands were now not to be allowed to leave their town or parish without licence from a deputy lieutenant; a command which underlined the requirement for them to be ready to rendezvous at one hour's notice. Officers and soldiers were to take the oaths of supremacy and allegiance. All able untrained men between 16 and 60 were to be enrolled so that they could be levied rapidly if necessary, these men were to be put under officers and provided with arms taken from recusants. The deputy lieutenants were only given a month to hold a review of all their trained forces and to report on their performance of all these additional orders.[16]

The orders of 21 May and 10 July were common to all counties, but on 15 July special orders were sent to Lord Russell on the action to be taken by his deputy lieutenants on the approach of an enemy.

They were to send 4,000 men to Falmouth, another 4,000 to Poole in addition to keeping 6,000 available to defend Plymouth. These numbers show that both the trained and untrained forces would have had to be mobilized. In addition, they were to be supported by 2,000 men from Cornwall, 3,000 from Dorset, 4,000 from Somerset and 4,000 from Wiltshire. Watches were to be kept and the coast was to be fortified.[17] The orders from the Privy Council had reached Devon before a number of JPs assembled in Exeter for the assizes and decided to send Chudleigh to the Council to argue the case for removing the troops from the county. Their letter detailed the 'many lets' which hindered 'that full performance' of the orders of the Council to review their trained bands and enrol the able untrained men. 'Amongst others shortness of time, the time of harvest, and the plagues everywhere dispersed', but it was 'the long continuance of His Majesty's army here without money' and 'justly discontented among us' which 'is such a terror to us'.[18] The JPs saw that the billeted troops were already hampering the ability of the deputy lieutenants to carry out the usual training of the militia and feared the effect of their presence if there should be an enemy landing.

Even while Chudleigh was labouring over billeting and the collection of the forced loan, he did not ignore his routine commitments as a deputy lieutenant. He was present at the meetings which ordered musters, requested artillery to be supplied to safeguard shore defences, and was even prepared to accept the minor task of reorganizing the watches at the beacons in his own hundred of Exminster. In 1628 he was among the deputy lieutenants who protested at the proposal to hold a muster of the troops of horse at Shaftesbury, nearly 100 miles away.[19] The following year the meetings to organize musters may also have been concerned with matters of wider significance. In September 1629 a rumour was circulating in the country at large that the deputy lieutenants of Devon intended to petition the King on behalf of the members arrested for opposing the dissolution of parliament and to ask him 'to halt innovations in the Commonwealth'.[20] It is not surprising if they petitioned on behalf of the arrested members, who included

William Strode, when the deputy lieutenants included both his father and Chudleigh, his brother-in-law. As regards innovations the one to which the deputy lieutenants are known to have objected was the Council's order to require the oath of supremacy as well as the oath of allegiance from participants at muster; this was an innovation to them as they did not conduct musters in 1626 when it was also required. In 1629 they maintained that the oath of supremacy was 'most unnecessary for the discovery of such as are ill affected' and considered that it should not be administered 'without an especial commission under seal'.[21] This refusal to require the oath of supremacy and the existence of a petition from the deputy lieutenants may be the background to part of an undated letter of Bishop Joseph Hall, which could well refer to repercussions from these two signs of protest. He wrote that, 'our western spirits are complained of as more stirring and apt to oppose the public ways of Authority, which is conceived as proceeding from some hidden leaven of puritanism.' There are grounds for dating this letter about this time and no other reason has been found to justify the comment.[22] Far from their opposition to the oath of supremacy being due to puritanism, it is as likely that the deputy lieutenants opposed it because of the Catholic associations of one of their number, Francis Courtenay, who was also a militia colonel. Whatever discontent the deputy lieutenants may have felt in 1629, it did not stop them organizing the musters efficiently. On 16 July Chudleigh and his colleagues ordered 'an exact view and muster of all trained forces of horse and foot before 10 September'. They then arranged to meet again at the Bear in Exeter on 17 September to compile the certificate of the muster to send to their lord lieutenant (who had now succeeded to the title as earl of Bedford). On this occasion they required the attendance of the captains of the horse with lists of their troops, the muster master with a perfect muster roll and list of all defaulters, and they also required the defaulters to be present. They reported to the earl of Bedford on 9 October that 6,403 men had mustered in seven regiments of foot, made up of 2,425 pikemen and 3,978 musketeers.[23] The achievements of the Devon deputy lieutenants was in marked contrast to those of

Cornwall where factious differences brought their office into disrepute and weakened their militia.[24]

For four years Chudleigh had given service to the King in support of his ill-judged foreign policy and combined this with attempts to minimise the effects of those policies on his county. After the strain of those years, Chudleigh enjoyed a comparatively quiet interlude in the early 1630s. The record of his attendance at quarter sessions and his signing of recognizances suggests that he was seldom out of the county and that his life revolved round the county government. At this time he was sometimes on the bench with Bishop Hall, dealing with problems such as the shortage of grain in 1630 and the relief of distress caused by plague in the Exmouth area in 1633.[25] There are no grounds for thinking that he would not have approved of Hall's efforts to prevent religious discord developing in the county, in contrast to the neighbouring bishopric of Bath and Wells where twenty-five clerics were suspended for not reading the Book of Sports. In his visitation charges Hall attacked schismatics but not puritans, he ordered the Book of Sports to be read but did not suspend anyone who did not do so, and he was more concerned with the state of church buildings than with the position of the communion table.[26] The 1630s were not, then, a period when Devonians were forced to show their religious colours. With that cause for controversy left to one side, the only murmur from the gentry leaders in the earlier part of the decade was over the Books of Orders, and here the complaint was in having to produce certificates, not over the actual orders which they were already largely fulfilling. As Chudleigh wrote with the other JPs of his sub-division, 'the diligence which we have formerly used in His Majesty's service cannot be much improved by the survey of any eyes besides those of our consciences.'[27]

Although England had been at peace since 1630, the King's hope of securing the restoration of his brother-in-law to the Palatinate drew England into alliances with countries who remained at war, in particular with Spain. Trading disputes with the Dutch increased the common ground with Spain and led the King to hope that development of the navy could serve three purposes; free the channel of pirates, curb the growing maritime power of the Dutch, and provide a bargaining counter for Spanish support for the Palatinate. Yonge's diary shows that it was common knowledge in 1632 that ships were being built to combat the Dutch fishing fleet; such information on possible conflict may have led Devon's deputy lieutenants to continue mustering their militia without specific orders from the Council. Churchwardens' accounts provide evidence of a general muster being held for three days in 1633. Their action was in marked contrast to that of the deputy lieutenants in twenty-one other counties who were berated in 1634 for not producing certificates or muster rolls for 'these three years past, whereat we cannot but much marvel'.[28] Yet with such a vulnerable coastline, the Devon deputy lieutenants had every reason to prepare to meet alarms such as the one which occurred in 1635 when a fleet of 12 men-of-war anchored in Torbay. They proved peaceable, but the deputy lieutenants had considered mobilizing six-or seven-hundred men and exercising them but they had hesitated to do so without express command. They sought instructions from the Council for similar occasions in the future.[29]

Their own assessment of the need for an improved navy might have reconciled the gentry leaders to a demand for ship money in its traditional form but not to the new form it took in a writ which reached Devon at the end of 1634. This caused the Epiphany quarter sessions 'to petition the Board about the business for the shipping'. Further evidence of this petition rests on the work of Lady Eliot-Drake, who, unfortunately, destroyed many of the Drake family papers when she had completed her work on the family. She claims that a letter was composed by Chudleigh and signed by fifteen gentlemen in protest at ship money being extended to inland towns. It asked 'that these towns might be spared the tax' which was a 'novelty'. This letter is said to have been 'very ill taken' by the Council who summoned Chudleigh and five other JPs before them. This statement is substantiated by the presence of Chudleigh and four other JPs at the Council meeting on 1 March 1635. They had been sent for by warrant and attended for some time before they were discharged on a petition being presented and signed by them.

Although Chudleigh and his colleagues objected to the extension of ship money beyond the port towns, there is no evidence of them actively opposing the later collections from the whole county, which were among the most complete in the country.[30]

The urgency implied in the demand for ship money may well have prepared Chudleigh for the tone of the muster orders of 27 April 1635. France had now entered into an alliance with the Dutch and was about to declare war on Spain, so it was not surprising that these orders were reminiscent of those at the beginning of the reign in citing the dangers from abroad. In addition to the usual orders for the trained men, it required the enrolment of untrained men aged between 16 and 60.[31] The Devon deputy lieutenants acted rapidly and were able to report on 19 June that musters had already taken place in Whitsun week (17–24 May). They had also ordered beacons to be strengthened and had assigned regiments of trained militia to their rendezvous in case of alarm, yet this was not just a routine report of orders sent out. The deputy lieutenants had gone into detail over the supply of soldiers with powder, match and bullets and found that this was short because the towns had neglected to renew their magazines after the fleet had taken their supplies. After the main report of the deputy lieutenants, a smaller group, including Chudleigh, sought Bedford's approval for changes they had made in the overall command of the militia to replace dead officers. Sir Ferdinando Gorges was Marshal of the Field, Sir Edward Giles colonel general and Sir George Chudleigh, sergeant major general (all deputy lieutenants); Walter Yonge was quarter-master general, and the corporals of the field were William Cary, Humphrey Prouz, Robert Savery and John Cloberry.[32] This is the only evidence found of Chudleigh holding a militia command, which would have made him third-in-command of the trained bands with two experienced soldiers, Sir Ferdinando Gorges and Sir Edward Giles senior to him. This is the only detail found of this command structure so Chudleigh may well have held the office for some time. Little is known of his early career but his period of education abroad may well have included some military service. This would have been in keeping with his appointment as the sergeant major general of militia and his later service as a parliamentarian general. In 1638 he added command of the regiment and horse troop of tinners to his other duties, this may imply that his lands included tin-mines.[33]

Devon's deputy lieutenants had a good record of carrying out Council orders to muster and exercise their trained bands yet, so far, they had not been in action. The possibility that this would change occurred with the King's decision, in the summer of 1638, to overcome Scottish opposition to his policies by an English conquest. News of preparations for war had reached Devon by July 1638, so the deputy lieutenants were well aware of the reason for the orders for a special muster, which they received on 24 November.[34] Chudleigh was the most experienced deputy lieu-tenant and the highest ranking militia officer present when they met on 27 November and so he had the major responsibility for drafting the succession of orders which came from this meeting. All trained forces were to be mustered on 11 December and any 'weak or insufficient officers and soldiers (if any be)' replaced; defective arms were to be repaired; officers were to see that their soldiers were 'well and carefully exercised monthly … according to wonted orders in that behalf'. Colonels were given the place of rendezvous for their regiments in the event of the firing of beacons or on orders from deputy lieutenants, who still geared their orders to repulsing a coastal attack even though Scotland was the immediate enemy. Other orders were sent to head constables to ensure that they had their beacons in good order and that they were ready to assist at the muster on 11 December, when they were to see that the petty constables brought lists of all fit, untrained men to the captains 'to make soldiers'. The next day the deputy lieutenants, led by Chudleigh, informed their lords lieutenant of the action they had taken and gave a report on the condition of the militia. The trained bands were in a reasonable state of readiness with able and well disciplined soldiers, the untrained men were listed under captains but they were not well armed, the magazines were 'indifferently well stored' and 'great complaint be made unto us both of the difficulties and prices in procuring of powder'.[35]

The deputy lieutenants arranged to meet on 22 February 1639 in case there were further orders from their lords lieutenant. Only Chudleigh and Bampfield attended, because of 'the present sickness of some of your deputies and the great occasions of others' but perhaps also because the urgency had lessened by then as 'the general intelligence' gave hope 'that none of the trained troops will be employed in the intended service'. Chudleigh and Bampfield were disturbed at the way their report on defaulters at the muster on 11 December had been handled. The worst offenders had been let off and instead those with enough money to pay fines had been charged. They felt

> This has rendered us of ill savour to our countrymen ... being accounted men who do our business with as little justice as fear of inconveniences. [They hope that] we ourselves may not wholely lose our powers to do his Majesty service by suffering too much shame and disgrace, we humbly implore the Lords' speedy endeavours to withdraw the messengers hence, lest we happen to impoverish the country instead of reforming it, and make them really unable that were before but unwilling.

The gentry leaders had claimed several times in the 1620s that they were losing credit with their countrymen because they had not the means to pay the billeting charges but it is difficult to find evidence that this was really the case, it may just have been part of their special pleading for funds. Their resentment now of being put in a position of 'ill favour with our countrymen' was different. They were the ones who had sent in the lists of defaulters and so might well be the ones blamed when feelings were so strong that doors were barricaded and mastiff dogs set on the royal messengers who were collecting the fines.[36]

Chudleigh and Bampfield's hope that the trained bands would not be needed outside the county was soon dashed. On 17 January 1639 the Council of the North had proposed that an army of 30,000 should be provided out of the trained bands; this was about one-third of the total number of the trained bands recorded in 1638. At the end of February Devon was told to have 2,000 men, roughly one-third of their trained bands ready to march to a rendezvous.[37] These forces were normally exempt from distant service so selection was another difficult task for the deputy lieutenants. In May 1639 Chudleigh and his colleagues reported to the Council that they had responded to the February orders and had 2,000 foot soldiers and 63 horsemen in readiness. In accordance with their instructions they had allowed pressed men to pay for a substitute, at the rate of about £5 each. They were distressed to learn from the Council that this had led to 'great and intollerable exactions' and they asked for the assistance of the Council's informants 'in a cause so near concerns us'.[38] Once again the deputy lieutenants were on the defensive, trying to clear their reputations. Chudleigh and Sir Thomas Drew investigated some of the accusations, one of which concerned Sir Hugh Pollard, a deputy lieutenant though not a JP but, possibly awkwardly, a distant relative of Chudleigh. Sir John Pole and John Bampfield later joined them in sending details of their findings to the Council. They wished their lordships to interrogate the informer as 'we yet groan under the bruit of this corruption'. They acknowledged that they would be 'very unworthy' of their places 'if we should prove any way guilty of this accusation'. They hoped that their lordships' justice would 'clear our reputes, cheer us in our duties and encourage others to observance . . .'.[39] In spite of the efforts of Chudleigh and his colleagues to detail men for the Scottish war in the spring of 1639, there is no evidence that any of them left the county before the first Bishops War ended in June with the Pacification of Berwick. An indication that Chudleigh had little enthusiasm for this war was his refusal 'to make trial of his good affection' by responding to the Council's request in April to contribute to the expenses of the northern expedition. He claimed he had contributed in another way, possibly by the personal expenses he incurred in raising the force in Devon.[40]

Soon after it was decided to renew the war against the Scots, writs went out in December for a parliament; not to consult with it, but 'to make trial of it' and trust that it would prove its loyalty with financial grants.[41] It is surprising, at first sight, that Chudleigh did

143

not seek a seat in this first parliament for eleven years, nor for the Long Parliament which followed in November 1640. Yet this was also true of nearly all Devon's leading gentry who had provided the strong county government of the last fifteen years. Walter Yonge was the only long-standing JP to serve in either parliament; many of those who did sit were sons or younger brothers of past or present JPs. Many well-known Devon names sat on the parliamentary benches for the county, William Strode, Edward Seymour, Thomas Wise, Sir John Northcott, Sir John Bampfield, John Maynard and Sir Francis Drake but these men had virtually no experience of county government. It is possible that the long years of service within the county had increased the sense of the importance of that duty for the leading governors of the county and reduced the desire to assume one that had become unfamiliar. Was this why Chudleigh did not seek a parliamentary seat or does his career up to 1640 reveal other reasons? When he had been a member in the early 1620s, he had followed a moderate line rather than pursuing any extremes; prepared to express a definite view over taxation but regarding policy as a matter for the King and Council. When he passed a vacant burgess seat on to his son for the parliament of 1626, he hoped that there would be 'such unanimity between the State and the House of Commons as from some private occasions I should now gladly be a spectator and give my son a little breeding there'. Evidently, he looked on parliament as a place for common endeavour not for conflict. When he was in London, during the heated debates on the Petition of Right, this view must have been shattered and he could well have felt that words were not achieving as much for his countrymen as his careful coordination of collecting the forced loan and paying the billeters. He objected to money being raised by forced loans rather than granted by parliament, he expected parliament to receive petitions but he was ready to trust the King's words. He may have felt that the opinion of Bishop Hall, expressed in a 'passionate' letter received by the Commons while Chudleigh was in London in May 1628, echoed his own view: 'fear not to trust a good king, who after the strictest laws made, must be trusted with execution'.[42]

Chudleigh's leading position in the county rested on the authority he had received from the King, the source of all secular authority. He owed his allegiance to the King and endeavoured to reconcile the welfare of his countrymen with the needs of the King. Whether as JP, deputy lieutenant, militia sergeant-major general or specially appointed commissioner, he had looked to the interests of his countrymen as well as his King. When grievances occurred he tried to overcome them; he petitioned against the unfair development of ship money in the first writ, he stopped unjust treatment of defaulters from musters and investigated heavy payments made to secure a substitute for impressment. Chudleigh with some of his colleagues tried to prevent secular grievances fermenting from neglect, while Bishop Hall smoothed over religious differences by not enforcing ecclesiastical innovations. As parliament was called to meet the King's financial needs for the Scottish war, Chudleigh's knowledge of earlier parliaments would have told him that there would be a demand for redress of grievances before supply. If he sat in parliament, his status within the county would make him the spokesman for Devon's grievances; could he reconcile this with the allegiance he owed the King, with his position as the King's most active servant in the county and with his labours to minimise grievances within the county?

If that was Chudleigh's standpoint in the spring of 1640, did it change during the next two years? Parliament was dissolved on 5 May but convocation continued and issued Canons on 16 June which Bishop Hall considered destroyed the 'peace and comfort' of his diocese, 'ending the general unanimity and loving correspondence of the clergy'. Chudleigh and his colleagues meeting at the summer assizes decided to petition the Council against the Canons and thirty-eight gentlemen, including Chudleigh, signed the petition.[43] Their objections centred on the oath which the clergy had to swear that they took willingly and without mental reservation, especially as an 'etc' implied more than was expressed. They accepted that the clergy should acknowledge that the doctrine of the Church contained 'all things necessary to Salvation', but strongly objected to the clergy being required to swear that they

145

would never consent to any alteration in the government of the Church as it was established. They maintained that this contradicted the oaths of allegiance and supremacy, which the clergy had already taken, as it deprived the King, in parliament, of the power to annul any part of ecclesiastical discipline. It was also:

> A flatt band against the power of Parliament because the Clergy can constitute no canons, much less make or impose new Oaths, unless the Parliament confirm them; and therefore they think it a Project to suppress all Parliaments for ever.

The Devon gentry did not only think this oath damaged the power of parliament but also that of the King; they argued 'that it clips the wings of royal prerogative and spiritual supremacy, barring his Majesty and his successors from altering anything in Church Government either by Synod or Convocation or Parliament'.[44] In supporting this petition Chudleigh was still the King's loyal servant but his support also shows that he placed great importance on parliament as an institution, even though he was not prepared to seek election himself. It was drawn up before the Long Parliament was summoned on 24 September, at a time when there must have been anxiety over the future of that institution after the prolonged period without parliament and the brief meeting of the Short Parliament.

The trained bands had been weakened in personnel and arms by pressing men from them, so Chudleigh and four other deputy lieutenants met on 2 September to order a general muster of these reformed trained bands. At the same meeting they wrote to the Earl Marshal raising a matter of great local concern: how would the trained bands, who were waiting to be ordered north, be paid once they had left the county? Clearly, they expected the King to pay these charges, 'according to custom and His Majesty's gracious promise by lords of His Majesty's Council'. The reply came from the Privy Council that it was the custom and law of the kingdom for every man to serve in the common defence in a time of actual invasion and as those in the north were doing so at their own charge, the men of Devon were expected to do the same.[45] This alarmed the deputy lieutenants who raised the matter at the Michaelmas sessions, showing again the close interlocking of the deputy lieutenants with the bench. Chudleigh was the first name among the twenty who signed the letter to the Council, they questioned both the precedents and statutes on which this Council order was based and also pleaded that the state of the county, 'much impaired by pirates and great impositions', would make it impossible for them to meet the cost of the trained bands which they estimated would be at least £3,000 weekly, not counting charges for horse troops. They hoped that as parliament was now meeting agreement would quiet all disputes 'about these necessary services'.[46] Chudleigh also supported another petition drawn up this autumn. This time it was from the freeholders of the county and had thirty-two signatures. It was presented in the Commons by the knight of the shire, Thomas Wise, who said that it contained some of the general grievances of the kingdom as well as some concerned with the Stanneries, another indication that Chudleigh may have had an interest in tin-mining.[47]

There is little evidence of Chudleigh's activities over the next eighteen months apart from his duties as a JP, yet it was apparent from the very first meeting of quarter sessions after the opening of the Long Parliament that these duties would now be affected by orders coming from the House of Commons rather than from the Council, evidence of where the decisions were now being taken. On 7 December the Commons ordered all JPs to require church-wardens to present the names of recusants to them so that they could proceed against them. On 29 December the Commons required them, 'to inquire into the great scarcity of preaching Ministers and to consider some way of removing Scandalous Ministers'. This was not a true description of the Exeter diocese under Bishop Hall, who allowed frequent lecturing and had had to answer for his actions on this matter to the King on three occasions. Even so, quarter sessions immediately set up a sub-committee of JPs, which included Chudleigh, to meet on 28 January to receive 'information sealed up' and pass on recommendations to the knights and burgesses. Future royalists and parliamentarians were prepared to serve on this committee, supporting the view that religion was not yet a divisive issue on the bench; one of Chudleigh's colleagues was William Peterson, Dean of Exeter and Hall's son-in-law, who had been threatened by Archbishop Laud when he tried to leave convocation before the Canons were issued.[48]

While Chudleigh appears to have remained quietly in Devon during 1641, his son James became involved in the army plots as a messenger for officers who were discontented over the Commons' decision to pay the threatening demands of the Scots army rather than pay the English one.[49] The activities of his son may have given Chudleigh some personal insight into the tortuous web of negotiations which went on before a treaty was ratified with the Scots during the King's visit to Edinburgh in August 1641. Scottish affairs were kept to the fore in Devon by the parliamentary order to have a solemn day on 7 September to celebrate the peace between England and Scotland. A sermon in Exeter Cathedral by Joseph Hall would always have drawn a large congregation and this occasion was one which would almost certainly have been attended by Chudleigh and his fellow gentry leaders. Hall drew the lesson that had been learnt from the bloodshed and cost of even 'this little glimpse of a dry war ... The anguish of this very touch is sufficient to make us sensible of the torment of the full shock of a destructive war'. After this reference to the Scottish war, Hall did not concentrate on celebration of a peace achieved but urged the need to pray and work for real peace for 'surely, if ever any nation had cause to complain, in the midst of a public peace, of the danger of private distractions and factious divisions, ours is it'. He appealed to his listeners:

> I know I speak to judicious Christians. Tell me whether you ever lived to see such an inundation of libellous, scandalous, malicious pamphlets, as have lately broke in upon us: not only against some particular persons, which may have been faulty enough; but against the lawful and established government itself; against the ancient, allowed, legal forms of divine worship.[50]

Propaganda from many sources must have left Devon's leaders confused over the national state of affairs and what actions they should take. The Protestation Returns had shown that recusancy was not a problem in Devon, yet rumours of popish plots evidently stirred them to act at the Michaelmas session, and they ordered the immediate disarming of popish recusants.[51] When news of the Irish rebellion reached Devon it therefore confirmed their fears of papist danger in the county. The passing of the Grand Remonstrance in November and the demonstrations in London in December led to the Epiphany session assembling in an atmosphere of petitioning. They knew that one petition had already been sent to parliament from the knights, gentlemen and yeomanry of Devon and they had before them petitions from Plymouth, Tavistock, Totnes and Dartmouth, so it is not surprising that they decided to send the towns' petitions with one from quarter sessions to the King and both houses of parliament. Chudleigh with Sir John Pole, John Bampfield and Arthur Basset were entrusted with the petition, one of the first of the thirty-eight county petitions sent to Westminster early in 1642.[52]

The petition to Parliament drew attention to the suffering of the port towns and to the effect on their trade of Turkish pirates, the Irish rebellion and 'London's Distraction'. Yet these were 'the least-feared Calamities' nor do:

> The Flocks of poor Protestants coming from that Kingdom ... so much affright them with the Charge of their Relief, as the threatening messages they bring from their wolvish Enemies, that the Bounds of that Kingdom shall not limit their malicious Tyranny. To these they add the Popish plots by your Wisdom and Vigilancy already discovered .

Quarter sessions laid the blame for this situation on 'the Practices of the Popish Lords and their constant Adherents in most of their Votes the Prelates, in the House of Peers', and begged that 'your Honours would ... employ your Endeavours to our most Gracious King, to exclude Papists from His great Affairs and His Prelates

149

from Temporal Jurisdiction'. They informed parliament that the bearers of this petition were also taking a similar one to the King, confident that the result would be:

> Instead of Distraction, Unity, for Remoras, Celerity; for Misunderstanding, Correspondency; And by the Mercy of God upon his Church and People, and upon the best of Kings their supreme Governor, Prerogative and Privilege will kiss each other, when His Majesty shall think it His greatest Honour to grant your just Privileges and you acknowledge it your best Privilege to enjoy the Benefit and Glory of His due and Princely Prerogative .[53]

As quarter session lasted from 11 to 14 January, this petition was almost certainly drawn up in the knowledge of the King's attempt to arrest the five members on 4 January; this would explain the need for the special plea for 'Prerogative and Privilege' to kiss each other in the face of the King's assault on parliamentary privilege. The petition of Devon's quarter sessions was an immediate reaction to the foremost news of the day, and to an event which had once more brought Chudleigh's brother-in-law, William Strode, into the centre of political controversy. Yet it was phrased in terms which, unlike most of the county petitions of this period, showed that Devon's governors saw the urgent need for the restoration of some trust between the King and the leaders at Westminster. Their decision to send a petition to both the King and parliament was another way in which their petitioning differed from other counties and this also underlines their objective of reconciliation.[54]

When Chudleigh and his fellow envoys reached London, they were admitted to the Commons on 24 January and Sir George made a short speech and then delivered two petitions to parliament, one from quarter sessions and the other from the city of Exeter. Devon's envoys sought the assistance of the new earl of Bedford to introduce their petition into the Lords. Bedford did this on 25 January and the Lords thanked the petitioners for their 'good Affections to the King, Kingdom and Parliament' and promised that they would take the petition into 'speedy consideration'. The King had retired to Windsor and no evidence has been found of Chudleigh delivering the quarter-session petition to him[55]

Chudleigh's presence in London at this time must have made him aware of how wide was the difference between the view of the political situation in the capital and in the country. In Devon they might fear the dangers to their coasts but there is no evidence that they had any thoughts of civil war; but in London Chudleigh found the forces of the city guarding parliament and that 'divers thousands' were coming out of Buckinghamshire to defend their member (John Hampden). With the capital under the control of forces which would not obey the King, Chudleigh must have seen that civil war was a real possibility.[56] He must also have heard of changes likely to come over the county militia, which would affect him personally. A Commons' committee had already resolved that lords lieutenant and deputy lieutenants should be named by ordinance in parliament and the earl of Bedford was nominated lord lieutenant of Devon and Exeter on 10 February.[57] With the passing of the militia ordinance on 5 March Bedford had the authority to appoint his deputies and send orders for the militia to be trained and put in readiness. While he awaited developments Chudleigh returned to his ordinary duties as a JP and was present at the Easter quarter sessions, attended by some who would soon find themselves fighting on opposite sides. He also acquired an additional task as a commissioner distributing funds collected for the relief of the Irish. With the 'flocks of poor Protestants' arriving from Ireland and now depending upon 'Christian charity', Devon gave generously and had contributed £3,000 by May 1642.[58]

The first clear evidence that Chudleigh was prepared to act upon the militia ordinance was on 31 May when Bedford informed the Lords that his deputies had met and prepared for the service. Among these deputies were Chudleigh, Sir Peter Prideaux, Sir John Pole, Sir Nicholas Martin, John Bampfield and his son, Sir John. They hoped that their progress would answer 'the loyal Defence of our dear Sovereign, His Parliaments and Kingdoms', yet the royal proclamation of 27 May had expressly forbidden any subject obeying the ordinance of parliament without the consent of the

King. Although these Devon deputy lieutenants had shown their readiness to obey the militia ordinance, the Commons decided to strengthen their hands. They had already required Bedford to appoint one of their number, Sir John Bampfield, as a deputy lieutenant, they now ordered him to remain in Devon. They followed this on 20 June by sending another MP of a Devon family, Sir John Northcott, to join them. On 4 July the Commons ordered these two MPs with Chudleigh and Sir Peter Prideaux to advance the Nineteen Propositions in Devon.[59]

On 12 July Chudleigh attended quarter sessions for the last time. Only eight JPs were present and, with the exception of Humphrey Prouz, they all, initially, supported parliament. This quarter session decided to present petitions to the King and to both Houses of Parliament. Their petition to the King voiced their regret that the breakdown in relations between the King and parliament,' have bereaved us of the fruit which we were ready to reap'. The one to both Houses of Parliament showed that they still hoped that differences could be reconciled 'by the unity of king and Parliament, unity in religion, unity in loyal affection to His Majesty's will, according to our protestation, by God's mercy keep us still in peace and charity'.[60] These petitioners were putting forward a final plea for peace, but this did not mean they would stand aside if war became inevitable. On the same day that he had attended quarter sessions, Chudleigh met with the two deputy lieutenants from the Commons and sent out orders for officers of the former trained bands to receive their commissions in the militia at the New Inn in Exeter on 14 July. When many did not attend then, these three were joined by six more deputy lieutenants on 15 July in sending another letter to the absent officers.[61] It is probable that the undated, unsigned letter from Devon's deputy lieutenants to the Gentlemen of Cornwall was compiled during these meetings at the New Inn. In this they showed their clear commitment to maintain the ordinances of parliament and oppose the Commission of Array which the King had issued for Devon on 15 June and enlarged on 19 July. The deputy lieutenants expressed their belief in the strength that would be gained by united action from the two counties: 'If we are linkt together we can hardly be ruined. Let us contract a mutual alliance.' Chudleigh was the most experienced deputy lieutenant at these meetings and later held high rank in the parliamentarian army so he was, almost certainly, the leader in these moves. This did not stop him, however, from being sincere in the hopes for peace proclaimed in the petitions of quarter sessions.[62]

Chudleigh cannot have been surprised when he was one of the six long-standing Devon JPs removed from the bench on 15 July.[62] This was the end of the authority from the King which he had wielded in the county of Devon and which, it seems, was the mainspring of his life. It was also the end of his power to serve a united Devon. His success in his service to the county was acknowledged in one of the petitions signed at the summer assizes by some of the lesser gentry: 'we miss so many of our ancient and well deserving Justices in the Commission of the Peace now read unto us and do fear what public damage may ensue thereby.'[63] What had now driven Chudleigh to the partisan actions which could only lead to his dismissal from the bench? He was not a sophisticated politician; he had once referred to 'the affairs of state' being 'in a distraction beyond the apprehension of so weak a mind as mine'. In 1640 he had not been prepared to seek election to parliament but by 1642 he felt that his 'lot fell to be cast on the Parliament side, by a strong opinion I had of the goodness of their cause'. His long career of service would have played its part in reaching this decision, not just the events of 1640 to 1642. All his struggles with the Council for payment for billeting or even for understanding answers to his letters, may well have convinced him of the wisdom of the first proposition of the nineteen: that the great offices of State and membership of the Privy Council should be filled by men who were approved of by both Houses of Parliament. In his religious views there is no evidence that Chudleigh wished to change the moderate, episcopalian Calvinism, common in the Jacobean period and undisturbed in Devon during the episcopate of Joseph Hall. But what would have been the effect on him when he heard of conflicts caused elsewhere by Laudian innovations, when he read the Canons of 1640 and heard rumours of popish plots? He may well have thought that it would be safer to accept the eighth proposition and restrict changes in the church to those advised by parliament, especially in the light of the very moderate declaration of the changes parliament intended in the church. He may well have a strong opinion of 'the loyal service I should do his Majesty in defending that His High Court from the manifest enemies that then to my judgement appeared against it: Religion and the Subjects lawful rights seemed in danger'. His presence in London in January 1642 could have convinced him of the reality of this danger and prepared him to accept a command under the militia ordinance, serving the 'loyal Defence of our dear Sovereign, His Parliaments and Kingdoms'. He had not changed his desire to serve the King only the means of doing so.[65]

The outbreak of war turned Chudleigh into a full-time soldier. The core of the parliamentary force in the county was the trained militia which Chudleigh had formerly commanded as the sergeant major general. A significant pointer to the confidence placed in Chudleigh at this time lies in a later account of the opening of the war. This referred to his appointment as governor of St Nicholas Island (now Drake's Island), which was regarded as essential to the defence of Plymouth, 'a most considerable place'. There is no evidence that Chudleigh actually took up the governorship of the island but he was given authority to appoint a deputy and chose Sir Alexander Carew, his nephew, the son of his sister Bridget.[66] Chudleigh's first experience of gunfire was at the siege of Sherborne in September 1642 but he was back in Devon the next month, stationed at Tavistock on Devon's western border to give support to Launceston, threatened by the advance of the royalist army, under Sir Ralph Hopton, out of Cornwall. Chudleigh had five or six full troops of horse, according to Clarendon, who referred to him as 'a man of good fortune and reputation in that county and very active for the militia'. Although Chudleigh's force nearby could not stop the parliamentarian garrison at Launceston from withdrawing towards Plymouth, Chudleigh continued to be held in high esteem by the people of Devon and Cornwall. In a petition to parliament they said he was 'fully resolved and determined not to yield to the demands and desires of the Cavaliers, but to stand it out to the last'.[67] His activity led to him being excluded from the offer of pardon made, on 9 November, to the citizens of Exeter. He was named as one of four 'against whom we shall proceed . . . as Traitors and Stirrers of sedition against Us'. On 31 December parliament responded by giving their protection to these four gentlemen 'who have carefully performed their duties in assisting the Parliament' and ordered their declaration to be printed and published in all churches in Devon.[68] The royalist paper, *Mercurius Aulicus*, referred to Chudleigh as governor of Exeter during the attacks on the city by Sir Ralph Hopton in late December. It accused him of imprisoning most of the well-affected in Exeter and 'with much inhumanity' requiring them to pay sums ranging from five to twenty shillings a week towards the costs of war. It reported the repulse, with casualties, of a sally which he led out of the city; but the parliamentary report of the siege makes no mention of Chudleigh as governor. On 17 January Sir George was appointed to a committee, established by parliament, to assess those in both Exeter and Devon who were able to contribute to the costs of the war; this lends support to the earlier report of him making such demands. The majority of the members of this committee were citizens of Exeter.[69]

Chudleigh must have looked back on his first four months of active service and felt that little had been achieved in the West Country, nor were matters any further advanced in the country as a whole. The drawn battle at Edgehill on 23 October had been a great disappointment to the many who had hoped that a single engagement would settle the war and peace parties began to be formed. Chudleigh was soon involved in attempts to secure peace in the west through negotiation. The first meeting near Plymouth on 29 January achieved nothing and was followed by a royalist siege of Plymouth, when Sir George showed he was still ready to fight. With Sir John Pole he led 'the forlorn hope' out of Plymouth and 'marching all night' joined other parliamentarian forces in a successful attack on the royalists at Modbury, which helped to secure the relief of Plymouth.[70] However, Sir George soon returned to negotiations. He and four others wrote from Plymouth to the

Parliamentary Committee for Safety on 3 March 1643 to explain their motives. They made a realistic appraisal of their situation:

> The great blessings of God upon our late endeavours, hath rendered the undisciplined forces of this country manageable to defend it against a small invasion. But consisting chiefly of Trained Bands altogether incapable to follow our victory into Cornwall . . . we have thought fit to accept our enemy's importunity for a treaty, hoping to increase our volunteers, and to get supplies, for our trained soldiers, whose affection to their families and husbandry carry them from us daily in very great number with their arms.

They also asked for arms and for power to use martial law.[71] The negotiations started the next day at Mount Edgecombe and were conducted in a more determined atmosphere than the earlier attempt. The participants received Communion, an indication of Chudleigh's own reverence for that sacrament, and took a solemn protestation 'to give assurance each to other and to all the world of their integrity and of the real intentions they had for peace'. They agreed a twenty-day cessation and considered proposals put forward by the royalists which would have neutralized the West Country. They also wanted to draw Somerset and Dorset into their projected accord and arranged a meeting for that purpose at the New Inn, Exeter for 14 March.[72]

The commitment to peace in the negotiations was different from the more opportunist line of Chudleigh's earlier letter to the Parliamentary Committee of Safety, but any hopes he had of peace were forestalled by the arrival in Exeter of Anthony Nicoll and Edmund Prideaux on 13 March with instructions from the Commons to prevent any meeting in the city over the treaty. Prideaux, a former Devon JP, used every argument he could to build up opposition to the treaty, in particular accusing the Cornish of invading the county. Even so, negotiations were continued across the Exe, in the parish of St Thomas. The different approach of Chudleigh and the parliamentarian spokesmen to these negotiations highlights the contrasting standpoint of the West Country leader and the Commons. Ultimately, on 12 April, the earl of Stamford and others signed a declaration accusing the Cornish of 'invading the County . . . that under the pretence of a Treaty, they did intend to pass through the County . . . to destroy all Parliaments by subverting them'. The royalist account of this declaration included Chudleigh among its signatories but the copy of it in Willoughby's papers does not.[73] Even though he did not sign it, intercepted letters had shown Chudleigh that the Cornish had ulterior motives in desiring a truce; both sides needed time to recruit and reorganize. On 17 April Chudleigh and the Devon Committee apologized to the Committee of Safety at Westminster for beginning the treaty but pleaded that it sprang from their desire to spare blood.[74] Although nothing came of these negotiations they reveal something of the way Chudleigh's ideas were moving, he had clearly been prepared to consider a neutralist position for the West Country as the best means of stopping bloodshed. The desire he had shown for peace in the spring of 1643 must not be forgotten when military and personal reasons may appear to be the immediate cause for him to resign his command later that summer.

One of Chudleigh's junior officers was his fifth son, James, who had rapidly made his mark in the county. In spite of his involvement with the army plots, he found himself neglected when he tried to join the royal army at Oxford 'for his family's sake, which was notoriously disaffected to the king'. He therefore offered his services to parliament and was sent to Devon where he proved to be one of the more effective commanders. Although he was only twenty-five years old and did not enjoy the support of the parliamentary commander, the earl of Stamford, he was promoted major-general. Stamford 'knowing Chudleigh's fire and heat' made his father, Sir George, 'lieutenant-general for his more [even] temper'.[75] Soon after the truce ended, young Chudleigh achieved a considerable victory against superior numbers at Sourton Down on 25 April. The earl of Stamford then took over command and ordered Sir George into Cornwall with the main body of the horse, giving him the task of dispersing the forces mustering at Bodmin and blocking any royalist retreat westward. This division of the parliamentary forces proved fatal. The main body with young Chudleigh as second in command was defeated at Stratton on 16 May. Sir George was left in an impossible position and retreated rapidly, leaving himself open to severe criticism from both friend and foe:

> With as much haste and disorder as so great a consternation could produce among a people not acquainted with the accidents of war, leaving many of his men and horses a prey to the country people, himself, with as many as he could get, and keep together, got into Plymouth; and thence, without interruption or hazard into Exeter.[76]

The reputation of Sir George was now injured by far more than his headlong retreat. His son was captured at Stratton and changed sides, 'convinced in his conscience and judgement of the errors he had committed'.[77] Sir Ralph Hopton hoped that a letter from James Chudleigh to his father in Exeter might lead Sir George, 'a man then much honour'd amongst them especially in matters of advice,' to advise Exeter to surrender.[78] Hopton sent a pass for Sir George to come to him and also passes for Sir Nicholas Martin and Sir John Bampfield who it was thought 'depended altogether on his counsels'. In this Chudleigh's influence was overrated as both Martin and Bampfield remained active supporters of the parliamentarian cause. As for Chudleigh he found himself being blamed by the earl of Stamford with 'betraying the Army by carrying away the Horse to Bodmin', and his son with allowing the ordinance and ammunition to fall into the hands of the enemy when he had been commanded to blow it up. In fact, Stamford was trying to shift the blame for his own failure in battle onto the Chudleighs.[79] For a man who had put so much stress on his reputation, criticism and any suggestion of dishonour would have been very hard to take. As the royalist army, including his son, approached Exeter, Sir George resigned his commission.

As Chudleigh's pardon was one of the terms for the surrender of Exeter on 4 September, he must have he remained within the besieged city until then. While he considered his own future,

Chudleigh would have heard news of other parliamentary defeats in nearby counties. Some elements of Stamford's horse, possibly some of Chudleigh's own command, had been among the beaten army at Roundaway Down; Bristol had surrendered and, perhaps influential on Chudleigh's thinking, a peace party was gaining support with the earl of Bedford among its leaders. The relationship of Chudleigh with the earls of Bedford had been one of conscientious, loyal service and it was the earl of Bedford who had invited Chudleigh's first step towards active service on the parliamentarian side, when he appointed him a deputy lieutenant early in 1642. Now in August 1643 Bedford was a leader of the peace party in the House of Lords and when their propositions were rejected by the Commons on 7 August, he was among those who went to the King at Oxford. The Commons discharged Bedford as lord lieutenant of Devon on 23 August, so this link with Chudleigh was now broken and Chudleigh may have seen his way eased to pursue his own desire for peace, which he had already sought earlier in the year.[80] After the surrender of Exeter the royalist newletter wrote of the parliamentarian leaders in Devon shuffling 'their final overthrow in the West from one to another, confessing they had lost the game but implying still, that they deserved to win; only Sir George Chudleigh remembers he is a gentleman, and therefore acknowledged the weakness not of their forces only but of their cause;' wherefore he purposed a declaration 'to satisfy his friends'.[81]

Chudleigh's personal declaration is a valuable commentary on his career. It provides insight into his view of the constitutional position, of the lengths to which it was permissible to carry opposition to the King, and his understanding of the religious issue. His political theory may be obvious, it may only reveal 'learning enough for a country Justice' but it is what one would expect of him. He considered that as 'the experience of all ages hath constantly taught' it was essential to maintain the balance between the three pillars of the kingdom (the Sovereign and the two houses of parliament).

The King hath Royal prerogative undeniable, without which he cannot govern as a King: the two Houses of Parliament have their peculiar privileges, wherein every Subject hath his interest; the end of all is that by a meet temper of their several rights a just frame of government may arise for the Common good, which may restrain all exorbitant affections and attempts, if any happen on either part.

This is the outlook of the efficient, conservative administrator who expected each organ of government to have its allotted place. He would have experienced this as a county governor and he had worked to achieve his position as a pillar of government in the county, maintaining another essential balance, that between the demands of the King and the needs of his countrymen. He protested at royal orders which he saw were in danger of destroying this balance; yet his protests were made as the King's servant, endeavouring to rule effectively in his name. He objected to being placed in the position of having to raise new forms of taxation in place of those established by precedent; he did not hesitate to remind the Council that the King's name would be damaged if they did not adhere to promises made in his name; and he was anxious lest his ability to serve the King in the county would be damaged if he and his colleagues lost their reputation with their countrymen.

Chudleigh had worked to prevent destructive differences grow- ing between royal commands and county government but he saw that the differences which did sometimes arise between King and parliament had never before been 'aggravated to that extremity as now'. He draws his career together in his comments on three stages in the development of parliamentary opposition. As one would expect, he declared that 'Petitions of Right are commendable'; for the Petition of Right targeted the abuses he combated over billeting soldiers and dealing with the forced loan. He thought 'Remon- strances not unlawful', which is not surprising as the Grand Remonstrance condemned many of the grievances he had struggled against in Devon; but the third stage of opposition, taking up 'Arms though defensive seem doubtful'. It is his emphasis on 'defensive' which is significant, later the Answer, to this declaration, used this phrase to condemn him as 'a doubtful man at first', yet he was not a man who had to be persuaded into taking up arms; he had done so in the belief that it would do the King loyal service to defend 'His high Court from the manifest enemies that then to my judgement appeared against it: Religion and the Subjects' lawful rights seemed in danger'. He stopped fighting when 'it hath gone too far; the destruction of a Kingdom cannot be the way to save it; the loss of Christian subjects, the subjects loss of their Estates by a double plunder or assessment concurs not with piety nor yet with propriety.' This could not be called a defence of the subjects' lawful rights, it was a destruction of them. But what of the danger of religion, 'which is the chief (and I confess in greatest danger)'; how did Chudleigh see the danger to religion and how did he justify stopping fighting to defend it?

In his support of the Devon petition of January 1642 he showed that he was convinced of the danger from popish plots, now in the autumn of 1643 he could accept that that danger had passed as 'his Majesty hath given us unquestionable security during his own time; for the rest the Lord of hosts with me hath determined the controversy, having done my utmost faithfully according to my Protestation'. The assurance from the King was given while Chudleigh was incarcerated in Exeter; Charles I was about to receive Communion at Oxford when he interrupted the service to make a solemn declaration of his intention to maintain the Protestant religion 'without any connivance of Popery'. Chudleigh may have trusted the King's word that England was secure from popery but what of the danger to religion from the parliamentary side? The proposal to reform 'according to the example of the best reformed Churches' in the Solemn League and Covenant, was agreed by parliament while Chudleigh was preparing his declaration; could he support this?[82] No evidence has been found that Chudleigh sought changes in religion, he was a defender of the *status quo* against innovations and popery, not an advocator of change in a puritan direction. He was at ease in his home parish of Ashton in the Teign valley, an area identified as conservative in religion.[83]

Chudleigh concluded his declaration: 'I will contend no more in word or deed', but thought it fit to declare 'the necessity I conceive there is of easing this destructive war, unless we will become the wilful Authors of the calamities we would decline ... making my prayer according to my hope for speedy peace.' There is no evidence that Chudleigh played an active part in affairs after 1643 though he was charged by the commission for compounding in 1650 that 'he deserted his trust in the Parliament service in 1643 and ever after aided the Late King against the parliament and was at Oxford with the late King at the Time of the Junto.'[84] His son, James, gave valuable service as a royalist colonel near Exeter in July 1643 but was killed later that year, impaled on a pike in the successful royalist attack on Dartmouth. Chudleigh's house at Ashton was damaged during the final campaigns in the county in 1645 and he surrendered to parliamentary forces in December.[85] He was brought before compounding commissioners in 1650 and 1651, when he was asked if he had taken the Engagement; the oath to be 'true and faithful to the Commonwealth of England as it is now established, without a king or House of Lords'.[86] He had not done this saying 'he was not therein satisfied'. No judgement was made on material collected against him before it was proposed, on 9 April 1652, that Chudleigh should be discharged of his delinquency in accordance with the act of general pardon of 5 April 1652.[87] One of the conditions of this discharge was that he should take the Engagement but no evidence has been found that he did so. The lenient treatment of Sir George with him escaping both sequestration of his estates and even the imposition of a fine may owe a good deal to the support his son and heir gave to the parliamentary cause. The younger George Chudleigh was acting as a JP in December 1646 and was included on the commissions of the peace from 1647–51.[88] Sir George died in 1657.

Chudleigh's apparent refusal to take the Engagement shows that he remained constant in his belief that the government of the country should rest on its three pillars, the King and both houses of parliament. There was, in fact, a general consistency in the career of Sir George Chudleigh. He always saw himself as serving the King,

FIGURE 7 Memorial to Sir George Chudleigh in Ashton Parish Church

even when his actions appear to conflict with that view. It is easy to assume that professions of serving the King, while actually fighting him was only a face-saving formula, but in the career of Sir George this rings true. He fought to restore the balance of the three 'Fundamentals' when he felt this was in danger. Equally, there had been no conflict in his purpose as a county governor, he was the King's servant but he endeavoured to carry out that duty in the interests of his countrymen, one does not have to determine whether the interests of the King or his county came first with him, he tried to be both Devon's leader and the King's servant. This is not an evasion of the issue but a true description of the situation in Devon and of the career of Sir George. The county did not show how divided it was, below the surface, until war destroyed the unity of the bench and turned their leaders, such as Sir George, from county governors to faction leaders.

Chapter 8

Richard Reynell of Creedy:
The Diligent Justice of the Peace

In contrast to Sir George Chudleigh, Richard Reynell of Creedy was not, at first sight, an obvious choice for a biographical study. He served on the bench for nearly thirty years and was conscientious in his attendance at quarter sessions but the minutes would not have singled him out for special attention. It was the extraneous quarter-session material in the numerous, rather intimidating boxes that revealed his work as outstanding. His signature occurs more frequently than any other JP on the many recognizances and examinations which survive. Moreover he stamped them with his individuality by often adding his own comments on some of the formal latin recognizances, thus providing some clues to the out-of-session work of an active JP. His assiduous attention to detail makes it possible to fill some of the gap caused by the absence of petitions and grand jury presentments among the Devon records. The other particular interest in making a study of Reynell's judicial work is that he died in 1631, so this chapter reveals a sub-division in action before the Books of Orders.

Like so many of the bench, the Reynell family had been long established in the county; the first Richard Reynell of note had been sheriff of Devon in 1191 and had held the custody of Exeter and Launceston castles.[1] By the sixteenth century the principal family seat was at East Ogwell, near Newton Abbot but Richard Reynell of

FAMILY OF RICHARD REYNELL OF CREEDY

Walter Reynell of Malston

Thomas Reynell (2) of Malston

- George Reynell of Malston = Joan d. of Lewis Fortescue (baron of Exchequer)
- John Periam
- Sir William Periam Chief Baron of Exchequer

Richard Reynell of Creedy, 4th son = Mary

- Jane = Walter Yonge
- Elizabeth = Sir Robert Bassett

John Reynell (1) heir of East Ogwell

Richard Reynell of East Ogwell

Sir Thomas Reynell d. 1618 — Sir Richard Reynell of Ford d. 1634

Jane = Sir William Waller

Sir Richard Reynell = Mary d. of Richard Reynell of Creedy

Sir Thomas Reynell

Sir William = Mary Pole

Sir John Pole

Arthur Bassett

Periam d. 1639

Burrough d. 1634

Mary = Sir Richard Reynell of Ogwell

Elizabeth = Thomas Tuckfield

Sara

Rebecca = Robert Hall son of Bishop Hall

Deborah

Trifena = (2) Sir John Davy son of John Davy

Creedy came from the junior branch of the family, established at Malston, near Kingsbridge. Two members of the senior, Ogwell, branch were also called Richard and as they were active during this period, this leads to some confusion in their early careers, but later they were clearly differentiated as of Ford, of Ogwell and of Creedy.[2] Richard Reynell of Creedy was probably born about 1565 as he was admitted to the Middle Temple on 26 November 1685 (as late of New Inn) and the normal age for entry to an Inn was between sixteen and twenty. He was called to the Bar on 8 February 1594, became a Bencher in 1614 and was Autumn Reader the same year.[3] He achieved wealth and standing in the county from his ability as a barrister and from a profitable marriage to Mary, daughter and co-heiress of John Periam esquire, twice mayor of Exeter, a burgess for the city and a leading member of the Merchant Adventurers of Exeter. Periam's brother, Sir William, had become chief Baron of the Exchequer in 1593, the same year as Reynell's marriage, and may have been a useful contact for the rising lawyer.[4]

Reynell's early professional career in Devon was concerned with corporate towns. As he acted in 1601 on behalf of Totnes in a dispute over the town's Magdalen charity, he may have been deputy recorder of Totnes while its recorder, Sir George Cary, was in Ireland from 1599 to 1601. However, correspondence with the mayor of Totnes shows that Reynell was already resident in Broadclyst in east Devon, where he had been given a property by his brother-in-law, Henry Borough.[5] He was closely concerned in the affairs of his parish and was one of the Eight Men of Broadclyst, at least from 1605 to 1609. They met each month and decided on parish business such as fixing the rates, deciding how many tipplers were needed in the town and dealing with vagrants. In 1609 Reynell asked to be released from these duties because of his commitments as a Counsellor-at-law and as a county JP, which he had been since 1603. He was released as 'if any of this parish have cause of complaint' they 'may show their grief' to this JP most conveniently living in the parish. Another claim on his time was his appointment as the first recorder of Bradninch in 1604, when the town received its Charter.[6] He was able to combine his duties as a county JP, centred on Broadclyst, with his duties as recorder of Bradninch (about five miles away) until his wife inherited her father's estates in the Crediton hundred on the other side of the Exe. John Periam had moved out of Exeter and was living at Creedywiger, in the parish of Upton Hellions. This house had been built by his brother, Sir William, who left it to his daughters who had then sold it to John Periam. Creedywiger became the home of the Reynells in 1618 on the death of John Periam. Over the next four years Reynell purchased more of Sir William's lands from his daughters and spent nearly £4,000 creating an extensive estate round Creedywiger.[7]

The first part of Chapter 4 described the judicial work of the Devon bench; a study of Reynell's work as a county JP makes it possible to give that an individual perspective. In spite of some gaps in the records, Reynell's outstanding work, especially out-of-sessions, deserves to be tabulated. This very impressive total of out-of-session work (682 recognizances and 59 examinations) gives some idea of the service given by Reynell, but it is the comments he added to the recognizances which give his work its special value. The legal format of a recognizance did not include the cause for it. If it was one for a suspected felon, this can usually be established by relating it to an examination and indictment but it has already been estimated that about 85 per cent of the recognizances tied up with those for suspected felons were not, in fact, for felonies.[10] In these cases there were no examinations and no indictments and it was only if the JP added a comment to the recognizance that the cause is revealed. There is also no ground for knowing the cause for a recognizance for good behaviour or to keep the peace, unless the JP added a comment. It is in this that Reynell stands out, not only did he sign an exceptionally large number of recognizances but wrote comments on more of them than any of his colleagues. His comments were often in his own hand and sometimes signed RR, a practice seldom adopted by any of his fellow JPs.

The comments on recognizances, tied up with those for suspected felons but actually for lesser offences can be drawn together under various headings. The largest group dealt with neglect of orders or duties, abuse of officials, including the JP himself, and attacks on officers. Twenty-nine of Reynell's comments concerned this type of offence. For example, 'for abusing the justices and also the constable of Crediton'; 'for beating William Pearse upon highway being then on HM service RR'; and five recognizances for

Table 7:
Reynell's attendance at quarter sessions and signing of recognizances or taking examinations from 1603–1631

	Epiphany	Easter	Midsummer	Michaelmas	Recognizances examinations
1603				*	2
1604	*	*	?8	*	no records
1605	*	*	*	*	8
1606	*	*	—	*	1 (few records)
1607	*	*	*	—	10
1608	—	?	*	—	6
1609	—	*	—	—	2 (few records)
1610	*	*	—	—	0 (few records)
1611	*	*	*	*	24
1612	?	*	*	—	3 (few records)
1613	—	—	*	—	21
1614	—	—	—	—	0 (few records)
1615	*	*	*	—	9
1616	—	*	—	*	no records
1617	*	*	—	—	26
1618	—	—	*?9	*?	14 (2 terms)
1619	*?	*	—	—	71
1620	*	*	*	*	92
1621	*	*	*	*	41 (2 terms)
1622	*	—	*	*	33 (2 terms)
1623	*	*	*	*	5 (few records)
1624	*	*	*	*	50
1625	*	*	*	?	46
1626	*	*	?	?	40
1627	?	—	*	?	100
1628	*	*	*	*	32
1629	*	*	*	*	45
1630	*	*	*	—	44
1631	*	died 27 April 1631			16
				Total	741

Table 8:
Analysis of recognizances signed by Richard Reynell

Recognizance	For suspected felons and other offenders	Good Behaviour & to keep peace	Evidence
Total signed by Reynell	236	353	93
Number signed with other JPs	140	102	35
Number of total with comments	161	107	7
Number of these with other JPs	81	44	

those who allowed 'three women negligently to escape being by me sent to the House of Correction at Honiton RR'.[11] Another substantial collection of comments concerned bastardy. This offence was usually dealt with by a recognizance for good behaviour, so these cases had some additional feature which required attendance at quarter sessions. Examples among Reynell's comments on bastardy include: 'she is the mother of a base child whereof she hath accused two', 'accused by Priscilla Squire of begetting her with child', and 'for willing his daughter to lay down her base child in the church at Rackenford and run away, which she did RR.'[12]

The alehouse was the site of some of the other offences causing recognizances bundled with those for suspected felons. Ten were for selling ale without licence and keeping ill-rule. One comment gave full details of the offence and punishment, 'keeping common tippling house without licence contrary to statute and hath paid fine of 20s and suffered imprisonment according to law.'[13] In several cases the offence was aggravated by keeping 'ill-rule on Sabbath day'.[14] Yet misbehaviour by a customer in the alehouse on Sunday might be covered by a recognizance for good behaviour; even one 'for gambling in an alehouse upon Sabbath day and inhumanly abusing the daughter of Mr John Pulton parson of Hittisleigh'.[15] Yet if an offence was in church, 'for hindering divine service and disturbing the minister in the church on the Sabbath day', it could lead to a recognizance to appear at quarter sessions; so could an over-zealous action in 'disturbing minister and congregation in time of divine service at Stockleigh Pomeroy by arresting Richard Venner in the churchyard, going into church, refusing bail and carrying him to ward by night.'[16]

Other comments by Reynell show him using this type of recognizance if someone failed to enforce prosecutions and also against anyone who made unfounded accusations; cases such as 'not prosecuting against Arthur Hearding for felony', and 'for arresting ... for felony where none was committed and relinquishing same again before me RR'.[17] Reynell and his colleagues showed that they would enforce their authority when faced with one 'affirming that he could and would accuse John Westaway of felony, but would not do it till at Sessions RR'; and also that they would uphold the probity of their clerks when it was said 'that Bt. Prideaux's clerk ... counterfeited the Baronet's hand to a recognizance'.[18]

The comments Reynell made on recognizances for the peace and good behaviour show his careful use of this means of maintaining order. For example, for being 'suspected of house breaking but not arrested, yet I thought good to bind him lest further matter might be proved.' He also played safe in another case binding over an unattractive, dubious character 'for living loosely and not above once this month in his own parish church and of ill manner, some doubt is had that he could be privy to a robbery ... but is not accused RR.' Another instance shows his care and also his caution 'for plotting a robbery which took not effect I determined to have examined him again and his accomplices but he being sick I would not and therefore think fit he should be continued till next. RR.' Reynell occasionally takes a promise of amendment into consideration; 'he hath by giving out slandering speeches, set great strife between sundry men ... and behaves himself very disorderly in the church of Broadclyst. But he hath promised amendment yet I think fit if the bench be so pleased that he be bound a Session now.' In another case, 'we have appointed to hear the same again and to order and end it according to equity and justice RR.'[19]

Some idea of the procedure followed by a JP can be gathered from Reynell's comments. Thirty-one of the recognizances were the result of warrants from another JP or an order from the quarter sessions or assizes. Reynell did not necessarily know the reason for these, for example: 'bailed out of gaol by an order from the Bench made at last Session', but in others the cause was clear, 'by order of bench for not paying the stock money'.[20] One comment showed the interesting use of constables as arbitrators: 'difference to be referred to Constable Lapell and Constable Bradford to be ended within 14 days next.'[21]

Other comments illustrate the range of cases which might come before a JP. Some concerned family relationships; 'it could not be denied by him that he had divers and sundry times beaten ... his wife ... Locking her out of his doors in the night season, in so much as she was constrained either to lie in the streets or by the hedges.'[22] That case was dealt with by a recognizance for good behaviour, as was by-passing parental authority by 'abusing body of Johanna Nime ... and for persuading her to marry him without her father's consent.'[23] The same was true for comprehensive threats without action even when they involved 'swearing to burn my lord bishop's palace and for burning his bedstead and saying his wife should whelp upon a burthen of straw RR'.[24] Only one comment has been found concerning suspicion of witchcraft, 'for striking of a poor old woman, pretending to fetch blood of her, believing that she had witched his dye vat which would not work.'[25] Other recognizances were used to enforce the game laws and laws on fasting.[26] In one case a recognizance was used against the risk of fire, 'for using fire in a room without chimney or mantel to the endangering of the town and for saying he would not ... forbear do what we could, he hath been often admonished by us RR.'[27]

It is not possible to draw any conclusions on the prevalence of certain offences when over half the recognizances, even from Reynell, had no comments on them. For example, only one has been found referring to forestalling the market, whereas this was the subject of fairly frequent orders in quarter sessions.[28] The recognizances to give evidence very seldom included any additional detail; Reynell only commented when cases involved extortion (four times) or perjury (three times). Even when Reynell signed some of these documents with other JPs, he still appears to have initiated the comment as it might be in his hand and with his initials. However, one of the other JPs of this sub-division, Northcott, has been found making comments on recognizances before Reynell moved to the Crediton area so Reynell did not introduce the practice there. Northcott and Davy also made comments on some of the recognizances they took alone.

The Crediton sub-division has already been shown to be the best example of the early development of petty sessions.[29] This started soon after Reynell's arrival in the Crediton area so it is pertinent to examine whether this was his initiative. From 1605 until 1616 a contrast can be discerned between the practice of the county JPs in Reynell's sub-division and the one he was to move to. On twelve occasions some east Devon JPs have been found acting together, but only once has a Crediton JP been found acting with a colleague. Reynell started signing recognizances in the Crediton area in 1617; he may have taken over managing his father-in-law's estate before his death. He was then one of a group of JPs making a fresh start in that sub-division. John Davy had just been appointed on 12 July 1617. John Northcott had been a JP since 1599 but had been briefly off the bench and then reappointed on 2 March 1618; the cause for this break in service is unknown but it may have ensured increased attention to his duties on his restoration.[30] Another member of this Crediton group, Sir Francis Fulford appointed in 1613, was less active. A fifth JP, Edward Cotton, rector of Shobrooke and son of the bishop of Exeter, was not appointed to the bench until 1620.[31]

Most of the quarter-session rolls of 1618 are missing but in 1619 the rolls show that there were twenty-eight occasions when two or three of the JPs of the Crediton sub-division signed recognizances together; Reynell and Davy were always present and on fifteen occasions Northcott as well. At the beginning of the year meetings took place on Saturdays but in June they started to meet on Thursdays and there were sixteen occasions when they met on that day during the rest of the year.[32] From this one must conclude that they had established a regular pattern for meeting. Evidence has already been detailed of the group of Reynell, Davy and Northcott gradually being recognized by quarter sessions as 'the JPs that meet at Crediton'.[33] As this development coincided with Reynell's arrival in the sub-division; as he was nearly always present when this group of JPs signed recognizances together; as he was the only one of the group who was a barrister and the only one with experience of working with other JPs out-of-sessions, he seems the most likely instigator of these regular meetings in the sub-division at Crediton, over a decade before it was ordered by the Council in the Book of Orders.

Although Reynells's activity within his sub-division was the principal reason for selecting him for individual consideration in this study, there were other aspects of his career where he can represent a feature common to some members of the county bench. Reynell had strong links with the city of Exeter which, at first, he may have owed to his relationship to John Periam, but he gradually secured his own position there; he was made a freeman of the city in 1607 and became a member of the Exeter Chamber in 1617.[34] He had a house in Exeter so he could have been available for any private or public professional work.[35] He was involved in the apprehension of papists on behalf of the city in 1621 which followed the arrest of a Catholic priest in Exeter on 14 November 1621. Reynell assured the mayor and JPs of the city that 'I will according to your advise send out warrants . . . The lord give a blessing unto our endeavours in his behalf.' A few days later he reported that when he had sent out his servant with warrants for the suspects 'they had notice of all the proceedings . . . and sent their papist friends to the Constables to learn whether they had received any warrants from me to search'.[36] This episode is an interesting indication of cooperation between the city and county as well as Reynell's own opinion of the danger from papists.

In 1623 Reynell acted as recorder of Exeter, with Richard Waltham, while the recorder of Exeter, Nicholas Ducke, was in London for several months. They were active in May and presented the charge to the quarter sessions of the city on 14 July 1623, the only meeting Ducke did not attend until he was replaced as recorder by Richard Waltham in October 1628.[37] In 1626 Reynell was one of the county JPs concerned in discussions with the mayor and magistrates of Exeter about the royal demand to supply two ships.[38] About the same time Reynell, with Sir Edward Giles, William Bastard, Arthur Champernowne, Ambrose Bellot and their followers were entertained at Totnes, where their help was sought 'at two sundry times about removing soldiers from us'. That Reynell was involved on this occasion, even though he was the only one of this group of JPs not to be resident near Totnes, suggest that he may have continued his earlier legal service to them. In July 1626 he supported their case against the billeting of soldiers by signing the letter from the bench to the Privy Council appealing for the removal of the army from the county.[39]

Recognizances and the slight diary of Sir Richard Reynell of Ogwell show that there were close contacts between the two Reynell families, with members of the Creedy branch among the godparents for most of the eight Ogwell children.[40] This contact was established before the marriage of Mary Reynell of Creedy to Richard Reynell of Ogwell with Reynell (of Creedy) signing recognizances with Sir Thomas Reynell in September and October 1611 for offenders near Ogwell. After Richard Reynell of Ogwell succeeded his father on the bench, the two Richard Reynells signed recognizances together on sixteen occasions. The dates of signings suggest that the families spent Christmas and the New Year together in 1619, 1620, 1628 and 1629; this close association, therefore, continued after the death in childbirth of Mary Reynell in 1626.

Sir Richard Reynell of Ogwell refers to his father-in-law as 'a wise religious gentleman' but there is not enough evidence to give him the label of any religious party. His anti-papist standpoint is obvious from his support of measures by the city of Exeter against Catholics and also from his membership, in 1606, of a commission appointed to enquire into the lands of recusants and to levy arrears of fines.[41] In his early years he may have been influenced by his brother-in-law, Henry Borough, who was sufficiently attached to him to give him a

175

FIGURE 8 Memorial to Richard Reynell and his wife (daughter of John Periam of Exeter) in the Parish Church of Upton Hellions

property in Broadclyst. Borough was a zealous Protestant who was involved in some scandalous but profitable deals as a collector of clerical tenths and subsidies under Bishop Bradbridge. Dr Vage, in writing of Borough, refers to Reynell as a puritan but gives no additional reference for this.[42] In spite of his obvious wealth Reynell has not been found giving financial support to any lectureship, whereas his father-in-law contributed towards the annual cost of a puritan preacher in Exeter, and a cousin, Laurence Bodley left money for a weekly preacher to be established in the city.[43] Reynell made only one charitable benefaction in his will, a gift of £21 to the poor of Upton Hellions, his parish church where he is buried; he died on 27 April 1631.[44] A significant indication of his religious views in 1631 was the marriage of his daughter, Rebecca, to Robert Hall, a canon of Exeter cathedral and eldest son of the bishop. This suggests that Reynell, like Chudleigh, accepted without difficulty the rule of that Calvinist bishop.

Richard Reynell's attention to detail has provided material to examine the work of a JP out-of-session. It was in this field, rather than quarter sessions, that his work was more comprehensive than his colleagues. This was probably due to two factors: firstly his profession as a barrister inclined him to use the legal method of recognizance to deal with problems brought before him and, secondly, his area of activity was uniquely suited to the development of a petty session. Crediton was the largest Devon town not to be a corporate town, it was also conveniently close to the residences of several JPs. His signature on documents throws some light on the nature of Reynell's life. After his move to Creedywiger there were few periods free of administration for long enough for him to have travelled far outside the county, or even for his wide movement within the county. His activity as a JP was concentrated in the triangle of Crediton, Newton Abbot and Exeter (none of these towns being more than twenty miles apart). Although his legal expertise was sometimes required by the city of Exeter or county of Devon,[45] most of his life was centred upon a small part of the county. His outlook, therefore, may have been predominantly absorbed with local rather than county interests. In this there is no reason to suppose that he was not typical of other members of the bench, who were not involved in the duties of sheriff or deputy lieutenant.

Chapter 9

Walter Yonge: The Puritan Diarist

Walter Yonge finds his place among these studies of gentry leaders as a diarist rather than as a ruler of the county. He was a conscientious JP but his service on the commission largely confirms the picture already drawn, it is his diaries which brings a fresh dimension. They fulfil a dual purpose, they show that Devon was no quiet backwater detached by distance from the controversies of the day and they reveal the development of one of the gentry governors. The diaries span forty years and so record not only Yonge's puritanism and his constant interest in politics but chart his increasingly partisan attitude to the affairs of the day. This adds a new feature to this description of the gentry government of the county, it shows that it could accommodate strong views on national affairs while maintaining the collegiate character of the county government. Yonge may well have shared these views with some of his colleagues in east Devon who, unlike Chudleigh and Reynell, were in closer contact with the strong political and puritanical views personified in Dorset by Sir Walter Erle and John White, vicar of Dorchester. In view of the interest in national affairs which Yonge shows in his diary, it is not surprising that he took the opportunity in 1641 to turn from county government to serve in the Long Parliament when the local seat at Honiton was restored. Yonge was the only one on the commission to make such a complete transfer of service from the county to Westminster.

Yonge had a different kind of background from Chudleigh and Reynell, he came from a family of prosperous merchants of

Colyton, rather than from a long tradition of gentry service. He was the only surviving son of John Yonge who achieved armigerous status soon after Walter's birth and gave his son the education common to a Devon gentry governor. He matriculated at Magdalen College, Oxford on 19 April 1599 'as aged 18' so was presumably born in 1581. He soon went on to the Middle Temple, where he was admitted on 26 October 1600.[1] He inherited considerable estates in east Devon from his father, with houses at Colyton, Axminster and Stedcombe near Axmouth in addition to a property at Upton Hellions in the Crediton hundred, which he enlarged with additional purchases in 1615.[2] His marriage in 1602 to Jane, daughter and co-heiress of John Periam of Exeter, brought him further wealth. Jane Yonge inherited lands in east Devon on her father's death in 1618 and a house in Exeter on the death of her step-mother in 1621. Although Yonge and Reynell were married to sisters, they moved in different circles and there is no evidence of them meeting outside the times of quarter sessions. Yonge gained other gentry connections from the Periam marriage which had a greater influence on him, namely relationship with the Pole and Prideaux families, two of the well-established gentry families in Yonge's immediate neighbourhood. He also came into contact with a leading puritan family from the opposite end of the county with the marriage of Yonge's son, John, to a daughter of Sir William Strode.[3]

Yonge was first appointed to the commission of the peace on 8 July 1622.[4] His financial status was sufficient for a JP as his subsidy rating was £20 but otherwise there was no obvious cause for his appointment.[5] Unlike some of his colleagues he had not served in any of the lesser county offices. Although he had been attentive to his duties as a JP, he had not the standing in the county to retain his place on the bench when the new Lord Chancellor set about his rigorous pruning of the commissions at the beginning of Charles I's reign. The crown office docket book does not record his removal from the bench but he was inactive after 7 November 1625 until his fresh appointment on 20 March 1626. His rapid restoration to the bench may well have been aided by his contribution of £20 to the forced loan on 3 March 1626. He remained on the bench until 15

FAMILY OF WALTER YONGE

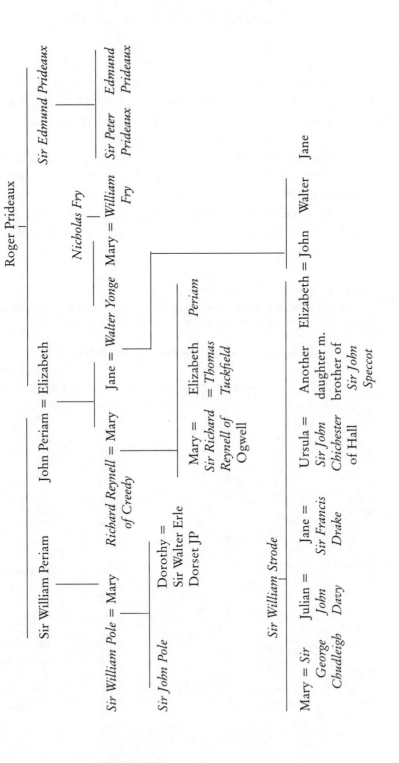

July 1642, when he was dropped for his commitment to the parliamentary cause, he was restored by 1647 and was still on it at his death in 1649.[6] A record of his service as a JP provides a useful comparison to Reynell's, especially as they cover different periods.[7]

In the 1620s Yonge was not as active as Reynell but the significant rise in the number of examinations and recognizances taken by Yonge from 1631 suggests that the Books of Orders may have stimulated him to increased activity. He was certainly very well informed on the Book of January 1631 as he copied a large part of it into his diary.[9] He showed his interest in the origin of some orders

Table 9:
Attendance at quarter sessions and signing recognizances or taking examinations. 8 July 1622–7, November 1625, 20 March 1626–15, July 1642.

	Epiphany	Easter	Midsummer	Michaelmas	Recognizances Examinations
1622	Not yet appointed		*		6
1623	*	*	*	*	2 (few records)
1624	*	*	–	*	16
1625	*	–	*	–	27
1626	out of commission	–	?[8]	?	22
1627	?	*	*	?	36
1628	sheriff	sheriff	sheriff	sheriff	–
1629	–	*	*	*	36
1630	*	–	–	*	73
1631	*	*	*	*	39
1632	*	*	–	*	66
1633	*	–	–	*	29 (few records)
1634	*	*	–	*	30
1635	*	–	*	?	69
1636	–	–	*	*	72
1637	*	*	–	–	43
1638	*	*	–	–	50
1639	?	–	–	–	76
1640	–	?	–	*	18
1641	member of parliament			*	3
1642	?	–	–	Removed	5

182

by adding more references to statutes in the margin of his diary than occur in the Book of Orders. Yonge's interest in the statutes which ruled his work as a JP was also shown by his compilation of a pamphlet titled, *Table containing such statutes wherein one or more JPs are enabled to act as well in Session as out of Session*. He probably drew it up at first to aid his own work as a JP as it was clearly only a practical guide and not in any sense a professional textbook. It is largely arranged as a table referring first to offences which could be dealt with by one JP and the penalties incurred, then a space was left for any additions to be included. A second section followed on cases requiring two JPs. A Commons' committee ordered it to be printed in May 1642 under the briefer title *A Vade Mecum*, for the public good.[10]

Apart from his service as a JP, Yonge carried out some orders at the behest of the deputy lieutenants and was the sheriff in 1628. The deputy lieutenants required him in October 1625 to serve on a committee to survey the coastal defences from Plymouth to Seaton, to order any necessary construction and to arrange for the cost to be met by the parishes and hundreds. As a result of this survey it was decided in June 1627 to fortify Seaton and to distribute the cost among the five nearest hundreds. Later in 1635 Yonge was named as quartermaster general of the militia and a member of the Devon council of war.[11] As he lived in the east division, Yonge was not closely concerned in the problems of billeting at the beginning of the reign, but he showed his opinion of the presence of the troops by putting his symbol signifying ' a plague of England' against the entry about them in his diary. When the soldiers returned in 1627, he was among the eighteen JPs who protested to the Council, on 26 October, at the effect on the county of the demands of billeting. A week later he was to have closer experience of the problems of billeting when he and some of his colleagues in east Devon were ordered by the earl of Holland to billet troops in their area instead of allowing them to proceed immediately to Plymouth. They evidently carried out these orders as they wrote to the Council three weeks later to complain that these men had not yet been moved.[12] Two letters at this time have the clerical acknowledgement on them that they were from deputy lieutenants but there is no other evidence to suggest that Yonge was ever a deputy lieutenant.[13]

Yonge served as sheriff in 1628 but the only direct reference to his duties in his diary was his receipt of a commission to enquire into the lands and goods of convicted popish recusants which he passed on to his undersheriff. On several other occasions he noted information relevant to his office, such as the summons of parliament to meet on 17 March 1628. He would have had to arrange for the return of members at the county court even though he did not have to deal with a contested election. He recorded the dates appointed for the payment of subsidy in 1628, in this he was reminding himself of another duty. Although the collectors of subsidy paid the money collected from the hundreds into the exchequer, the sheriff appears to have been responsible for paying in clerical subsidy. There are six entries in 1628 of Yonge paying in the subsidy from various rectors. He also had to pay fines due into the exchequer, even after the end of his year of office. His duties stretched on to 25 February 1631 when he paid in the last recusancy fine of £154 11s 3d.[14]

Yonge's two diaries reveal the development of his interest in national and international affairs. The first one shows that he had not yet become deeply interested in national affairs. It could be considered a pocket diary (about four inches by seven inches), it started just before the gunpowder plot and continued until the spring of 1628, ending soon after the mutiny at Plymouth. This is a more personal diary than the second one; he mentions Sir William Strode giving his wife, Jane, a piece of a thunderbolt found in Plymouth and indicates that his circle of friends included John Drake and Sir John Pole. His diary reveals him as actively involved in agriculture, often mentioning the state of the weather and the effect this had on the harvest and price of corn. He was not above taking a hand in the harvesting and in 1609 records that, 'I myself had to turn oats some four, some five times before I could save it' because of the 'extreme wet'. He records storms at unusual seasons, one so violent in August 1622 that over £200 worth of damage was done at Axmouth. This same year when economic distress was

FIGURE 9 The house of Walter Yonge at Colyton

severe he reports on unemployed weavers seeking relief in Exeter and others without work complaining to the JPs in Wiltshire and Gloucestershire.[15] This would have been of particular interest to him as this was the year he became a JP.

This first diary reveals Yonge's puritan convictions and one later sees them influencing his selection of news in the second diary. He was clearly apprehensive of papist influence, but although this was common to puritans it was not confined to them; Chudleigh, Reynell and Bishop Hall all shared this fear with Yonge, but how did these men, who have not been described as puritan in this study, differ from Yonge?[16] Yonge was an admirer of some of the leading puritan writers, including John Dod, Richard Greenham and William Perkins. Greenham was a pioneer of sabbatarianism and Perkins was one of the outstanding Calvinist writers of the late Elizabethan period whose books were still in print in the 1630s.[17] Yonge was an opponent of Arminianism and Pelagianism which 'do

185

much spread abroad in divers parts of the realm and many bishops infected herewith'. Both Arminianism and Pelagianism rejected predestination, the cornerstone of Calvinism. Yet belief in pre-destination, like anti-papism, was not a sure means of identifying a puritan; Hall believed in it but strongly rejected the charge of allowing puritanism to flourish in his diocese.[18] A clearer indication of Yonge's puritanism was his comment on a book of Dr Cosin which 'containeth many points of popery and 7 sacraments, which he termeth sacramentals'. His association of popery and sacraments shows his distrust of the increased emphasis being placed on the sacraments in the Caroline church. Yonge evidently considered that preaching, rather than the liturgy and sacraments was the most important feature of church services. In 1622 he recorded with equal distrust that there was a report that 'Papists shall have a toleration here in England, and that Protestant ministers shall preach but once a Sabbath'.[19] He was also clearly a sabbatarian, he regretted in 1624 that 'a good bill past both houses against revels, and for sanctifying of the Sabbath; but the King would not pass it'. Later he gave a local example of the dire consequences of ignoring the sanctity of the sabbath. The fate of one of those playing dice in the churchyard at Tiverton on a Sunday in 1635 when a stone fell off the church and dashed out his brains, was taken as a warning to those who abused the Lord's day.[20] All these factors, belief in predestination, in sabbatarianism, and in preaching, rather than sacraments build-up a convincing picture of Yonge as a puritan which is strengthened by the certainty of his occasional inter-pretation of God's will. He did this in 1622 when he saw the failure of the Spanish fleet to sail because of a great famine as God fighting for his Church when others neglected it. Later, in August 1626, he saw 'here God's hand upon the contemners of his ordinances' when four people died and four went mad after ignoring an order to fast.[21]

Yonge scribbled a note at the corner of the fly-leaf of his first diary that he would mark the plagues of England by adding a figure in the margin. He may have added this note when he started to use this device in February 1622, when he heard that it was proposed to remove all puritan JPs from the commission of the peace, this at a time when he was just about to be included on it. In 1625 he put a rose in the margin against the arrival in Plymouth of 10,000 soldiers.[22] These symbols, usually of a rose, suggest that he was now becoming more critical of the way national affairs were developing and this is confirmed by his decision to start a much larger diary to record some of the issues of the day. The two diaries overlap until May 1628, and for this period the smaller diary continued to record local events with a brief summary of wider affairs while the larger diary covered twenty pages with considerable extracts, probably from newsletters or separates (which included news with business and private matters).[23] It may well be that the account of the trial of the five knights, followed by the pre-Easter session of parliament was not written until the first diary became full in May 1628, and Yonge decided that the importance of these events demanded far more detailed treatment. From May 1628 news gathered from local sources is interspersed with material copied from newsletters so it is easier to determine whether this national news was included at the time it occurred.

Yonge prefaced his second diary with a reference to the commission for the forced loan which was received in Devon in the spring of 1627. He noted that some gentlemen refused to sit on this commission, but there is no evidence that any actively refused to do so in Devon. Yonge's own practice appears to have been to absent himself from meetings of the commission. He did not sign either of the letters sent to the Council, which were signed by a number of Devon commissioners.[24] He may therefore have felt a common cause with the five knights who were imprisoned for their refusal, especially with Sir Walter Erle who was his occasional neighbour at Bindon House near Axmouth, which belonged to Erle's wife. The first nine pages of this large diary are devoted to an account of the trial of the five knights who were imprisoned for nine months for refusing to pay the forced loan before they were ultimately brought to court on a *habeas corpus*. Yonge recorded the case for each defendant in detail and so obviously understood that the significance of their case had changed from being concerned with their refusal to act as commissioners for the forced loan and had become one of much greater importance. He underlined points which he considered the core of the case: that 'no cause of imprisonment is showed' on the return, that the prisoner 'is committed by the commandment of the king'. Later, after copying references to Magna Carta and statutes of Edward III, he underlined the opinion that if proceedings were not according to the 'old laws of the land ... then the subject shall be disinherited of the laws which is his birth-right'. Finally, he recorded the judgement that the prisoners remain in prison 'until the king enlarged them', this was at odds with the opinion he had underlined earlier that a prisoner 'ought not to be perpetually imprisoned, but ought to come in due time to his trial'.[25]

In the early days of the third parliament of the reign, Yonge detailed speeches which referred to matters with which Devon was very familiar, the raising of loans and the 'lamentable' effects of billeting soldiers. In a reference to billeting he underlined a reference to 'these upstart lieutenants', a confirmation that he was not one of them and also an indication that Devon's deputy lieutenants may have had to face some criticism from their fellow gentry governors. Yonge also noted the Commons' reaction to the case of the five knights, their resolution that no free man ought to be committed or detained in prison unless the cause was shown. Thus from these first days of the parliament he recorded three of the matters which were later to be part of the Petition of Right. When the petition was presented to the King in May, Yonge went into considerable detail on the actual petition, the King's answer to it on 2 June, and the debate which followed that answer which was 'no way answerable'. He also recounted the King's visit to the Lords on 7 June and the joyful response which greeted his undertaking to give a 'more clear and satisfactory answer'. Finally, Yonge used bigger print than usual and underlined part of the King's statement on 26 June: '*I neither repented nor mean to recede* from anything I have promised you', and later he wrote, again in bigger print, that in '*no time to come in the word of a king* you shall not have the like cause to complain'.[26] Yonge's detailed account confirms that full information on the debates was reaching Devon and it shows that he now had a clear benchmark against which to weigh up the King's future actions.

Yonge's description of the first session of this parliament was definitely based on secondhand material as he was sheriff during 1628 and so had to remain in Devon but he may well have been an eyewitness to the session of January and February 1629.[27] He showed that he shared the opinion of the members that religion should take precedence in the debates over tonnage and poundage, giving a far fuller account of the religious fears of Arminianism and Popery than of the conflict over the customs.[28] Yonge's description of this session shows that he would clearly have approved of the first of the three resolutions, that anyone introducing innovations in religion or attempting to extend Popery or Arminianism 'shall be reputed a capital enemy of this kingdom'.[29] His comment on the adjournment on 25 February shows that he was aware of the constitutional issue. In an observation which has the ring of one in close contact with some members, he wrote:

> It is said that the king sent a message unto the house of parliament that they should not intermeddle with Jesuits or priests, nor tonnage but he resolved to take tonnage by his prerogative. Upon this message the house was by themselves adjourned for that being forbidden to speak they thought unfit for themselves to sit as having nothing to do.[30]

When parliament was dissolved a week later, Yonge commented that it was 'in great discontent'. He listed the members arrested and referred to their detention 'for some notable cause against the king and his government and for stirring up sedition', and noted their places of imprisonment.[31] His son's marriage to Elizabeth Strode would have given him a personal interest in the case of her brother, William Strode.

Yonge's caution in using symbols to show his opinions would have seemed even more justified in 1629 when a royal proclamation was issued against mutterings over the dissolution of parliament. In the same year, the imprisonment of Devon's lord lieutenant, the earl of Bedford, for having 'a pestilential tract' found in his possession, may well have underlined the need for caution.[32] Yonge often showed his opinions by his selection of news rather than by direct comments. He confirms in the second diary the earlier impression of his puritanism. He shows his esteem for John White, the puritan vicar of Dorchester, who opposed the Book of Sports and was sent for in October 1635 to be questioned, presumably before the Court of High Commission. He noted at that time that 'the King is very violent against all such as will not take satisfaction from Dr White's book (being bishop of Ely) concerning recreation on the Lord's day.'[33] Yonge was already familiar with John White, possibly through his other Dorset friend, Sir Walter Erle, who was a stern critic of the King and a supporter of White. Yonge was one of the 119 investors in the Dorchester Company, an enterprise of White and Erle which hoped to combine profit with the propagation of religion in the New World. Yonge's enthusiasm for the project may be measured by the number of his family who also invested: his son John, his brothers-in-law Richard Mallack and William Fry and five of wife's Pole connections. Yonge also showed his confidence in John White by appointing a kinsman of his, William Walton, to the parish of Beer and Seaton.[34]

In spite of his caution, Yonge did reveal his views on some issues. He thought that it was wrong that 'many are fined £200 some at £100' for knighthood composition. He claimed that 'a fine should be only a recompense proportionable unto the fault or wrong committed but I conceive that His Majesty is not demnified by any subject for his not attending to seek the honour of knighthood and therefore such fines are rather grievances than fines.' The figures mentioned are higher than any paid in Devon but Yonge may have gathered news of more widespread discontent when he paid his own composition at the exchequer on 4 April 1631.[35] He showed his growing resentment of Lord Wentworth when he noted his activity in collecting fines for knighthood, some on lands valued under £40 and that he 'made some widows to compound also the fines for knighthood'.[36]

When another form of taxation, ship money, was revived he did not need convincing of the need for an increased navy. The dangers to the Devon coasts were a recurrent theme in the diary, dangers from Dunkirkers and from the fleets of France and Holland.[37] He had noted in 1632 that there were 'divers ships now building and many carts taken up for carriage of timber out of New Forest', but he was doubtful of the purpose of these ships. He had heard that they were 'to beat off the Hollanders from trading for fish upon the north parts of this kingdom', yet he questioned if 'we be able to do so that could not be master of our own coasts or our port towns of Dunkirkers. This business smells of Spanish fight.' Yonge appears to have suspected in 1632 that the fleet might be used in support of the Spanish, even before Charles had negotiated a treaty to this effect.[38] When he heard from his local head constable that Axminster and Axmouth were to be charged under the ship money writ of 1634, he protested that they were decayed towns not port towns and had no man of worth living in them. He attended the Epiphany quarter session and would no doubt have supported their protest to the Council at the extension of the charge beyond the port towns. Later he noted each ship money writ as it was sent out but did not express opposition to the principle of the later levies although he did note examples of men in Nottinghamshire, Wiltshire, Berkshire, Northamptonshire, Hertfordshire, Essex, Gloucestershire, Somerset and London refusing to pay ship money.[39] His own attitude may be suggested by his slowness to pay the charge in 1637; he recorded the various stages of the Hampden case and may have awaited the judgement before paying.[39] He makes no comment in 1637 on the decision in the ship money case but in the autumn of 1639 he refers to the judges being partial, an indication that his opposition was growing.[40]

Yonge reveals his interests and sympathies in his selection of some of the news reaching Devon. He wrote periodically on the progress of the Thirty Years War, much of it just reporting actions, but his pen portrait of Gustavus Adolphus reveals his admiration for that Protestant hero.

He constantly riseth about midnight and visiteth his guards until the morning, seldom sleeping above four hours in twenty-four. He often makes use of the ground for his bed and a gray felt hat (which he commonly weareth) filled with earth for his pillow. He is frequently alone at midnight writing with his own hand, what he hath done in the day and sending dispatches, making orders and giving instructions to his chief commanders, all with his own pen.[42]

Another area where Yonge's selection of news reveals his sympathies was his account of affairs in Scotland. He recorded the King's presence in Edinburgh on 15 June 1633 to hold a parliament and council there. Charles was granted six subsidies and was given power to alter, add, make and ordain any ceremonies in their church. Yonge was critical of the apparent eagerness of the Scots to welcome the King appropriately, he records that they 'were so gorgeous in apparel that it's conceived they put two whole years revenue upon their back before their other charges.' In 1633 Yonge may have thought that the Scots were prepared to accept changes in their church to bring it into line with the English one but he was able to report a very different attitude when a new prayer book was imposed on the Scots by a proclamation based on the Royal Supremacy.[43]

The new prayer book was first used in St Giles Cathedral on 23 July 1637 and in October Yonge wrote: 'the Scots do much oppose the receiving of the English liturgies, and will not admit of our ceremonies into their churches nor the actual government of church by bishop etc. after the English manner.' He then copied out the petition sent from 'the nobility of Scotland and others to the Privy Council' which was drawn up on 18 October. It opposed the prayer book and the Canons and claimed that the proceedings were contrary to the preservation of the true religion which Charles 'hath ratified ... in his parliament of 1633' (a point Yonge underlined).[44] Yonge may have been in London during the summer of 1638 as there is no evidence of his presence in Devon between 18 May and 5 October. This is supported by his comment on 26 May that 'this day Marquis Hamilton sets forward in his journey for Scotland to declare unto them the king's pleasure'. Hamilton went to face Scots who 'continue resolute of no alteration, no innovation either in points of religion or government'. His next news of Scotland was a letter of 20 July that he had heard about but had not been able to copy, suggesting that he was learning of affairs in London, rather than awaiting newsletters. This letter apparently referred to the concessions which had been granted by Hamilton but that the 'Scottish Lords and others of the Covenant will abate nothing of their demands'. At the same time Yonge became aware that pre-parations for war were going on in London and that soldiers were being pressed for a war against Scotland.[45] Soldiers were also being pressed in Devon in September 1638 but Yonge wrote on 15 October that 'the business between the king and the Scots is ended'; this optimistic assumption must have been based on the pro-clamation of 19 September which revoked the prayer book, Canons and Court of High Commission and suspended the Articles of Perth, it also promised that a General Assembly should meet in November 1638 and the Scottish Parliament in May 1639.[46] Although Yonge does not chart the moves towards the first Bishops' War he does give a sense of the apprehension at the time; in November there was a portent of 'a very great light ... with sudden flashing about seven of the clock at night', and when the King moved north in March to engage the Scots, he reported omens from other counties—the noise of many horses but nothing appearing in Wiltshire and a river in Essex which 'runs half water and half blood'.[47]

Yonge's account of Scottish affairs, like his presentation of the arguments in the five knights case and the detail on all the steps towards the Petition of Right show what was moulding the political ideas of this future parliamentarian. Both his diaries reveal Yonge's puritan standpoint but his second diary suggests the development of views, increasingly critical, of royal policy. This is not something which is apparent in the study of Chudleigh, who only became a party figure when conflict became inevitable, and even then he strikes one as a reluctant partisan. There were other gentry leaders in Devon who shared Yonge's views, including several of his neighbours in east Devon, an area which has been described as particularly susceptible to puritan zeal. Three of Yonge's fellow JPs, Sir Peter Prideaux, Edmund Prideaux and Sir Henry Rosewell were summoned before the Court of High Commission and they with Sir John Pole and Yonge himself were all dropped from the Devon commission by 1643.[48] From the other end of the county Sir William Strode would have shared Yonge's religious and political views. It is a significant fact that the Devon bench could accommodate strong and differing standpoints without them disrupting the peaceful government of the county. The diaries also add an extra dimension to this study of Devon's gentry leaders as a whole. There is nothing unique in Yonge's sources. The information he records could have been available to all his fellows on the bench, so they provide the national background for the activities within the county. They enable one to dismiss any idea of the county being isolated from mainstream affairs, either through ignorance or indifference. If Devon was more peaceful and law abiding than some other areas then it was not because it was isolated from knowledge of discontent elsewhere.

Yonge concluded his most detailed diary in the summer of 1641 and left it at his house of Stedcombe when he took his seat in the Long Parliament as member for Honiton. His diary was found by Sir Edmund Fortescue when he captured Stedcombe on 22 April 1644. At that time Yonge's home was the principal outlying garrison for the besieged port of Lyme Regis.[49] After the sequestration of his estate Yonge was one of the MPs granted £4 a week to maintain themselves in the service of the Commons.[50]

Although Yonge's career as a gentry governor of Devon had ended, a brief epilogue on the last years of his life is relevant to this study. Nearly twenty years of service on the bench led to seven years of service in parliament. His successful transfer from Devon to Westminster, from local administration to national politics, confirms the impression of his main diary that a Devon JP could have his finger on the national pulse. Yonge's puritan sympathies may well have been the principal reason for his support for the parliamentary cause but his experience as a gentry governor must

money in Devon with sketches of five more of the governing body of the county.

Sir Thomas Drew

The Drew family had been long established at Sharpham in south Devon but their prosperity had greatly increased with the success of Edward Drew, father of Sir Thomas, who become a serjeant-at-law in 1589 and the Queen's serjeant in 1596. The wealth he accumulated enabled him to purchase large estates in east Devon, at Broadhembury and Broadclyst, where he built his house at Killerton. Thomas Drew followed his father to the Inner Temple but did not become a barrister, instead he went on to Oxford where he was one of the few Devon gentry to achieve a degree. After his father's death in 1598 he sold the Killerton estate to the Acland family and built his own house, The Grange, at Broadhembury.[5] He was appointed to the bench in 1603 and was a conscientious JP, attending quarter sessions, on average, about twice a year and was one of the more active JPs in signing recognizances and conducting examinations in his home area.[6] He was knighted at the coronation of King Charles but did not make his individual mark on county affairs until he was appointed sheriff in his late fifties.

The usual day for the King to prick the sheriffs was the morrow of All Souls Day (3 November), so Sir Thomas was immediately faced with the task of dealing with the first ship money writ issued on 20 October 1634. He was expected to organize assessments within thirteen days of receiving the writ but the first evidence of Drew doing so was his order to the head constable of Axminster for the parishioners of Axminster and Axmouth to appear before him at the Guildhall in Exeter on Wednesday 10 December 1634. He had also summoned 'the mayor of Exeter and the other mayor commissioners for the setting forth of two ships one of 700 tons and the other of 400 tons'. Parishioners were 'to bring the rates of the poor with them for the proportioning of £9,000 to be taxed upon them towards the said service'. At this meeting it was agreed that £5,401 should be paid 'for the setting forth of one ship by Exeter'.[7] The Privy Council had expected a more rapid response to

199

the writ and wrote to Drew on 9 December 1634 stating that the magistrates 'had deprived themselves of the benefit of setting their own rates' by their slowness. Drew was now ordered to assess the rates himself and was told that Plympton, Plymouth, Tiverton, Bideford and Barnstaple were to provide a ship of 500 tons collectively at a cost of £4,621; and Exeter, Clifton-Dartmouth-Hardness and Totnes were jointly to provide one of 700 tons at a cost of £6,615.[8] This letter, with figures contrary to those mentioned in Yonge's diary, caused the town officials so much concern that they hurriedly sent representatives to London to appear before the Privy Council. They maintained that their delay in making rates had been due to the slowness of the messengers taking the writs to them. In spite of this the Council's next letter to Drew, dated 24 December, repeated their order for him to act in accordance with their letter of 9 December.[9] If Yonge's figures are correct Sir Thomas was faced with the unfortunate task of having to increase arbitrarily the assessments agreed at the Guildhall meeting of 10 December. The meeting concerned with assessments for the smaller ship was held at Plymouth on 2 January 1635 and the assessments agreed were only a round £22 short of the figure in that letter, although the reference was to a ship of 400 rather than 500 tons.[10]

This demand for ship money was very different from the traditional demand for ships from port towns. This order of 1634 for Exeter and seven corporate towns to combine to produce two ships could only be met by a financial levy, even if the ships could be found locally. The two meetings in Devon at Exeter and Plymouth, which assessed the towns and parishes, imposed charges on a wider area than one would understand as the sea coast; towns such as Tavistock and South Molton lying over ten miles from the sea being included. A later letter of Sir Thomas Drew says that 'seven score parishes or thereabouts were involved in this first collection', that is about a third of the county. As it was the sheriff's agent who sent the order to outlying areas, such as Axminster, it was presumably Sir Thomas himself who decided which parishes should be regarded as sea coast areas.[11] Sir Thomas Drew was obviously faced with a complicated task; an unaccustomed form of an old demand, involving wide but selective collection, these were factors which were an invitation to opposition. Yonge's complaint that Axminster and Axmouth had no merchants living in them, that they were not port towns and that Axminster was a decayed town probably reflected typical discontent.[12] Sir Thomas must have felt isolated in the position he held as the King's agent when he noted the intention of both the Epiphany quarter session and the Exeter City Council to petition the Lords of the Council 'in the business concerning shipping'.[13] He was detached by his office from the collegiality of the bench and could only observe the support given by fifteen JPs to the letter of protest over ship money being extended to inland towns, which was 'a novelty'.[14] In spite of this opposition from the county and Exeter, it was Barnstaple which caused Drew his greatest difficulty when the mayor tried to bypass his authority by writing directly to the Council. His defiance led to a strong Council letter criticizing his 'great neglect and backwardness in the execution of His Majesty's writ' to which he had added 'contemptuous demeanour in menacing the said high sheriff that you would complain of him to this Board'.[15]

In spite of the opposition he faced Drew achieved a rapid collection and made five payments to the treasurer of the navy between 5 April and 29 May 1635 totalling £11,236.[16] The receipts make reference to ships of 700 and 500 tons which the King was graciously pleased to provide for them, showing that the full amount for the tonnage laid down in the Council's letter of 9 December 1634 had been collected, rather than the lesser figures named in Yonge's diary. Sir Thomas Drew had proved more successful than his fellow sheriffs in some other counties who still had arrears to collect on 30 June 1635. It is a feature of the ship money collection that coastal counties tended to respond better than other counties, Cornwall had completed their return in full by 1 April 1635.[17] Devon was very well aware of the need for an improved navy and this may have aided Drew's first collection aimed at combating 'thieves, pirates and robbers of the sea, as well Turks, enemies of the Christian name', but opposition was to grow with the repetition of the charge. The success of the later collections in Devon owed more to the labours of the sheriffs collecting it than to belief of the people that it would relieve the dangers to their coasts.[18]

Sir Thomas only had a brief respite from the problems of ship money before a new writ was despatched on 4 August 1635.[19] This time a smaller amount, £9,000, was to be levied and the whole county was to be assessed. The Council had learnt from the experience of the first writ and now sent detailed instructions to the sheriffs and corporations outlining the method of collection and suggesting the amount to be paid by each corporation. Similar instructions have been found for the next two years with only small differences.[20] They emphasize the lonely position of the sheriff in collecting this tax; unlike all the other taxes of the period, whether parliamentary or extra-parliamentary, he was in sole charge. The sheriff was to summon the mayors of the corporate towns to meet within thirty days (forty days in 1636 and 1637) and decide on their contributions. As the sheriff was 'presumed to stand alike affected to all the corporate towns' he would ensure that no unfair burden was placed on any town. The amount laid down for each town in the instructions could be varied if the majority of mayors and the sheriff agreed, as 'we are so far content to give way to your judge-ment (who are upon the place)'. When this was decided the sheriff was to divide the rest of the charge between the hundreds 'in such sort as other common payments upon the county'. The sheriff then had to get the constables to select some of the 'most discreet and sufficient men' to decide how the charge should be assessed and send details of this to him as soon as possible. Some discretion was allowed to assess men with 'gainful trades . . . according to their worth and ability' even if they had little or no land and so would not be taxed in 'ordinary land scot'. This would make it possible to free the frail or those with large families from the charge but it created problems for the sheriff by giving alternative principles for assessment: the ability to pay or the amount of land held. The instructions clarified some matters but created other difficulties, in particular the decision to divide the payment between the divisions on the same principle as for common payments. This led Sir

Thomas to assess the three divisions equally. Evidently, he had no doubt that this was the correct method, although he commented on its unfairness in a letter to the Council in October 1635 and requested the assistance of the deputy lieutenants for re-rating.[21] As he had no hesitation in adopting this method, one must assume that this was the normal procedure with the common payments in spite of its obvious inequality for divisions of varied population and wealth.[22] He clarified the exact position over the rates in a letter of 26 November 1635 by stating that each division was to pay £2,573 6s 8d, exactly one third of the amount due from the county (£7,720) after deducting the payments due from the corporations.[23]

Sir Thomas Drew acted rapidly on receipt of the writ of 4 August 1635 and by 12 September had organized a conference at Exeter with the mayors of the corporate towns.[24] They maintained the overall division of the assessment between the towns and county included in the instructions but varied the amount from some of the towns. This led to complaints by Barnstaple and Plymouth at the increase of their rate for the 1635 levy, while Totnes had a lower charge.[25] The instructions had given Sir Thomas authority to agree to changes in the towns' assessment but had not stated that he could use his discretion over the rating of parishes. He wrote to the Council, on behalf of the conference meeting in Exeter on 12 September, asking for permission to be more generous to parishes which had been charged highly in the 1634 collection in contrast to those who had, so far, paid no ship money.[26] He thought this concession would make the maritime parishes pay the 1635 assessment 'with cheerfulness'. The Council's reply ignored this query over rating though it did commend 'his diligence'.[27] Meanwhile, he proceeded with the assessment and sent warrants to the head constables who were to meet in each division, make an assessment for every parish and return it to him. This was not a straightforward task, and Drew toured his extensive county holding many meetings and dealing with 'sundry complaints of wrong doing through the malice or favour of the constables' before he could approve the assessments. He succeeded in doing so by 13 October but his efforts had been greatly handicapped by 'the inequality of the ancient rates of the county in general' which the Council's instructions had required him to follow. He had met with 'many refractory people from all parts of the county' who would delay the collection but he would use his authority 'to destrain and imprison' and so had 'no doubt of the accomplishment and will (God willing) make payment of the money with all possible speed'.[28] Clearly, Drew was being faced with considerable opposition, although there is no evidence how far he had to carry out his threat 'to destrain and imprison'. This second imposition of ship money affected far more of the population than any other national tax; people who had previously only paid local taxes now found themselves subjected to a new, national tax.[29]

In spite of his difficulties Sir Thomas achieved a rapid collection within the county. He had received £7,000 by 26 November 1635 and on 12 December was able to report that the 'service was now near despatched'. He had sent the undersheriff and his bailiffs among the slow and refractory and only £500 remained to be collected. The towns were proving slow to respond and he had 'called on them by my letters'.[30] A sheriff normally handed over to his successor in November but this year all sheriffs appointed in November 1634 remained in office until January 1636. In Somerset the new sheriff acted with the old one for the 1635 collection but in Devon Sir Thomas Drew completed his collection alone. On 10 February 1636 he paid £7,930 to Sir William Russell, the treasurer of the navy, this included money from some of the towns though Exeter, Plymouth, Barnstaple, Totnes, Torrington and Bideford sent their payments separately and this brought the total from Devon up to £8,840 by 24 March 1636.[31] This means that Drew's collection of ship money compares very favourably with those of other counties. Fifty-three counties were charged ship money in 1635 and Devon was one of the twenty counties who had collected at least 90 per cent of the charge by 1 April 1636.[32] There is no detail of a final payment from Devon but on 8 June 1636 Drew wrote to Edward Nicholas, clerk to the Council, that 'the money has been wholely paid to Sir William Russell . . . though I have not received so much by £24 as I paid him in.'[33] So Sir Thomas was personally out of pocket for all his labour.

Sir Thomas Drew deserves much credit for the successful collections of ship money in Devon, not only for those of 1634 and 1635 but also for establishing the pattern for future ones. This was in contrast to the situation in Somerset where the first ship money sheriff adjusted assessments to his own and his friends' benefit and so caused justifiable complaints which destroyed confidence in the sheriff, confidence which his more conscientious successors could not restore.[34] The fact that Devon's response was conspicuously better than that of many counties showed Edward Nicholas the value of Drew's opinions and influenced the notes he compiled on the ship money collection. He wrote that in Devon refusals stemmed from the very unequal rates and that steps should be taken to rectify this. He gave the example of one parish with a rate of 8d per pound and another with only 4d and commented 'no wonder the inhabitants there very obstinate and reluctant to pay in more after so unequal a tax'.[35] This report, however, had no effect on the instructions over rating for the next ship money collection.

After his hectic term as sheriff, Sir Thomas had a quiet period, signing recognizances but not attending quarter sessions until after he became a deputy lieutenant in 1639. Although he ignored a request to show his 'good affection' by contributing money to the expenses of the northern expedition in April 1639, he was very active as a deputy lieutenant impressing forces for the northern campaign in July 1640.[36] The surviving indentures show that he was concerned in two stages of the process. He impressed men out of the regiments of the east division and also delivered those impressed in other divisions to the officers of the lord general. He signed all the surviving indentures for the Devon conscripts, these concern about 1,250 of the 2,000 to be enlisted in Devon. As these nearly all came from the east and south divisions, there is no evidence that Drew was involved in raising the men from the north division who mutinied at Wellington on 12 July. It is clear, however, that when Drew and his colleague, Sir John Pole, delivered recruits to their officers between 7 and 16 July, they were facing a very inflammable situation. There must have been considerable risk of the mutiny spreading to these recruits. They wrote on 17 July that they were dealing with troops acting 'in a tumultuous manner having disbanded themselves'. They considered the position with the men's officers and decided that, in view of 'their mutinous and uncivil disposition ... it was most safe to send them home in lesser numbers'.[37] So the effort to collect 2,000 men in east Devon to send north in early July 1640 came to nothing and it was not until 2 September that Drew and his fellow deputy lieutenants met to give these men fresh orders to be ready to march at sixteen days notice. This was the same meeting which protested to the Earl Marshal at the county being expected to meet the charge of these trained bands once they left the county and so, naturally, Drew was a signatory to the petition against that.[38]

The loyalty of Sir Thomas was assumed in his appointment to the Commission of Array in July 1642. This, however, was a false assumption as a parliamentarian in east Devon reported in August that 'Sir Thomas Drew is very much against this Array'. This view is confirmed by his nomination on 18 October by the Commons as a deputy lieutenant.[39] He did not take up arms but showed his sympathy for the parliamentarians by signing the declaration to be published in churches in April 1643 condemning the suffering caused by the forces of Sir Ralph Hopton. These parliamentary leanings led to his removal from the bench in May 1643.[40] When the royalist forces moved successfully through the county in the summer of 1643, he evidently considered himself too closely associated with the parliamentarian cause to remain at large and took refuge in Exeter. He was in Exeter when it surrendered on 7 September 1643 and so would have been pardoned in accordance with the terms of surrender. At this time the parliamentarian cause in the South West, if not in the country as a whole, must have seemed lost to Drew and he lent £1,000 to the governor of Exeter and Prince Maurice to pay the King's army. Sir Thomas was now sixty-five years old and took no further part in affairs. The fact that he had contributed to royal funds and later sued for pardon under the great seal at Oxford led to information being laid against him as a delinquent, but no evidence has been found of him being fined before he died in 1651 at Broadhembury.[41]

Sir Thomas Drew was the longest serving JP among the ship money sheriffs. He spent nearly forty years on the bench, living in what is still the picture postcard idea of a Devon village. It was only during his demanding term as a ship money sheriff and later as a deputy lieutenant coping with impressment of recruits for Scotland that he had to fulfil duties beyond the routine ones of a JP. Although one cannot isolate the effect of his term as a ship money sheriff from the other influences upon him, it is clear that after that time he was reluctant to act outside his own neighbourhood and that, when war came, his sympathy was with the parliamentarian cause.

Dennis Rolle

Dennis Rolle was a complete contrast to his predecessor as sheriff. He was only twenty-three years old and new to any administrative responsibilities. Prince gives a glowing account of his character and says that he was 'the darling of his county in his time, adorn'd with all the desirable qualities that make a compleat gentleman. He was, though young, of a ready wit, a generous mind and a large soul.' When he became sheriff 'his state and parade at that time was so great and splendid (his attendance being mostly gentlemen by birth, in rich and costly liveries lined with velvet) that the glory thereof is not yet forgotten in these parts.'[42] That he should have left such a reputation as sheriff when he had had to collect ship money, speaks well of his ability in that task.

He was the wealthiest landowner in Devon having succeeded to the estates of his grandfather Sir Henry Rolle of Stevenstone in north Devon in 1625 and those of his mother at Bicton in east Devon. He was married to Margaret, daughter of Lord Poulet, one of the most powerful men in Somerset. With this background he probably expected that it would be his lot to serve a term as sheriff. Even so he must have felt that he had drawn the short straw when he received the instructions for collecting ship money. One of Drew's difficulties was clarified and he was given the authority to alter the hundred assessments. He was also given powers to act against uncooperative officials but he was warned that 'even if they neglect their business you are to do yours'. If anyone delayed or refused payment he was 'to proceed roundly with them (of what quality or condition soever they are)', and certainly not leave them till last so that the 'refractory gained time above those that were well affected to the said service'. Finally, the responsibility for this collection was firmly placed on Rolle, if he had not raised it all by the end of his year of office he would have to collect the rest under warrant from his successor.

Rolle began his formidable task with a meeting of the mayors of Exeter and the corporate towns at Exeter on 9 November 1636.[43] This meeting accepted the assessments in the Council's instructions, although Barnstaple again objected to their rating but were out-voted.[44] Rolle then assessed the county according to their hundred rates but not without many complaints 'of the inequalities thereof which I have laboured to accord'. He ended his report to the Council on 27 December 1636, 'humbly entreating your lordships' pardon for those errors which through want of practice and experience in these great affairs may be committed by me'. Although Rolle was diffident of his ability he was most conscientious and sent the Council an assessment covering forty-four pages.[45] The detail supplied shows that the three divisions were no longer being assessed exactly equally. The north was now charged £2,559 19s 9d, the south £2,617 8s 2d and the east £2,544 12s 4d. This difference is not substantial enough to suggest that there was any extensive re-rating; rather that it was the result of Rolle's labours to deal with inequalities. Collection followed rapidly on assessment and Rolle sent up an indenture for £6,300 on 9 February. He anticipated difficulty over the rest of the collection and had issued warrants to distrain those who refused to pay. He ordered the head constables to bring the rest of their collections to the assizes, this was presumably the £1,789 that he despatched on 25 March 1637. He then informed the Council that Exeter (£350) and Plymouth (£190) had undertaken to make their payments so a total of £8,629 had been collected, leaving only £371 outstanding for which 'there shall want no pains nor care on my part to collect'.[46]

After achieving so much, it must have been galling to Rolle that he was included in a rebuke which the Council meted out to most of the sheriffs for not responding promptly to the writ.[47] He therefore added to his letter of 25 March 1637, that 'it grieves me to receive your Lordships reprehension by your letter for keeping His Majesty's money too long in my hands or for being slack in my service.' He was still smarting from the Council letter when he wrote to Nicholas, three days later, underlining his achievement in collecting such a large sum so quickly. He had managed this without any 'complaint made to their lordships against my service or murmurings in the county, that I can learn of at my carriage.' He then shows that there had been considerable opposition, 'many suffering distresses to be taken of their goods . . . and some base people have not spared to spatter the officers employed by me with base scandalous language and some there are that have published their resolution to bring their actions against the constables taking distress.'[48] Opposition to the collection was growing at this third repetition of the charge. If Devonians had hoped that ship money would give them greater security they were much disappointed in the late summer of 1636 when ships from Exeter, Topsham, Plymouth and the Newfoundland fleet were lost to Turkish pirates. The JPs wrote to the Council about these losses, as well as seeking a certificate from the Lord Keeper for a collection to ransom the crews of five barques from Salcombe who had been carried off to Sallee in North Africa.[49]

A final letter from Rolle was dated 19 November 1637. He had collected a further £130 with great difficulty and ordered his servant to pay the residue of £111 to Sir William Russell, requesting that it should be certified that Devon had paid the full amount.[50] Rolle may have received some of the arrears before his death in June 1638 but it is more likely that he bore this extra charge for his work as sheriff.

Thomas Wise

Thomas Wise moved in a different circle from the other ship money sheriffs and, indeed, from the other Devon gentry included in these biographical studies. His family had long been established at Sydenham, near Tavistock, in the far west of the county, beyond Dartmoor. His family, therefore, had closer family ties with some of the gentry of east Cornwall, rather than with those of Devon. His father, Sir Thomas, was a first cousin of Sir Richard Buller and the two families shared the same puritan outlook. Both Thomas Wise and Francis Buller were sent to Sidney Sussex, one of the Cambridge colleges with a puritan reputation and they developed a firm friendship.[51] Thomas Wise then went on to the Middle Temple in 1622. He was a member of three parliaments for the nearby Cornish seat of Callington in 1625 and for the equally nearby Devon seat of Bere Alston in 1626 and 1628, where his fellow member was William Strode. No evidence has been found of him playing an active part in debates.

When Wise was appointed sheriff in the autumn of 1637, it was the first time he was involved in the gentry government, even though his father, who died in 1630, had served as a sheriff, a JP and a deputy lieutenant as well as being one of the commissioners for billeting at the beginning of Charles' reign. Thomas Wise took up his task as a ship money sheriff just as his uncle, Sir Richard Buller, completed his term as sheriff for Cornwall. Sheriffs were pricked unusually early in 1637, probably because of the need to have them in office for the new ship money writ. Wise received the writ and instructions on 15 October, at the same time as he was notified of his appointment as sheriff. He immediately summoned all the mayors to a meeting on 26 October when they agreed on unchanged contributions.[52] No detail has been found of the assessments of the county's charge of £7,720 but Wise had sent £5,000 to London by 9 February, and on 14 February he entered the amount still owing from each hundred in his family estate records. This amounted to £2,695 0s 4½d, which Wise carefully noted was an error of 2s 2½d as the amount still owing from the county was actually £2,695 2s 7d.[53] Although money was clearly coming in more slowly than in the collections by Drew and Rolle, this was a feature common to the collection nationally but at least Devon was one of the sixteen counties who had managed to make a substantial payment within six months of the writ.[54] The slow collection of the rest of the charge may have been partly due to Wise's own attitude, he did not set a good example himself and had not paid his own contribution of £4 7s in April 1638. He was later criticized as unworthy to be knight of the shire 'as he did not levy the ship money', but Rolle's reports show that Wise took on the task when resistance was growing as the charge lost its novelty and so its sense of urgency.[55] It was thought in Cornwall that the release of sailors held at Sallee would aid the collection but the returning sailors may well have brought news that it was Moorish land fighting rather than the naval blockade which had secured their release.[56] A greater talking point than a naval success could have been the fact that so many of them had become Moslems during their captivity that Bishop Hall had to create a series of services, spread over three weeks, for the reception of such apostates back into the church.[57]

Some reasons for delay in this fourth collection of ship money were outside the control of Wise. The legality of the charge was being questioned in the Hampden case. Yonge detailed this long drawn out affair which started in the Michaelmas term, just as the collection for the 1637 writ was beginning, continued throughout the Easter Term and was not adjudged 'for the king in the Exchequer Chamber at the king's pleasure and that he only is the judge thereof' until the Trinity term.[58] The arguments in the case and the realization that the judges for Hampden were speaking *pro patria* could have caused many to delay their payments, possibly Wise himself, although the final decision, even by a close margin, removed the justification to refuse them. Another reason for the slow collection by Wise was the problem created by re-rating. Complaints over the unfairness of the rating system had been raised by both Sir Thomas Drew and Dennis Rolle.[59] In May and October 1637 the Council discussed a general re-rating and in October, just as the writs were despatched, the judges of assize were ordered to confer with the JPs of all counties about this.[60] Action was taken in

Devon and Thomas Wise informed the Council in May 1638 that new rates had been confirmed for 'every hundred and division of a hundred' by the deputy lieutenants in their meeting and the JPs at quarter sessions. However, the Council replied on 30 June that in their view the old rates were best though the sheriff had latitude to alter them in particular cases.[61] The inequitable basis for rating was the most frequently repeated complaint of each sheriff but even so the trouble caused in the one known case of considerable re-rating suggests that changes, even if fairer, would also be a source of difficulty. The dispute was over the 'great inequalities of rates for His Majesty' within the Exminster hundred. The three parishes which complained had had their rates increased by almost as much as six other parishes had had their rates decreased. After a reference to the consideration of five head constables, a petition to the Council and an explanation from Wise, the new rates were eventually confirmed.[62] This dispute illustrates the effect of the Council's indecision in advocating the ancient rates in the instructions, yet also proposing re-rating. Such conflicting orders must have made all rates open to question and increased the difficulties of the sheriff.

When the Council had made its decision against re-rating on 30 June 1638 it also examined the state of the ship money returns and urged the sheriffs to quicken their efforts, Devon was then £2,025 in arrears. Other counties were more backward in the summer of 1638 and Wise was not one of those summoned before the Council on 29 July for their neglect.[63] There is no evidence that Wise made any more payments before he was succeeded as sheriff by Sir John Pole in November 1638 and yet another ship money writ was issued. This gave Wise the excuse that he could not act unless Pole provided him with 'a warrant of assistance' to the head and petty constables wherever arrears still existed. As Pole thought he could not do that, Wise was 'disabled from collecting'. He asked the Council to give fresh orders and excuse him from obeying their instruction to attend the Council on 3 February 1639. More than one letter was sent before Pole produced the warrants but the threat that he must do so or collect the arrears himself proved effective.[64]

Wise and Pole had other commitments at this time, Wise had become a militia colonel and Pole was a deputy lieutenant, both were concerned with preparing the trained bands for the possibility of active service against Scotland.[65] This was the background to the apparent dilatoriness of Wise in collecting the arrears of ship money. On 10 April 1639 the Council required Wise to attend the Council with details of the arrears and to give reasons for the remissness of the county but he excused himself from attending because of the need to ensure his 'account may be framed by my receivers as may be fit for their Lordships' perusal'. He put the blame for the slowness of the collection on the constables and informed the Council that the arrears had now been reduced to £1,200 of which about £400 was due from the corporations; £340 of the arrears were already in his receivers hands in Exeter but he was having difficulty in obtaining bills of exchange to transfer this money 'in these times'.[66]

The delays in the Devon collection were not taken as distrust of the loyalty of Wise as he was appointed to the commission of the peace in July 1639.[67] When the Council wrote, on 20 October, requiring either payment of the arrears or for Wise to appear before the Council on 24 November, Wise maintained that he had not received their letter until 3 December. He again blamed the delay in collecting the arrears on the remissness of the head and petty constables in executing the warrants he had got from Sir John Pole. As there was now a new sheriff, Sir Nicholas Martin, he asked for instructions to be sent to him to assist him. He also asked for information on how those being proceeded against for arrears should pay charges to the officials as the absence of such instructions in the last letter had been 'a great hindrance to this employment'.[68] This is the first reference found to commission being paid to those executing the warrants. Wise now included detailed accounts with this letter of 5 December 1639. It is not surprising that he was reluctant to attend the Council as these show that the total paid to the treasurer of the navy was £7,790 14s (£6,948 12s from the county and £842 2s from the corporations). This left arrears of £1,209 4s which were more than the round figure he had given on 30 April 1639. He had not despatched any more money to the Council, not even the £340 he then had in hand. He now said that the amount collected and held by various officials was £534 16s 9½d, so he had collected just over £200 in nine months. Wise then covered 35 pages with the amounts owing from individuals, some for as little as 3d. Wise himself had paid what he owed. This account of 5 December 1639 is the last one found for the writ of 1637, which suggests that the arrears remained at £674 9s 2½d.[69]

At first sight one might assume that the delays and excuses of Thomas Wise show that he was not prepared to make the same effort as Sir Thomas Drew and Dennis Rolle, but circumstances had changed. Discontent at the repetition of the charge, delays over re-rating and the Hampden case may have accounted for the slower initial response but this meant that the fresh demands caused by the Scottish war faced the county when Wise tried to collect his arrears. It was not only that additional charges were now expected from the parishes to equip and pay soldiers but that these charges had to be collected by the same parish officials who were also involved in collecting ship money. Wise might put the blame for this failure on the parish officials but they were the ones at the sharp end of the collection, having to seek payments of ship money from their neighbours. It is not surprising that some of them failed to do so, especially when they were also in charge of collecting coat and conduct money and organizing impressment.[70]

There is no evidence that Wise was active in the affairs of the county after he presented his final account in December 1639, probably because of his commitments as knight of the shire for Devon in the Short and Long Parliaments. He showed his support for the feeling in the county by presenting two petitions in the autumn of 1640; the first to the Council against the oath required by the clergy in favour of the current discipline of the church and the second to parliament over 'the general grievances of this Kingdom' as well as some concerned with the Stannaries.[71] Wise died of smallpox in March 1641 and was succeeded as member for the county by his brother-in-law and fellow JP, Sir Samuel Rolle, who was later an active supporter of parliament.

Sir John Pole

Sir John Pole's family was another with a long background of life in Devon, and like that of Richard Reynell and Walter Yonge it had recently gained in wealth through marriage to a Periam, the prosperous merchant family of Exeter. Sir John's mother was Mary, daughter and co-heiress of Sir William Periam who had been Chief Baron of the Exchequer.[72] John Pole was appointed to the commission shortly before he was created a baronet on 12 September 1628, he took the place of his father who was then sixty-seven years old and had served for over forty years. He was more active in the county government than his father, with whom he shared an antiquarian interest in Devon.[73] He had the widest range of experience of any of the ship money sheriffs having served as a knight of the shire in 1626, as a militia captain and later as lieutenant colonel of a militia regiment, and by 1638 he was a deputy lieutenant. As a JP his attendance at quarter sessions and activity out-of-sessions was comparable to that of Sir Thomas Drew. The occasional mention of the place where a recognizance was taken suggests that his principal home was at Colcombe, near Colyton, which had been built by Sir William, but after his father's death he was sometimes resident at Shute, which was also in east Devon.

The ship money writ which Sir John received in November 1638 required only a third of the sum demanded in previous years; the county was to pay £3,150 and the towns £481.[74] This reduction was because the chief need, in 1639, was likely to be for troops against Scotland rather than for ships to counter maritime dangers. As a deputy lieutenant as well as sheriff, Sir John found himself faced with a dual commitment: to raise the reduced amount of ship money and to press soldiers out of the trained bands for service in the north. His letters over the conduct of the collection suggest that, like Thomas Wise, he had no enthusiasm for his task. He had to be pressed to give assistance to Wise over the collection of arrears (including £4 2s due from Pole himself) and he did not send any immediate report on his own progress as all his predecessors had done. It was not until 6 April 1639 that Sir John produced his first account in response to a letter from Nicholas which required an

account of the 'shipping business' as well as assessments for each
parish and a separate assessment of the clergy (which had been
required since 1636). Sir John's reply informed Nicholas that he had
collected £1,700 from the county and that the corporations had
promised to pay their charges. As for the assessments he obviously
considered his delay fully justified. He wrote: 'I could not possibly
effect it now, having been employed by myself and another deputy
lieutenant of this county in impressing soldiers out of the trained
bands for His Majesty's service in the northern parts.' He promised
to send the assessment of the clergy shortly but as for the parish
assessments, 'I do not see how I can speedily return them', and
there is no evidence that he ever did so. He then went on to give
Nicholas the reasons for his difficulties over the collection and his
advice on how the position could be improved. Obstruction to the
collection was caused 'by the murmur and discontent of the people
at the disproportion of the hundred rates'. He shows his antiquarian
interest in the background to these proportions, saying that
they had long been used but their 'disproportions' only recently
perceived; presumably because they had never before been used for
such large and repeated payments. As a JP and deputy lieutenant he
may well have been involved in the re-rating which occurred in 1638
and was set aside by the Council but he now offered fresh advice
that the Council should, 'for the time to come ... direct their
letters to deputy lieutenants and justices of the peace for the making
of more equal proportions upon the hundreds of the county, which
are indeed so unequal as in some places men pay as much for £20 *per
annum* as other in other places pay for £40 other for £60 and other
for £80'. Pole hoped that he would be able to complete his full
collection, 'having by all fair ways and means pressed the country
with the consideration of His Majesty's special occasions'. He ends
his letter by declaring that, 'if there be any jealousy in making the
assessments that I have assessed more than I ought, I assure you
upon my credit that I have not varied from the direction I received
from the Lords to the value of one penny which I shall be ready to
make good whensoever I shall be called thereunto'.[75] This letter of
Pole's shows a different approach to the collection from the sheriff

of Northamptonshire, who was also having to press men for Scotland and felt that he could no longer put pressure on subordinates to collect ship money.[76] Whatever Pole might have thought of the order to impress men for Scotland that did not lead him to relax his efforts to collect ship money, it only made him unwilling to do the bureaucratic task of producing assessments.

As Pole was meeting opposition to the collection in the county it might have been expected that Sir Richard Strode would be successful when he tried to get the support of the summer assize grand jury for a presentment against ship money. However, Lord Chief Justice Finch harangued the jury for an hour, giving them the clear reasons for the judgement against Hampden before he allowed Sir Richard to speak, and he then made such a poor impression that the grand jury did not support him. Strode's limited standing in the county and his cantankerous reputation may have contributed to his failure.[77] Meanwhile, Pole was making every effort to complete his collection, though without making any further reports to the Council. His silence led them to summon him on 20 October to attend them but instead of attending he reported on 18 November 1639 that he had sent the full amount, apart from £43 9s 10d, to the treasurer of the navy. He informed them that attendance at the Council would 'rather retard than further the service' because he was having to use his own servants to levy distresses for non-payment as the constables were afraid to do so lest they had actions brought against them. Opposition had grown since Rolle found that constables were being threatened, now Pole found them too fearful to act.[78] Although Pole did not attend the Council he sent his undersheriff to seek advice on how to deal with collection from those who had died and divided their estate and those who had left the county. On 3 January 1640 he wrote to Nicholas acknowledging 'gratulatory' letters sent by the Lords with a command for the arrears. He had got warrants from the new sheriff to try to obtain them, 'but it will not be effected without great difficulty'. He then made it clear that 'this work hath been full of trouble and of very great charge and expense unto me, otherwise I could not have brought in my accounts so shortly'. He therefore expected

Nicholas to put his case to the Council for 'an allowance for collecting and levying of the same as I understand His Majesty is pleased to allow the now present sheriff of this county'.[79] Pole's letters show how the attitude of the sheriff to his task had changed since Drew and Rolle were ready to cover the shortfall in the account. Even Wise had not expected any commission for himself when he had asked that officials collecting arrears should receive it.

In January 1640 Pole returned to his commitments as a JP and, as a deputy lieutenant, had to press more forces for the northern campaign during the summer.[80] Pole showed the characteristic efficiency of the gentry body as a whole in that regardless of what he thought of the policy which led to the orders he received, he still carried them out loyally. Pole's sympathies may well have been with the Scots; he certainly shared Yonge's interest over their opposition to the new prayer book, as he supplied the document about it which Yonge copied into his diary. He would have understood their standpoint because of his own puritan views. He had shown this earlier as a member of the Dorchester Company which aimed to develop puritan trading settlements in New England, and in 1635 he saw his brother William and sister Elizabeth sail for the settlement (Elizabeth is remembered as the foundress of Taunton, Massachusetts). In the Epiphany quarter session of 1641 he was included on the committee on preaching ministers set up in response to a parliamentary order.[81] Pole supported the various critical letters and petitions to the Council in 1640 and in 1642 he was one of the delegation which presented petitions from quarter sessions to the King and parliament.[82]

As the conflict came nearer Pole continued to attend quarter sessions and so supported the petition of midsummer 1642 which pleaded for unity even though he had already committed himself, in May, to support parliament's militia ordinance.[83] As the quarter sessions ended he met with Chudleigh and other deputy lieutenants to invite the officers of the trained bands to command their companies in the parliamentary cause.[84] Although Pole gave his full support to parliament during the early months of the war, he was not immediately dropped from the commission of the peace and

FIGURE 10 Memorial to Sir John Pole in Colyton Parish Church

219

continued with his out-of-session commitments until mid-October 1642. He was concerned in raising properly equipped horses and riders for parliament as well as serving with his own command.[85] In February 1643 he and Chudleigh led the 'forlorn hope' out of Plymouth and marched all night to attack the enemy at Modbury. However, he was also ready to examine the possibility of peace in the West Country and joined Chudleigh as one of the commissioners for Devon at the conference held near Plymouth early in March. He went on to the next stage of the negotiations at Exeter but then returned to Plymouth when the envoys of parliament ordered that they should be broken off.[86] Once again he acted with Chudleigh and joined his force of horse which was sent to take Bodmin and so was not present at the battle of Stratton.[87] No further evidence has been found of Pole on active service, yet he is referred to as 'in arms for the Parliament' when to his 'great grief' his son Sir William was in the royal army but no date is attached to that statement among the compounding papers.[88] Pole's estates suffered severely from both belligerents, his castle at Colcombe was badly damaged by royalists in 1644 and his estate at Shute suffered £5,000 worth of damage in a parliamentarian raid.[89] He had been dropped from the commission of the peace in May 1643 but was active again from May 1646 until 1651 when he may have left Devon as he died in 1658 in Bromley, Middlesex, the home of his second wife.[90]

Sir Nicholas Martin

Sir Nicholas Martin was the first member of his family to be numbered among the county gentry. Earlier generations had been notable as leading citizens of Exeter, one of them serving as mayor in 1533 and his three sons later in the sixteenth century. Their wealth had increased with marriage to another leading Exeter family, the Hursts, who had obtained the manor of Oxton, near Kenton on the western side of the Exe estuary. This estate was inherited by William Martin, recorder of Exeter and father of Nicholas. He gave his son the education common to a gentry governor but also determined that he should uphold his own severe religious standards. William Martin dedicated his book of moral precepts, titled *Youth's Instruction,* to his son, while he was at Oxford in 1612; Nicholas later went on to the Middle Temple. He was appointed to the commission of the peace in July 1630 and was a conscientious member of the bench, attending quarter sessions on average twice a year.[91]

The sixth demand for ship money must have reached Sir Nicholas soon after he assumed the office of sheriff as the instructions for the collection were dated 1 December 1639. Once again the sum required from Devon was £9,000 and, at first, sheriffs were only given a very short time to meet their charge before they would have to appear before the Council. The unreasonable deadline of 20 February was soon extended to 1 April 1640 and on 29 February Martin reported that the towns had agreed to the amounts included in the instructions. He had assessed the county rapidly enough to have already collected £3,303 16s 8d and the following month he sent a copy of his assessments to the Council.[92] This makes it possible to compare the rates of 1639 with those of 1636. There were widespread minor variations, only twenty-seven of over 400 parishes had identical assessments in these two years; the differences ranging from 1d to £7. This suggests that these parish assessments may have been adjusted each year entailing considerable work for the head and petty constables and for the sheriff who would have had to approve each assessment before collection began.[93]

Sir Nicholas continued with his efforts and on 27 June 1640 reported having raised a further £992 7s 5d, making a total of £4,296 4s 1d, but not without 'difficulty and affronts'.[94] On 28 July 1640 the escheator of Devon and Cornwall, William King, was ordered by the Council to assist the sheriffs of Devon and Cornwall in their collection of ship money. He met Martin in Exeter on 3 August and found he had collected £200 more. He instructed him to use bailiffs as well as constables to distrain to try to raise the rest of the charge but there is no evidence that any more was collected.[95] Although Martin had raised only half the sum demanded, this was a great achievement compared with the feeble effort of the sheriff of

Somerset who collected just £200 of the £8,000 expected of his county that year.[96]

Sir Nicholas returned to service as a JP and was present at the last two quarter sessions before the outbreak of war, so he would have supported the final petitions of the peacetime bench. On 15 July he, like Sir Thomas Drew, found himself appointed to the Commission of Array, possibly on the assumption that conscientious service as a ship money sheriff would be followed by active support of the royal cause. This was a consequence that did not follow in Devon nor in other counties; there was no certainty that a diligent ship money sheriff would be a royalist nor that a critical one would be a supporter of parliament.[97] Clearly little was known of individual opinion in Devon and Martin was soon acting as a deputy lieutenant in Exeter for the parliamentary cause, sending out orders for money, horses and equipment. His activities led to him being excluded from a proposed pardon from the King to Exeter on 9 November 1642, he was named with Sir George Chudleigh, Sir John Northcott and Sir Samuel Rolle as 'Traitors and Stirrers of sedition against us'. Parliament responded to the royal condemnation with a declaration of protection for Sir Nicholas and the other three. They commanded that this protection should be printed and published in all parish churches in Devon.[98]

In March 1643 Martin joined Chudleigh and Pole as Devon commissioners at the truce negotiations near Plymouth. The next month he was on the county committee organizing the weekly assessments for parliament but at the same time he was still acting as a JP, though he was to be dropped from the commission in May. He was in the besieged city of Exeter in July and his pardon was included in the terms of surrender of Exeter in September 1643, with the others originally named as traitors.[99] It seems probable that Martin left the county after the surrender of Exeter and did not return until after the royalist defeats in 1645. His wife, Lady Elizabeth, was involved in a fracas with a constable of Kenton in the spring of 1644 which suggests that Sir Nicholas was not then in the county. When the constable, acting on the orders of the King's commissioners arrested a certain Archillis Shipley, she 'did beat and abuse the said constable and by herself and others whom she invited therewith rescued the said Shipley from custody'. She was required to appear at the next quarter sessions but unfortunately the minutes do not give any further information.[100]

The very unsettled state of the county prevented quarter sessions meeting for a year after midsummer 1645 but some parliamentarian supporters in the county, such as Martin and Pole began to act as JPs, signing recognizances, before quarter sessions met again on 14 July 1646 with an almost complete change of personnel.[101] In this year Martin was recruited as the MP for Devon in place of Edward Seymour who had been disabled in 1643. Martin remained in the Commons until he was one of those excluded as part of Pride's Purge on 12 December 1648.[102] The fact that he tried to be present when parliament reassembled, after forty-one members had already been excluded on 6 December, reveals the strength of his political views. He clearly supported the stance of the parliamentary majority and opposed the policy of the army. It also suggests that his puritanism lay in a Presbyterian form of worship rather than independency. He returned to Devon after Pride's Purge and remained a JP but has not been found taking an active part in affairs.[103] He died at Kenton in March 1654.

Conclusion

The approach of Devon's five ship money sheriffs to their task changed as the charge was repeated year after year. When Sir Thomas Drew started with this unaccustomed duty, he raised his difficulties with the Council, but when he received no constructive response, he struggled on without criticism. Young Rolle also assiduously followed all the instructions he received but even he, starting with diffidence from his inexperience, felt justified in expressing his distress at not receiving greater consideration and commendation for his efforts. The next two ship money sheriffs were faced with a different situation. Thomas Wise had to deal with a changed attitude to the charge in the county; at first Hampden's case and the projected re-rating made the response slower and then the Scottish war made the demand for ship money a lower priority.

Pole made the collection on his own terms. He was not prepared to produce a speedy assessment of the parishes and he firmly offered advice to the Council to order fairer rating. His final letter to the Council made it clear that he would be making a claim for his expenses in levying ship money. The material on the last ship money collection does not provide insight into the attitude of Sir Nicholas Martin but his efforts ensured that Devon was one of seven areas which did produce over 40 per cent of their charge.[104]

There can be no doubt that ship money was a success nationally, producing more than all the subsidies collected during Charles' reign. The reasons for this response of the counties have not been fully explored, yet one generalization is often made, namely that maritime counties were more ready to pay ship money because they recognized the need for an improved navy.[105] This account of the return in Devon suggests that this assumption underestimates the achievement of their ship money sheriffs. They managed to make the collections with only Barnstaple complaining to the Council of the conduct of the sheriff; their success with the other corporate towns and with the city and county of Exeter suggests that they moved with sufficient diplomacy and equity to prevent petitions to the Council; petitions which hampered the collection in many other counties, such as Warwickshire and Norfolk. If a petition was allowed from one town, it soon promoted others leading to the need for reassessment and undermining the sheriff's authority.[106] The success of the Devon sheriffs masks the difficulties they faced, ranging from the criticism of JPs at the 'novelty' of the charge being extended to inland towns to the break down of the sheriff's chain of command in the county, when constables refused to distrain. These Devon sheriffs were very much part of the gentry government of the county, whereas in Essex few sheriffs were also JPs, while in Herefordshire, Lincolnshire and Worcestershire the office tended to be held by newcomers to the county.[107] The sheriffs' collection of ship money was characteristic of the gentry government as a whole; they were the King's servants and so fulfilled his orders but did not hesitate to express their criticisms to another of the King's servants, the clerk of his Council. The juxtaposition of the experiences of the ship money sheriffs with their later careers underlines the fact that competent local administration did not equate with support for royal policy, even though the appointment of two of them to the Commission of Array in 1642 suggests that the King assumed that it did.

Chapter 11

John Willoughby:
A New Class of Justice of the Peace

A biographical study of John Willoughby enlarges the scope of this history of country government. Willoughby's career reveals the type of esquire who might fill some of the supporting roles in the county such as treasurer of maimed soldiers and militia captain but was not a man of sufficient standing to aspire to a place on the bench in normal times. Yet in 1642 this member of the second rank of gentry leaders was appointed to the bench showing that a widening of the membership of that body occurred earlier than generally assumed. This was only one of the changes which came over the county government at this time; the outbreak of war destroyed its collegiate character as many of its leading members were dropped from the bench, the new leaders who arose in the county concentrated on military affairs and paid little attention to county government. What then was the role of a JP who was not also an army commander or a commissioner? This is the value of this study of John Willoughby as a JP, it reveals how far normal county government continued to exist in wartime. The quarter-session records are so slight for the years of Civil War that it would be easy to think that the routine of county government was submerged by the needs and movements of armies. The papers of John Willoughby correct this balance.[1] A study of his career reveals some of the problems of serving as a JP during these years. They show

how difficult it was for him to avoid being drawn into active support of the warring parties, and they suggest that he only found this possible until the end of 1643, thus underlining the changes which then occurred in the administration of the county.

The wealth of the Willoughby family stemmed from the cloth trade. John Willoughby's grandfather was termed 'clothier' when he obtained the manor of Seaton in 1557 but his father had become known as 'gentleman' by the time he purchased lands at Payhembury in east Devon for £750 in 1580. He had married Agnes Culme from Canonsleigh, within ten miles of Payhembury, and his heir John Willoughby was born on 27 September 1571. When John inherited the estate in 1602, the mansion of Leyhill had been built at Payhembury; its kitchen and the solar with its ornamental frieze survive, still providing peaceful views over the surrounding countryside.[2] Although Willoughby also held the manors of Seaton, Whitewell and Farway in Colyton hundred, his estate does not compare with those of Reynell or Yonge. He was less affluent than earlier appointments to the bench, a point borne out by his subsidy assessment of £10 which was only half that considered suitable for a JP. His household of only twelve servants also suggests a lower standard of living than two JPs whose households were enumerated in 1622: Nicholas Gilbert had a household of thirty-six persons and William Bastard, a bachelor, one of twenty-two.[4] Willoughby's genealogical table shows that he moved in a different social circle and, unlike Chudleigh, Reynell and Yonge, was not related to many other gentry governors.[5] He was not only less wealthy and well-connected but also less educated than most members of the Caroline bench in Devon; he did not go to the university or an Inn of Court.

Willoughby married Margaret, daughter of Philip Steynings of Holmscott, in West Somerset in 1598. In this marriage he was allying himself with a far more established gentry family; wealthy enough to build the fine south aisle (dated 1538) in their parish church of Selworthy. The marriage brought Willoughby into relationship with Dr George Montgomery, a useful contact for possible advancement as he was a chaplain to James I and became

FAMILY OF JOHN WILLOUGHBY

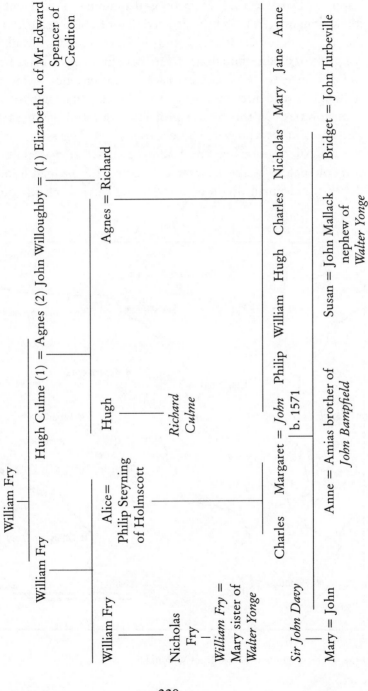

bishop of Derry in 1605. He proposed a number of different offices for Willoughby; in 1608 he suggested that he could make him one of the surveyors for the Prince's lands in Devon and Cornwall, 'which is a place of credit, though no greate benefit, onely it maye be a step and entrance to some better place hereafter', but it seems that Willoughby had little ambition to take the first step to greater opportunities.[6] In this he was probably typical of many of the less wealthy esquires who were content to manage their estates and leave any official positions to the leading gentry. He was almost fifty years old before he spent a year as treasurer for maimed soldiers for the east and north divisions in 1620, he carried out his duties as

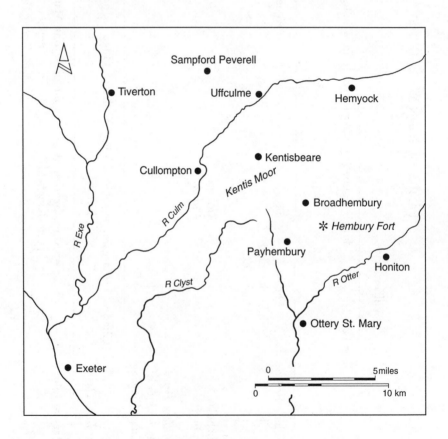

MAP 6 The neighbourhood of John Willoughby

230

treasurer competently and his accounts throw some light on the collection of funds to pay pensions to soldiers maimed in royal service.[7]

Willoughby did not hold any other county office until 1634 when he was made a captain in the militia regiment of the deputy lieutenant, Francis Courtenay.[8] He was perhaps ready to take on this task as it gave him a position of some authority in his home area. The care he showed in keeping copies of the orders he sent out suggests that he was impressed with the importance of his duties. His papers reveal some features of interest about a militia company. A comparison of Willoughby's muster book (of 4 June 1634) with that of his predecessor, Henry Walrond, three months earlier, shows that more than half the men were newcomers. Nearly all these men continued to serve for at least the next five years, suggesting that a considerable personal bond must have developed between the captain and the rank and file of his trained band. The officers remained unchanged from Walrond's command and twenty-one gentlemen also served in the company.[9] Willoughby rapidly got into the routine of organizing musters. In 1635 he ordered the head and petty constables to see that all his company appeared before him at Kentismoor (near Kentisbeare) on Tuesday in Whitsunweek by 8 a.m. They were to appear in complete armour to be reviewed, trained and taught the 'militariness' of their moves that day. On the Wednesday, Thursday and Friday the musketeers were to be provided with one and a half pounds of powder and enough match from the store: 'The best men were there and then to be exercised'.[10] The next two years Willoughby mustered his company at Hembury fort, about two miles from his home.

The demands upon a militia captain increased when it seemed likely that the trained bands would be required for war with Scotland. On 27 November 1638 the deputy lieutenants, acting on orders from the Privy Council, required all company commanders to hold a special muster on 11 December. Willoughby's new colonel, Henry Ashford, expanded on these orders and promised to be ready to assist him 'in these affairs'. Willoughby's orders to his company show how the commands of the deputy lieutenants, led by

Chudleigh, were now put into effect.[12] His company were to report to him at Kentisbeare on 11 December between 8 and 9 a.m., this order included the gentlemen who were to attend armed with sword, gorget and pike. The petty constables were to bring a list of all able men in their parish between the ages of 16 and 60 years and a list of all the powder, match and bullets in the parish store. They were also to see that a good store of carriages, horses and furniture were ready for the transport of 'necessaries'. The warrant for this muster ended with the proviso: 'no favour at this time to be expected', an indication of the urgency of the situation and perhaps of the latitude given to the constables on other occasions.

Any hope that the trained bands would not be needed outside the county was destroyed at the end of February 1639 when Devon was ordered to have 2,000 members of the trained band ready to serve. Willoughby's muster book of 11 September 1638 shows that impressment had already begun and fifty-one of his company were marked as 'prest', although they were still expected to muster in the trained band. In March 1639 further impressment took place and the details show that, contrary to the orders sent to the deputy lieutenants, the contingent of pressed men was only partly drawn from the trained bands. Seventy-five men were pressed but twenty-three of them had not served in Willoughby's company.[13] The pressed men were allowed to provide substitutes and a few of Willoughby's company were prepared to pay 6d a day for a replacement. The best arms of the trained soldiers were allocated to the pressed men and the owners of these arms were to be compensated. Willoughby himself provided the arms for two pressed soldiers from Payhembury. He now had the added responsibility of seeing that the pressed men were exercised each week, being 'exceeding careful and industrious therein to the end they may be perfect soldiers before they may be presented before His Majesty'; such training was obviously necessary as a third of the contingent were raw recruits.[14]

Willoughby was still expected to hold a normal muster for the whole company, in addition to organizing the weekly training for the pressed men. It must have become a taxing task to command the company for their two days training in June 1639, a company which included both those 'select and stand still imprest for HM present service as the rest not impressed'. The arms intended for the impressed men could be used for the muster but then had to be returned to the store. For the two days of muster Willoughby's soldiers were to 'be made acquainted with the most necessary discipline' with 'rounders' checking that the sentries were alert during the night hours. Willoughby was to camp with them in 'a tent set up in the most eminent place where your company is lodged'. It looks as though sleeping out in the field was a new hazard for the sixty-eight-year-old captain as he was advised that if he could not provide a tent soon, 'you are to have one of cloth which you may safely get from the colour makers'. Each soldier was to bring a knapsack with enough food to last him during the muster as no sutler or victualler was to be allowed near them; although they could have one or two sellers of beer at a suitable distance.[15] The list of defective arms compiled at this muster shows that Willoughby was now ranked as sergeant-major, that is third in seniority in the regiment.[16]

The pressed men continued to be part of Willoughby's company until 28 April 1640 when steps were taken to replace them. Presumably these men now became part of one of the contingents assembling in east Devon and awaiting orders to march north, though their names have not been found in the surviving indentures.[17] As 2,000 pressed soldiers from all parts of the county moved into east Devon, Willoughby and his militia company must have been well aware of the murmurings among them. On 11 July, 600 conscripts assembled at Tiverton and 160 of them were immediately taken on to Wellington where they mutinied the next day. They had noticed that one of their officers, Lieutenant Evers, had not attended church that Sunday and so, suspecting him of being a papist, they murdered him. This contingent would have passed through part of the catchment area of Willoughby's company as they marched to Wellington and when they came back boasting of the murder. Other pressed contingents assembling in the area also became unruly and were disbanded by the deputy lieutenants.[18]

These events in Willoughby's neighbourhood may have made Colonel Ashford anxious of discontent spreading to his militia companies. Recruiting fresh men to replace the pressed ones had evidently led to men from the same parish serving in different companies, which resulted in 'great trouble' and led Colonel Ashford to reorganize his regiment. In this unsettled state of the county it is not surprising that the summer musters were not held until 15 September in 1640.[19]

The threat of war brought personal worries to Willoughby as he feared that two proclamations issued in August 1640 might make him liable for active service or at least for extra taxation. The proclamation of 20 August revived knighthood composition (which Willoughby had paid in 1631) but allowed the option of being ready to serve the King by 20 September. The second proclamation, of 31 August, seemed to conflict with this as it required all in command of trained bands to be ready to serve 'His Majestie for defence of the Kingdome'.[20] Willoughby wrote to his new son-in-law, John Turbeville, on 19 September to seek his advice on the matter. Turbeville, a barrister, replied within a week but was uncertain of the position himself though he had sought the opinion of the 'greatest lawyers'. He reassured Willoughby that, 'few or none at all do either go in person or compound; for it there be a parliament, all those grievances will be redressed.' Willoughby had also sought Turbeville's assistance on a more practical problem; he evidently wanted to be well equipped in case he should be forced into active service and asked his son-in-law to find out the cost of a buff coat and a belt. He was told that a buff coat was 'exceeding dear, not a good one to be gotten under ten pounds ... but for your belt, you may have a substantial one reasonably'. Turbeville also gave Willoughby news of the Scots in Durham but after some details he added that as it 'is now in print and hath been this five or six days' this would save him the trouble of writing.[21] Clearly Turbeville assumed that newsletters would be reaching his father-in-law's quiet corner of east Devon.

Willoughby soon had a greater anxiety than possible military commitment, he suspected that his name was one of the three to be presented to the King for him to prick the sheriff for Devon. In order counties the unpopularity of the office had already led to nominations from a lower level of gentry. The recommendation of Willoughby for the office suggests that this was now happening in Devon, where all the Caroline sheriffs had, so far, been JPs or men of similar status.[22] When Chudleigh had wished to avoid the position, some years earlier, he used his friendship with the Secretary of State, Sir John Coke, to free himself from the task, but a man of Willoughby's standing did not have these connections and had to use different means. He commissioned his nephew William Davy to find out the truth of the matter and when he discovered that his uncle was indeed the first of the three names to be presented to the King, he started 'labouring' to get his uncle off. He made many journeys, 'yet found the matter difficult, till I engaged myself for £10 which I believe my friend will accept, and think me extremely obliged to him besides, . . . for if I had gone any other way, I could not have got you off for £20'.[23] The one appointed, Nicholas Putt, was of similar standing to Willoughby, so the office was now being filled by men of lower gentry status. The next year Willoughby wrote to Robert Starr, whose family held Willoughby's manor at Seaton, to find someone who would save him from the office. Starr was ultimately able to give him the good news that his cousin, Richard Culme, was appointed sheriff instead of him and 'so you are spared for this time'. He would let Willoughby know to whose help he owed this relief and 'what you are to gratify him for it'.[24]

When Willoughby sought to avoid the office of sheriff in 1640 he would have feared that it would involve another collection of ship money, a formidable task for a man of limited financial resources and little standing outside his immediate neighbourhood. When he was in danger of the office the next year, he may well have felt that he did not want to be put in the difficult position of being the King's principal official in the county. He was being kept in touch with national affairs through correspondence with John Turbeville, who wrote: 'I know you expect to hear of the proceedings in Parliament, and to deny you that, were to deny you the love and service I owe you.' Willoughby also had news from London from William Davy, and once heard from a soldier billeted in Yorkshire (possibly one pressed from his company). The correspondence which survives underlines the amount of political information reaching a fairly isolated part of east Devon. Some of the printed matter enclosed must indeed have prepared Willoughby's 'thoughts for the change which is like to be.[25]

One of the acts which Willoughby received news of from his nephew was one imposing a poll tax on all males over sixteen years of age. This was to provide the money for 'disarming the armies and settling the peace of the two kingdoms of England and Scotland'. This poll tax was publicized by a proclamation on 6 July 1641 which required all persons to make speedy payment on a scale from £100 to 6d. The detail of the tax in Willoughby's papers is the only information found on this collection in Devon.[26] It is also of interest in revealing something of the composition to Willoughby's home village. The restriction of the tax to males was evidently not understood by those compiling the book for Payhembury as it lists 276 persons of whom 130 were women. All but thirty-two parishioners were to pay at the basic rate of 6d and the total sum produced was £31 15s 6d (Willoughby paid £10). The nearby JP, Henry Ashford, and his son Arthur authorized the constable, overseer and two parishioners to make the collection and to distrain goods, if necessary, to enforce prompt payment. The list of poll tax payers shows that there were at least forty households in Payhembury, including those of two gentlemen and six yeomen, who all paid above the basic rate, so did four farmers, two clothiers and the local butcher, blacksmith and carpenter.

In January 1642, just as the 'Flocks of poor Protestants' were reaching Devon from Ireland and underlining the fear of the influence of the popish lords in parliament, Willoughby heard from his brother in Ireland. Nicholas Willoughby wrote from Dublin of the great losses he had suffered in the rebellion, he was 'robbed of all we had and with great danger, my wife, myself and two of my daughters came to Dublin, and left our son and three daughters more in the country amongst the rebels and what is become of them

I know not'. Nicholas' first thought was to come to Devon relying on his brother's 'love and charity' but there is no evidence that he did so though John did send him financial assistance.[27] At the same time as he was getting first-hand news of the Irish rebellion, Willoughby received a letter from his son-in-law in London which expressed the doubt about the future that all must have been feeling: 'How the times are, every man knows, what the times will be, no man knows.' It was during this period of general uncertainty that Willoughby was appointed to the commission of the peace and so became one of the gentry governors of the county, a position which surely, must have seemed beyond his reach.[28] He may well have felt apprehensive of what demands and decisions his new position might require of him. Turbeville wrote in June that, 'the King and parliament did never so much disagree as now they do', he heard that parliament was likely 'to raise more money out of the kingdom' and that a report had it 'that the king hath a very strong guard both foot and horse now attending upon his person at York and 40,000 more upon an hour's warning and that he is full of money but from what place he hath it, is not yet certainly known'.[29]

Willoughby's service as a JP was restricted, almost entirely, to his home area and he first signed recognizances there in April 1642.[30] There is no evidence that he ever attended quarter sessions, though the brief wartime minutes of quarter sessions seldom included a list of those present. It is not surprising if Willoughby did not venture to attend quarter sessions when troop movements could well force a change of venue. The session of Michaelmas 1642 began at Tiverton on 3 October and was then transferred to Exeter where it met in a city fortifying itself on the news that cavalier forces had moved westward from Sherborne.[31] The danger of a visit to Exeter at the time of the Epiphany sessions would have been obvious to Willoughby from the fate of his near neighbours, Richard Culme (the sheriff) and Henry Ashford, who were arrested when they were in Exeter for the sessions. According to a parliamentary newsletter, they were among many 'Delinquents' required to pay ransoms ranging from £100 to £800 for their freedom.[32] The Easter sessions of 1643 were held in Exeter during the time of the truce, but by the midsummer sessions the city was held by a beleaguered parliamentarian garrison and so inaccessible. Quarter sessions was first summoned to meet in Tiverton on 11 July (about ten miles to the north of Willoughby's home), but only two JPs were present and the meeting was adjourned to meet the next day at Topsham (about ten miles to the southwest of Willoughby), when three different JPs were present. Three further adjournments followed at Topsham in August and September. By the last one, on 12 September, Exeter had been surrendered by the parliamentary commander, the earl of Stamford, and quarter sessions ordered the sheriff to summon the Michaelmas session to meet in Exeter. Now that the eastern part of the county was securely in royalist hands, Willoughby attended to his duties in Exeter. He was present at the goal delivery on 13 December 1643, when he signed a number of recognizances with Peter Sainthill.[33]

Although Willoughby may not have attended quarter sessions, he was active in the out-of-session work of a JP. The quarter-session rolls as well as the minutes are very slight for the war years but even so they do provide the material to make some assessment of the work carried out by the JPs and to compare Willoughby's record with those of other members of the bench. These assessments concern the sixty-five JPs who were on the commissions of the peace of 1643 or have been found acting as JPs until the summer of 1645, when any effective rule broke down in the face of the lawlessness of Goring's troopers. These gentlemen can be divided into four groups, according to the number of acts of county administration carried out or expected from them; that is, attendance at quarter sessions, being assigned specific duties in their localities, taking examinations and issuing recognizances. The most active were seven esquires who carried out between fifty-five and eighty-eight tasks during this period. Eight more JPs can be credited with twenty-five to fifty duties, though Willoughby's own tally of fifty is swollen by twenty-two recognizances taken at a single gaol delivery. Of the remaining JPs thirty-three carried out some county duties and so only seventeen appear to have been inactive in county administration. A survey of the home areas of the most active JPs shows that Willoughby's own hundred of Hayridge was the best served with Peter Sainthill and John Were (of Silverton) as well as Willoughby himself, but it also shows that no area apart from Plymouth was completely beyond quarter-session rule. Orders were still sent to the JPs in distant hundreds; for example, William Cary in Clovelly and Arthur Champernowne in Dartington could be required to arrange for the repair of a bridge, Sir John Chichester of Hall near Barnstaple and Sir Richard Reynell near Newton Abbot could be asked to swear new head or petty constables. JPs still met together to issue alehouse licences, indenture apprentices and take recognizances, though their meetings were now too seldom to suggest any regular pattern of petty sessions.[34]

Willoughby's papers fill one gap left in the survey of the varied duties of a JP which were outlined in the chapter on administration and continued in the study of Reynell's use of recognizances; they show a JP supervizing parochial officers. On 29 March 1643 the head constable of Hayridge, acting on the instructions of Henry Ashford and John Willoughby, required the constables of Feniton, Payhembury and Broadhembury to order the churchwardens and overseers for the poor of their parishes to make up a perfect account and bring it to these JPs at the house of Mr Anthony Merson at Kentisbeare by 8 a.m. on the 4 April. They were then to nominate new overseers of the poor for their parishes for the next year, and to see that those nominated were present. They were also to warn all innkeepers, alehousehkeepers, tipplers and taverners in their parishes to be present and bring with them two sureties to be bound with them by recognizances for the next year. Another duty Willoughby fulfilled was to bind apprentices and to call before him any who had not paid their poor rate.[35] Although Willoughby was not present at quarter sessions, he was clearly not neglecting his other functions as a JP. He was ready to fulfil them whichever party was in control in Devon, but he tried to avoid action when he was required to give support to the warring forces in the county.

Willoughby had remained in command of his militia company after the last known musters of 15 September 1640 and so was faced with making a decision on his future allegiance when three deputy lieutenants required him to come to the New Inn Exeter on 14 July to receive a commission from the parliamentary lord lieutenant, the earl of Bedford. He evidently did not attend as another letter was sent on 15 July, informing him that they held a commission for him to command the same company as that 'formerly commanded by you'. Willoughby was required to give his answer to the deputy lieutenants at Honiton on 23 July.[36] He did not accept the command of his trained band in the parliamentary cause and instead was present at the attempt to publish the Commission of Array at Cullompton on 22 August.[37] His cousin Richard Culme, the sheriff, and two other JPs were present but the petty constable of Cullompton refused to read the commission and Willoughby left the gathering before warrants could be issued to stop parliamentary forces from mustering. As a JP he would have been involved if warrants were issued in his presence. Evidently he was not prepared to act against the parliamentary forces who were being mustered on this same day, 22 August.[38] He had not thrown in his lot irretrievably with either side and the parliamentary deputy lieutenants valued his advice enough to summon him to meet them at the Bear in Exeter, on 21 October, to discuss the dangerous state of the county with troops passing through it.[39] There is no evidence that he attended this meeting. The next order from the deputy lieutenants was of a different kind; it came from their meeting in Exeter on 8 November and required a number of gentlemen of the Hayridge hundred, including Willoughby, to provide a light horse and rider fully armed for the service of parliament. This order was sent to some who had already shown themselves active royalists (such as Henry Ashford and Peter Sainthill) and so was no indication of parliamentary support. Willoughby was slow to obey this command and was criticized in January 1643 by Sir Samuel Rolle for his 'backwardness'. When he did send a horse with a relative, John Fry, as the rider, he still had not supplied the necessary arms. He did, however, make sufficient financial contributions to the parliamentary cause to avoid being charged extra for dilatoriness.[40]

There is no evidence that Willoughby left his home area during the disturbed early months of 1643. While he was busy apprenticing the son of a very poor woman of Culmstock on 13 May, the rival armies were approaching Stratton, on the northern border of Devon and Cornwall, where the royalists were victorious over the earl of Stamford on 16 May 1643. This brought the war into Willoughby's home area as the royalists pursued the defeated parliamentarians eastwards and took Bradninch, Cullompton and Tiverton in the first week of June and began the siege of Exeter.[41] Both sides tried to raise forces in east Devon so their efforts give an indication of the allegiance of Willoughby's neighbourhood. The downhearted parliamentarian party failed to get the support of the trained bands and while they tried to summon the 'Arms of the East', the royalists summoned a *posse comitatus* from the east division. Although the trained bands were not prepared to fight for parliament at this time, the indictments of those who did not respond to a summons to the posse suggest that many were equally reluctant to fight for the King.[42] Two of the indictments differ from the rest as they have attached to them a list of those summoned; these lists name 196 from Tiverton hundred and the same number from some of the parishes in Hayridge and Hemyock hundreds including forty-eight who had served in Willoughby's trained band in 1639. Deletions on the Tiverton list make it clear that thirty-seven refused to respond to the summons but the list for the Hayridge and Hemyock parishes is unmarked and so it is impossible to determine how many actually refused to serve. There are seven more indictments concerning men from Willoughby's area who failed to answer a summons to the *posse comitatus* in July 1643, though each of these indictments involved only one or two men. The reluctance of some of Willoughby's neighbours to respond to a summons to a posse must have shown him the feeling of his neighbourhood. Although a letter from Peter Sainthill at this time assumed that Willoughby was a royal supporter, he had not done much to prove it and this inaction was in keeping with the signs of reluctance to serve the King in his area.[43]

A new body of commissioners was emerging in the county during this summer of 1643. Their prime concern was with the royal army and their finances but they began to usurp the functions of some of the traditional offices; four commissioners rather than the customary sheriff issued an indictment on 18 July for those who failed to answer a summons to a posse.[44] The historian of the royalist war effort has noted the establishment of new commissions for guarding five counties (Worcestershire, Gloucestershire, Herefordshire, Oxfordshire and Wiltshire) between March and June 1643, but he thought that the commissioners in the West Country were a continuation of the original Commission of Array. Although no commissions have been found for the West Country, the commissioners acting from June 1643 were a different body from those appointed in the original Commission of Array. Twenty-six Devon commissioners have been identified by their signature on letters or from mention in compounding papers; only ten of them being among the twenty-seven members of the Commission of Array of July 1642. The current army commanders were included, otherwise they were mostly, but not exclusively, JPs. Willoughby was not among them.[45] The first evidence of them in action was a declaration of commissioners and JPs 'now in His Majesties Army', dated 26 June 1643. Four of them expressed their trust in the King's promise to maintain parliament and the Protestant religion. They then proposed that all justices, gentlemen and freeholders of Devon who desired peace with security of religion, law and liberty should meet on 3 July at Crediton and there agree that Devon and Cornwall petition the King and both houses of parliament to free both counties from further charges and the ruin caused by war. The commissioners hoped that the King's commanders, the sheriff, justices of the peace, ministers and two of the ablest men of every parish would attend this meeting. Willoughby filed the declaration among his papers but there is no evidence of who attended the meeting.[46]

The royalists increased their hold on the county during the autumn as Exeter and all the other centres of parliamentary resistance, except Plymouth, fell to the army commanded by Prince Maurice. Plymouth was now the principal objective of the royalist forces in the county, though, for those who lived in east Devon, Lyme Regis, just across the Dorset border, must have seemed the more immediate target. All this military activity had its repercus-

sions in increased work for all the JPs, including those, like
Willoughby, who were not commissioners. JPs began to find
themselves expected to enforce the orders of commissioners who
were now exercising the authority previously belonging to the
deputy lieutenants. The head constables of Willoughby's group of
hundreds were required to report to commissioners at Cullompton
on 27 September 1643 bringing with them lists of all trained
soldiers, all able men and all who had recently fought against the
King. It was thought, optimistically, that these former opponents
would now fight for the King. Constant watch was to be kept to
arrest spies and rumour-mongers and bring them before the nearest
JP to be dealt with. Those who had previously supplied arms were
to have them ready and others who had, so far, been free of this
charge were now to supply them, according to the value of their
land.[47] Willoughby soon found himself involved in extra work on
this score when two commissioners ordered the constables of
Awliscombe to see that 'all owners of arms and all other able and
sufficient men' of their parish appeared before him at Payhembury
on 2 October at 1 p.m.[48]

The dividing line between the military and civil authorities was
becoming clouded. The 1643 Michaelmas quarter sessions tried to
define this line. They said that they were ready to obey Prince
Maurice and the chief officers of the army, the governors of towns
and to execute all reasonable warrants from them but, 'we are
unwilling that the county should be subject to the extravagant and
illegal commands of inferior officers'. They would not execute any
warrants from such inferior officers and it would be lawful for any
man to refuse to obey such a warrant. They made it clear that any
one acting unlawfully would be arrested and tried according to the
laws of the land, this would include both actions by soldiers and
against soldiers.[49] Clearly, quarter sessions were still attempting to
rule by the normal law of the land. This protest in quarter sessions
may have influenced the careful wording of the instructions to
Captain Cockayne when he was sent with his troop on 27 October
'to attend and assist' Willoughby and four other JPs of the
east division in collecting arrears of martial rates. Even so, the

commissioners were actually usurping the role of quarter sessions when they authorized the JPs to grant warrants to arrest those who refused to pay the rates and have them brought before the commissioners in Exeter. The JPs were to pay the money to the treasurer of the royal army in the west and to be accountable to the commissioners in doing this.[50]

Willoughby was about to be required to be more active in the royalist cause. The commissioners of Devon and Cornwall met at Tavistock on 1 November to decide on recruiting 6,000 men 'to go through with the business of Plymouth'. They required 1,500 men from the east division and ordered the JPs and commissioners of that division to select men from posses to be raised at Cullompton on 6 November and at Ottery on 8 November.[51] This order was among Willoughby's papers and he could have had no doubt that the purpose of raising the posse was to attack Plymouth, yet he pleaded in his petition to the committee for delinquents late in 1645 that he was unaware of the purpose of the posse until he reached Ottery and that he then refused to join in raising it.[52] So far Willoughby had managed to maintain an ambivalent attitude towards the struggle in the county. He had paid the contributions to both sides and acted on orders he received from the sheriff or commissioners, who were often fellow JPs, but he could claim that this was not open defiance of parliament. These new posses, however, were intended to attack parliamentarian forces. Whatever may have been claimed in his petition in 1645, Willoughby did take part in raising the posse in November 1643. Conclusive evidence lies in a letter of 20 November from Willoughby and George Parry to the head constables of Axminster, Clyston, East Budleigh and Ottery. In this they state that they were: 'present at Ottery St Mary about the execution of the warrant upon the said posse'. They ordered the head constables to common 'all able men as were warned and . . . there made default of their appearance' to attend quarter sessions on 28 November at Exeter castle. In another warrant these two JPs required those who had defaulted to appear 'before us and other JPs' at the quarter sessions, so Willoughby may have attended on this occasion.[53]

The summoning of the posses in November 1643 was a turning point for Willoughby. In 1645, with memory dimmed, perhaps by wishful thinking, and supported by a plea of his near eighty years (he was actually seventy-five), he falsely claimed that he had withdrawn from this action when he had discovered its purpose. Yet he had gone on to attend the gaol delivery on 13 December 1643, which was a Commission of Oyer and Terminer, although he also contended in 1645 that he had utterly refused at any time 'to meddle in the Commission of Oyer and Terminer'.[54] Willoughby's petition to the committee for delinquents in the autumn of 1645 suggests that he was under pressure in the winter of 1643 to become one of the commissioners. He claimed that for 'about a year and a half while the king's party in that county was at their greatest height [he] being named in several commissions for his Majesty was threatened by order [of] His Majesty's commissioners for refusing to join with them'.[55] November and December 1643 were a time of great uncertainty for Willoughby; at first he obeyed the commissioners and he may well have contemplated becoming one of them, but he then decided against such action and ignored a plea from Peter Sainthill to attend an urgent meeting at Cullompton on 19 December 1643 on 'business of high warrant'. This meeting was to arrange support for the King's forces and ordered soldiers to be conveyed to join Prince Maurice before Plymouth.[56]

Willoughby continued to act as a JP and thus far he was the King's servant, but he had now separated himself from his colleagues on the bench who gave their wholehearted support to the royal cause as commissioners. Each fresh demand of the commissioners for support must have made Willoughby more uncertain of his own position. It became apparent in March 1644 that the commissioners were prepared to use force to raise money for the royal cause. Whereas Captain Cockayne had been ordered to aid and assist Willoughby and his colleagues in October 1643, in March 1644 royalist forces were used to compel payment of taxes by the people of Hemyock, about eight miles from Willoughby's home. The men of Hemyock had been encouraged in their opposition by the parliamentarian success in holding Lyme. They had first seized

Hemyock castle with assistance from the Lyme garrison but then they had been attacked by royalist forces who hung the three ringleaders and took 200 prisoners to Exeter.[57] Willoughby may well have known some of those involved as it was the recruiting ground of his former trained band. After the outbreak at Hemyock, John Acland, the sheriff and also a commissioner, sent Willoughby an order on 24 April to investigate a report that Mr Humphrey Sanders, the parson of Hemyock, had been trying to persuade people that 'they should now stir, for now was the time to regain their liberties'. Sanders had also advised those collecting the martial rates at Uffculme, 'to leave that business and rise likewise'.[58] This was to prove the last order Willoughby was sent in the belief that he would act in the royal interest.

It was six months since Willoughby had first shown his reluctance to give active support to the royalist cause. His doubts may well have increased when he heard of the royalist troops suppressing the rising among his neighbours at Hemyock, but the final breaking point was the letter of 17 May 1644, from five commissioners in Exeter:

Although we find your name in several commissions as a person in whom his Majesty resposeth trust and confidence, yet we find not your personal performance which you owe to your sovereign, whereby you do not only give an ill example to others, to absent themselves but do much retard His Majesty's service. And if you shall hereafter neglect your business, as hitherto you have done, we shall have right cause to suspect that you are but lukewarm, if not worse, we leave this to your consideration and rest your affectionate friends, Peter Ball, Henry Ashford, Peter Sainthill, John Were, John Davy.[59]

It had obviously become impossible to continue to act on the Devon bench unless one gave active support to the royal army; after this date there is no evidence of Willoughby fulfilling any duties as a J.P. He was, however, ready to join with three others in complaining to Sir John Berkeley at the abuses suffered by the officers and soldiers of Hayridge and Hemyock from French horse and other troopers.[60] As these French forces had been among those used to suppress the rising he was showing his concern for the suffering in his neighbourhood.

When Willoughby drafted his petition to the committee for delinquents in the autumn of 1645 he claimed that when he was threatened for refusing to join the commission he had 'preferred rather to forsake his house than comply'.[61] This had some truth in it as Willoughby did ultimately leave his home but not until March 1645, so one must question whether this pressure from the commissioners was as severe as his petition was intended to suggest. A list of 'all my linen', dated 25 March 1645, was evidently part of his packing before he left for Holmscott, the home of his brother-in-law, Charles Steyning.[62] He may well have found that he shared a common political standpoint with Charles Steyning, who was regarded as a royalist but was lukewarm enough to become a JP after the King's defeat.[63] An account of Willoughby's expenses while he was away from home until March 1646 show that he reached Holmscott before Easter 1645 when he paid the minister of nearby Porlock 2s 6d to make his Communion. He seems to have enjoyed his 'holiday', making a number of small monetary gifts to his Steyning relatives and perhaps sharing with them the cherries which he records purchasing on four occasions. In August he made a rather surprising excursion to Wales, sailing from Minehead on 9 August and returning to Holmscott on 10 September. It is possible that the journey was too much for this seventy-five-year-old as he later claimed in his petition not to have 'thoroughly recovered from his late sickness'. However, he was well enough to leave Holmscott early in November 1645, though possibly still an invalid as he went to his daughter, Bridget Turbeville, whose home at Sampford Peverell was on his direct route back from Somerset, but near enough to Payhembury for him to be in touch with conditions there.[64] Sir Thomas Fairfax and the parliamentary army were established in the county by the time Willoughby returned. He 'rendered himself' to the committee of parliament in Devon (which included Sir John Bampfield, the brother of his son-in-law) on 19 November and the same day Fairfax made an order protecting him from any officers or soldiers under his command plundering his house, taking away his horses, cattle or other goods or to offering any other violence or injury to his person or family, provided that he obeyed all orders and ordinances of parliament.[65]

Willoughby was now prepared to take every step possible to salvage his position with parliament. As he had lived within an area subject to the King's forces and, arguably, assisted those forces, he was required to take 'the negative oath'. After some delay because of the disturbed state of the county, Willoughby took his oath at Ilchester on 24 December, swearing not to 'willingly assist the King in this war . . . nor any forces raised without the consent of the two Houses of Parliament'. He also signed the National League and Covenant. He used the occasion of the enforced journey to Ilchester to move from one member of his family to another. After six weeks with his Turbeville daughter he moved to his daughter Anne, married to Amias Bampfield at Weston, in south Devon between Seaton and Sidmouth, where he remained for twelve weeks.[66] In an petition to explain his delay in taking the negative oath, he had claimed that he had no knowledge of any crimes he had committed against the State, saying that he had utterly refused to have any hand in the Commission of Array or at any time meddled in the Commission of Oyer and Terminer. This was only the first of several petitions from Willoughby, two drafts among his papers appear to be alternatives for the next petition submitted after he had taken the oath at Ilchester; these drafts denied that he had had any hand in raising the posse once he realized it was to go against Plymouth. It has already been shown that these petitions of Willoughby were a mixture of truth, half-truths and falsehoods; a useful reminder that statements among the compounding papers cannot all be taken at face value.[67] He was allowed to compound for £500 and in 1652 was included in the general pardon provided he took the Engagement.[68] This was probably no obstacle to him, for as his relative Charles Steyning rhymed:

248

Then lets subscribe and go through stitch
As long as we are governed by a soldier's switch.[69]

John Willoughby died in 1658 aged 87.

It would be unsatisfactory to end a biographic study of Willoughby without some attempt to gauge his religious standpoint, yet his papers throw little light on this matter. No evidence has been found of pre-war puritan groups in Payhembury but equally the traditional church ales were no longer held there.[70] Just as Willoughby's home village showed no evidence of either extreme in religion, neither did he. His choice of Wadham rather than the more puritan Exeter College for his son suggests that he had no strong puritan sympathies, so does a letter which his son wrote to him from Oxford which reassured the elder Willoughby that he did not mix with 'lewd company', but did not think it necessary to make any reference to religious observance. The books listed in the study at Payhembury included works of Shakespeare, Bacon and Sidney but only one of sermons, Latimer's; a great contrast to the reading matter favoured by Walter Yonge.[71] On the other hand, Willoughby's will of 1651 begins with the confident resignation of 'my soul into the hands of my dearest saviour Jesus Christ . . . who hath Redeemed it in love, who hath preserved it in mercy who hath nourished in with grace. And I rest assured will crown it with glory'. At this time he obviously regarded himself as one of the Elect.[72]

John Willoughby belonged to the second rank of the county gentry; more centred in his locality, less affluent and less educated than the majority of the bench, but a suitable choice to hold the lesser offices in the county. What led to him breaking into the more élite group of justices of the peace? His appointment was not the only instance of JPs of this lower group joining the bench in 1642. Other examples include Nicholas Putt, sheriff in 1640, Robert Duke, a militia captain, Hugh Fortescue, a captain of the militia horse troop, and John Courtenay, once summoned as a grand juror at quarter sessions. There was nothing in the careers of these four men, appointed about the same time as Willoughby, to suggest that they had been selected as proven loyal servants of the King as two of them, Fortescue and Duke, were dropped from the commission by 1643. It seems that the appointment of JPs of lower standing than usual had become inevitable because there were few suitable candidates of the higher gentry. This was partly for political reasons: neither of the sons of Sir William Strode were suitable; Sir Richard tried to arouse the assize grand jury against ship money in 1639, and his brother William was one of the King's most outspoken opponents. The chance concentration of the death of eight JPs between 1641 and 1642 may also have forced replacements from a lower rank of gentry.[73]

This chapter has shown that Willoughby fulfilled his duties as a JP out-of-session; but one must ask if his absence from quarter sessions was solely due to the disturbed state of the county. Quarter sessions has been shown to be a gathering of equals and so gentry of the second rank may not have felt at ease there. Willoughby may have differed socially from the other subjects of these biographical studies but did this difference go deeper? The higher gentry's standing in the county led them to expect that they would be required to hold county office, whereas Willoughby had no such conviction; until circumstances forced him into a wider sphere, he was satisfied with his life as the leading figure of his village. Unlike Chudleigh and those who ruled the county in the difficult years before the war, he did not seek credit with his countrymen, though he did care for the welfare of his neighbours; that perhaps measures the difference in attitude of the different ranks of gentry. Although Willoughby was eager to have information on the political events of the day, this knowledge did not mould his actions. Yonge received similar news and sought election to the Long Parliament, but Willoughby's interest in affairs was as a spectator rather than as a participant, and so when he was forced to act he was reluctant to commit himself fully to either side. In this he may well have represented a strand of county opinion. John Willoughby is the only subject of these biographical studies who would not have been given a place among these gentry governors because of the service or leadership he gave to King and county. He stands among them because of the chance survival of his papers which reveal one whose service to the county was not conspicuous, but whose career adds to our knowledge of the character of the gentry government of Devon.

Chapter 12

The Character of the Gentry Government of Devon

The outstanding feature of Devon's gentry government lay in the quality of its leading members. It is that which underlines the difference between this county study and many others. The administration of the county is described but it is the personal element in the government which is emphasized. One is conscious that these gentry governors understood the problems of those they governed and shared their dangers and frustrations. Their prosperity rested on the same foundations and they were all, to a greater or lesser extent, affected by any new demands or orders made to them by the royal government. Yet they were also the efficient executants of that royal policy, more effective in some fields than the gentry governors of other counties. It remains to draw together an overall impression of this gentry government. How did they reconcile their responsibilities to their county and to the King? In this the period for examination is before the Civil War, but the continuation of this study into the war years makes it possible to assess how far the gentry governors' concern for their countrymen continued under the pressures of war. The second need in this concluding chapter is to attempt some survey of the political opinions of the gentry governors. How far did they reveal such opinions in their peacetime government; at what point did the unity of the bench break down; and how far was their support for the

253

royal or parliamentarian cause affected by their care for their countrymen? This study has been carried into the war years to establish a connection between the peacetime and wartime ethos of the gentry governors and so its conclusions concentrate on the men who had borne the major burden of government in peacetime and ignores those who only rose to prominence in the different circumstances of the war.

The quality of the gentry governors stands out not only in the individual studies but also in their collective work at quarter sessions and on special commissions. They were flexible enough to develop sub-divisions that straddled the hundred boundaries and so were better able to serve the administrative needs of the county. They showed the initiative to introduce new methods even in the circumscribed field of their judicial work. They would respond to the needs of the county, in times of economic crisis, without waiting for any royal proclamation. Yet their readiness to take independent action did not conflict with their belief that they were the King's servants, charged with ruling the county effectively; it was a part of that service. They did not see the dual role of serving the King and their countrymen as conflicting but as complementary. Their response to Council orders or royal proclamations confirms this whether the orders were designed to stimulate them to greater efficiency in their routine administration, or to demand their assistance in raising extra-parliamentary taxation or to command their support in the military field. When the orders concerned local administration, they were received with attention but as they were usually in line with existing practice in the county, they caused little change, only a slight increase of impetus. This built up a homogeneous approach to county government which followed the orders of the royal government but also accorded with the gentry governors' own ideas of how their county should be governed.

Alignment of the King's interest with the welfare of Devonians was more difficult when it concerned financial demands and orders to billet troops. When faced with orders for extra-parliamentary taxation the gentry governors either raised it efficiently or rejected it completely; there were no half measures. When they refused to act they expressed their view that to persist in the charge would endanger His Majesty's honour. They felt that it would do so to risk a repulse to the demands for ships in 1626 and to the demand for ship money in 1628. Both these demands followed the second forced loan when they did 'according to His Majesty's proclamations and instructions . . . engage our faithful promise to our countrymen that if they willingly yielded to His Majesty's necessities at this time, we would never more be instruments in the levy of that kind'.[1] So to accede to the King's demands on these occasions would affect not only the King's honour but that of the gentry rulers of the county; he and they would be shown to be false to their word.

The response of the gentry leaders to military orders also reveals something of the character of Devon's government. The deputy lieutenants were among the most conscientious in the country in holding musters and taking steps to improve the efficiency of the militia; even so they could show their independence in refusing to require the Oath of Supremacy from their soldiers, considering that quite unnecessary as a test of loyalty.[2] They pressed soldiers for overseas campaigns but they did so reluctantly because of the 'great number of seamen which the county ever yieldeth to His Majesty's service'.[3] In the task of billeting expeditionary forces the gentry leaders fulfilled their instructions from the Council but their relationship with that body changed. They obeyed the orders to billet troops but they gradually realized that they could not rely on the promises of the Council to pay the billeters; they saw that they would have to act themselves to reduce the suffering of the billeters. First they negotiated the direct use of the forced loan for the billeting costs, later they raised a county rate to meet the costs while they awaited direct payment and ultimately they went even further and refused to billet unless the expenses were met by the duke of Buckingham.[4] This change from confidence in central government to a belief in the need for their own independent action must have strengthened the corporate sense of the gentry body; it must also have undermined each gentry leader's confidence in the royal government.

Diaries and letters leave no doubt that the gentry governors were well aware of the political disputes of the day; they were not an inward-looking body, concerned only with the interests of their own county, but they have not been found identifying themselves in strong criticism of royal policy. They were outspoken on the difficulties they met in responding to royal orders but seldom questioned the policy behind those orders. Except for the sheriff, they had some safety in numbers and in the fact that local government could not be carried on without justices of the peace and deputy lieutenants. Even so, when a letter did imply some criticism of royal policy, it was tentatively phrased. The deputy lieutenants in 1625 hoped that their 'diligence to this service ... may not be a means to invite His Majesty to an often recourse to this kind of supply.' In 1627 the loan commissioners showed their approval of the King's intention not to make it a precedent 'to the prejudice of the ancient approved way of parliament'.[5] The nearest they came to direct criticism was their 'complaint of the intollerable burden laid on Devon and Cornwall by billeting soldiers upon them and not paying money'. Internal evidence shows this to belong to November 1627, but as it was unsigned, undirected and refers to the Council in the third person it may never have been sent. Instead, it could be material for the earl of Bedford to argue Devon's case for relief at the Council Board. This would account for its more outspoken tone.[6] The gentry governors might speak with a single voice in the face of the problems of the early years of the reign but there are no such collective expressions for gauging whether their accord continued during the Personal Rule. One obvious possible cause of difference, religion, was not exacerbated in Devon under a bishop of Exeter, Joseph Hall, who did not try to enforce Laudian conformity. Any political differences among the members of the county government, if they existed, were not strong enough to make their mark on the county records during the first fifteen years of the reign. If this picture of apparent harmony on the bench is a true one, did it survive until war forced division on the county?

The euphoria expressed by the JP, John Bampfield to Edward Seymour, the Devon knight of the shire, shows the sense of optimism in the county in January 1641, during the early months of the Long Parliament:

> The news of these times are so excellent that he deserves not to breathe this British air who prayeth not God heartily for them, and is not in himself very well pleased with them, hence you may perceive how acceptable your missives are ... For ever be this Parliament renowned for so great achievements, for we dream now of nothing more than of a golden age.[7]

Bampfield and Seymour seemed to be in perfect accord and yet in less than two years they were supporting opposing sides. What of quarter sessions, did men still act together who would soon fight each other? The unity of the county government seemed still unbroken when fifteen JPs met after Easter 1642. They could still sit on the same bench, although eight of them were soon to be dropped as active parliamentarians and six of the seven who continued to serve were later commissioners for the royal army.[8] The situation changed before the midsummer quarter session assembled. The earl of Bedford, now nominated as lord lieutenant by parliament, had made fresh appointments of deputy lieutenants and sent them orders to put the militia ordinance into execution on 1 July. Two MPs from Devon families, Sir John Northcott and Sir John Bampfield, had been sent down to see that the ordinance was carried out. Meanwhile, the first Commission of Array had been issued on 15 June.[9] Under these circumstances it is not surprising that quarter sessions showed that the unity of the bench had disintegrated. Only eight JPs met for quarter sessions on 12 July 1642, four of them were Bedford's newly appointed deputy lieutenants, another was parliament's envoy, Sir John Northcott, two others would soon ignore an appointment to the Commission of Array and actively support parliament, so the only royalist present was Humphrey Prouz.[10] Although this quarter session represented, almost entirely, active adherents of the parliamentary cause, they were still talking the language of peace and unity in the petitions they sent to the King and to both Houses of Parliament:

Distractions are amongst us through various commands hardly to
be reconciled but by the unity of king and Parliament, unity in
religion, unity in loyal affection to His Majesty's will, according to
our protestation, by God's mercy keep us still in peace and charity.[11]

Although the petitions show an overwhelming desire for peace and
unity, this does not mean that the petitioners intended to be inactive
or neutral if war came; indeed, some of them were already obeying
the militia ordinance. But nor should it be thought to be merely lip
service to an ideal. The petitioners' words were expressive of the
character of the gentry government of Devon. They had enjoyed
greater peace and unity on their bench during the peacetime years
than many other counties. This unity was represented by their
ability to work together for the benefit of the county even though
they held the varying political and religious opinions which would
ultimately lead to division on the outbreak of war. This longing for
peace must be remembered when some of the petitioners sought a
separate peace in the West Country once they saw the effects of war
on their own county.

The county government had been deprived of some of its most
active members who gave their support to parliament; how far did
those who remained on the bench now continue to serve the county
as well as the King? The biographical study of Willoughby has
revealed how far the machinery of county government remained in
force and has underlined the problems of a JP who tried to avoid
full commitment to the royal cause but he was only a newcomer to
the bench. His activities, or lack of them, cannot show how far the
spirit of the peacetime government was maintained in the very
different circumstances of war. However, two episodes involving
long-serving members of the bench reveal that something of
that spirit remained. The first concerns Henry Ashford from
Burlescombe, near the Somerset border, who had served for over
twenty years as a JP, acted as sheriff in 1628 and become a deputy
lieutenant by 1637.[12] He was named on the Commission of Array in
1642 and was present when it was published on 13 August but he
was not prepared to remain in his militia command and never took

up arms against parliament.[13] Instead he continued to work in his locality as a JP and became one of the royal commissioners dealing with the financial and administrative needs of the King's army. He was not one of the more active commissioners but he joined them when the King was in the West Country on the Lostwithiel campaign, and in the spring of 1645 he took up residence in Exeter.[14] He was one of the signatories to a letter, of 12 September 1644, to the War Council, which was actually opened by the King himself, probably when he reached Exeter on 17 September.[15] Ashford and his fellow commissioners were courageously outspoken in seeking relief for their fellow countrymen:

> We humbly desire your lordships that you will forthwith move His Majesty to send strict order to the Horse who since their coming into this county have plundered all the parts they come to so much that will utterly disable them to pay contributions or to till their grounds next year, which will be so great a mischief that if not speedily prevented this county will be ruined and the people's poverty insupportable.

This letter shows that concern for their fellow countrymen clearly continued during the hazards of war. Something else which survived the conflict was friendship among the leading gentry. When Ashford died in 1649 his will referred to his 'well beloved friends' including two who had served with him on the bench, Sir George Chudleigh and Sir Ralph Sidenham, and the sons of two other former colleagues, John Bampfield and John Northcott. These friends, one royalist, two parliamentarians and one who changed allegiance, defy any party label and show that friendship could surmount political differences, a fact which is a reflection of the strength of the peacetime bench.[16]

Further evidence of the continuance of some of the earlier spirit of the bench lies in the career of Sir Francis Fulford, who served as a Devon JP from 1613, but was also a JP in Dorset, where his wife had inherited extensive estates, so there were times when he was absent from Devon.[17] His one major task in Devon, in addition to those as a JP, was as one of the two county collectors of knighthood composition, this required his attention for two years from 1630 to 1632. It was in Dorset that Fulford became a deputy lieutenant and it was probably there that he began his active service before returning to Devon, late in 1642, under the command of Sir Ralph Hopton. In 1643 he suffered capture and imprisonment and the looting of his home of Great Fulford; he also suffered bereavement when his son, a royalist colonel, was killed during the final days of the siege of Exeter.[18] In spite of his personal suffering at the hands of parliamentarians, he was ready to risk his own life to aid the town of Crediton when it was endangered by undisciplined royal troops, even though men of Crediton had been among the earlier looters at his own home. Fulford's activity as a JP and as a commissioner for the King's army in Devon show that he was at Great Fulford through most of 1645, so it was presumably at this time that he earned the gratitude of Crediton.[19] They later certified to the compounding commissions that Fulford had:

> Caused divers troops of the king's army that had plundered many in this county to be punished for their misdemeandours. And at that time when many commanders and officers of the king's Army came unto our town in warlike manner with 200 foot soldiers and near a 100 horse to Plunder and burn our town and to bring us subject unto other violence of the soldiers upon information that our town . . . had risen to resist the king's forces. The said Sir Francis Fulford came unto our town of purpose and so behaved himself for the preservation of our poor town from all that intended violence (and not without danger of his own person) as took off all that intended mischief and thereby our town escaped. And we do also humbly certify (that to our knowledge) the said Sir Francis Fulford did many good offices for the county as we believe the whole county will likewise certify.

This certificate was supported by seventy-three names, some of them signatures and some with additional comments such as 'I do believe that Sir Francis Fulford was the special means under God to preserve our town'.[20]

These examples of Ashford and Fulford being ready to speak and act in their countrymen's interests even in the midst of conflict show that they continued to demonstrate the concern which had been a characteristic of the peacetime bench. The wartime quarter sessions maintained, to some extent, the dual service of the gentry government; they still acted in the name of the King and they still tried to serve their county by preventing the civil administration being completely dominated by military demands. Although the balance of the peacetime bench was destroyed when the active parliamentarians were removed, it did not become a completely partisan body. In spite of continuous military activity in the county, the gentry managed to maintain their established form of government. The bench had sufficient independence not to be absorbed by the commission for the royal army, the really partisan body in the county. Quarter sessions carefully defined the extent to which JPs would obey the commands of royalist officers, making it clear that the soldiers were subject to the law of the land. As the minutes only occasionally list those present one cannot judge how many JPs attended, but it has been shown that many of them did still fulfil their duties in their localities. Quarter sessions maintained the established practices of county government until the summer of 1645, but then the activities of Goring's rapacious cavalry and later the siege of Exeter, by the army of Fairfax, ended any pretence of normal government.

The gentry who had given long service to the county and then supported the royal cause in the war were still part of the gentry government of the county and could still show their concern for the interests of their countrymen. But what of the other part of the peacetime gentry government, the leaders who had been excluded from quarter sessions because of their support for parliament, how far did their wartime service show that they still upheld the concerns they had shown in peacetime? The deputy lieutenants, Chudleigh and Pole, now appointed with the approval of parliament, continued to command trained bands, but Chudleigh soon

261

recognized that they were of limited value in the kind of war that was developing.[21] What was needed was a volunteer force which would be ready to leave the county and would not be so liable to drift back to their homes. This army would not be built on the traditional relationship between the trained band and their gentry leaders, so what would be the future role for those gentry officers? As the demands of war made clear the need for a different type of army it also revealed the suffering brought about by Civil War. In these circumstances some of the gentry leaders clearly felt that they would best serve the interest of the county by seeking a regional truce. Chudleigh's resignation from his army command occurred when it did because of the defeat at Stratton and his son's change of allegiance but all his experience of wartime command must have been in his mind when he drew up his declaration. His was the most conspicuous withdrawal from active service but the service of other gentry leaders, who began the war as parliamentarians, diminished or ended as the successful royalist forces swept through the county in the summer of 1643. Few long-serving Devon governors were prepared to leave their county to continue the fight, instead they seem to have retired quietly to their estates. In deciding that the conflict had 'gone too far', Chudleigh may well have voiced an opinion of many of his former colleagues.

The emphasis of this county study on its individual leaders is not just an original way of portraying a county history, it is the most effective means of revealing its character. The ability of the gentry leaders to work together without conflicts aroused by personal ambition or inflamed by political or religious faction allowed them to rule in the interests of both the Crown and the county. They achieved success in this task by compromise, striving to fulfil most royal orders while also pleading for the interest of their countrymen in doing so. The continuation of the biographical studies into the war years has made it possible to trace some continuity between the peacetime and wartime ethos of those who had been the most active gentry leaders of Devon before the Civil War. The unity of the pre-war county government is underlined by the fact that it did not break down until the moment when the gentry governors were forced into opposing parties by external pressures. Once that unity was broken, the county government became a weaker body, exerting some influence and showing some care for its countrymen, but not capable of directing the county. As the war dragged on and many of the longest-serving gentry governors withdrew to their estates, many new features determined what happened in Devon. Some gentry continued to play their part but they found they had to contend with new forces welling up from among the lower ranks of the people, with invading armies and with marauding troops. All that is a different tale, largely told elsewhere. The gentry who had led the county in peacetime no longer ruled it in war.

Notes

Preface

1. A. M. Wolffe, 'The Gentry Government of Devon, 1625–1640' (University of Exeter Ph.D., 1992).
2. Alan Everitt, *The Community of Kent and the Great Rebellion 1640–1660* (Leicester, 1973).
3. G. Roberts (ed). *The Diary of Walter Yonge* (Camden Society 1st Series, 41, 1848), p. 111.
4. Ann Hughes, *The Causes of the English Civil War* (New York, 1991), pp. 33–5.

Chapter I

1. William, J. Blake, 'Hooker's Synopsis Chorographical of Devonshire', *TDA*, LVII (1915) p. 339.
2. I am grateful to Dr Jonathan Barry for allowing me to quote figures from Chapter VII of *Historical Atlas of South West England*, (eds) Roger Kain and Bill Ravenhill (Exeter, forthcoming); see pp. 44–5 for a detailed table; William Hunt, *Puritan Moment* (Harvard, 1983), p. 3.
3. Blake, 'Hooker's Synopsis', p. 338.
4. Paul Slack, 'Mortality, Crises and Epidemic Disease in England 1485–1610'. Reprinted from *Health, Medicine and Mortality in the Sixteenth Century*, (ed.) Charles Webster (Cambridge, 1979), p. 34–6.
5. Thomas Westcote, *A View of Devonshire in 1630* (eds) G. Oliver and P. Jones (Exeter, 1845) p. 35.
6. Anthony Fletcher, *A County Community in Peace and War, Sussex 1600–1660* (1975), p. 134; T. G. Barnes, *Somerset 1625–1640* (Cambridge, Mass., 1961), p. 69.
7. See Part I, Chapter 3.
8. M. Weinbaum (ed.), *British Borough Charters 1307–1660* (Cambridge, 1943), p. 25.
9. J.D. Morrill, *The Nature of the English Revolution* (1993), pp. 196–8; M.D.G. Wanklyn, 'Landed Society and Allegiance in Cheshire and Shropshire in the First Civil War' (University of Manchester Ph.D., 1976), pp. 77, 92, 116, 121–2, 124, 126, 130.
10. All the sources used: PRO, C181/3.4.5; C192/1; C231/4,5; E179/102; SP16/70/18, 150/76, /153/113,114, 199/29,32,33, 241/55; DRO, QS1/6,7,8; A.J. Howard (ed.), *The Devon Protestation Returns 1641*, 2 vol (1971). At their highest rank the 379 consisted 13 baronets, 54 knights and 312 gentlemen.
11. 814 from the subsidy rolls and 315 from the Protestation Returns. It also includes, 58 termed 'Mister' which appears to be interchangeable with 'gent'.
12. DRO, QS1/6,7, QS Rolls boxes, 28–45; PRO, SP16/70/18, 150/76, /153/113,114, 199/29,32,33, 241/55; SP16/435/33, E179/102; J.S. Cockburn (ed.), *Western Circuit Assize Orders 1629–1648*, (Camden 4th series, 17, 1976). These were drawn from twenty-four appointments to lesser county offices, forty-seven appointments of junior militia officers, seven collectors of subsidies, 123 references to head constables and, finally, 643 empanelled for the grand jury at quarter sessions.
13. These lesser county offices were not restricted to this rank, forty-five gentlemen have been found holding them.
14. W.G. Hoskins, *Devon* (1954), p. 79.

15. Joyce Youings, *Devon Monastic Lands: Calendars of Particulars from Grants 1536–1558* (Devon and Cornwall Record Society, New Series I, 1955).

16. J.L. Vivian, *The Visitations of the County of Devon, Comprising the Heralds Visitations of 1531, 1564 and 1620* (Exeter, 1895).

17. Ibid. Only the first marriage or the marriage to the mother of the heir, if different, is counted.

18. Alan Everitt, *Change in the Provinces* (Leicester, 1969), pp. 10–11; J.S. Morrill, *Cheshire 1630–1660* (Oxford, 1974), p. 4; Anne Duffin, *Faction and Faith* (Exeter, 1996), p. 30; Fletcher, *Sussex*, p. 44; Clive Holmes, *Seventeenth-Century Lincolnshire* (The Lincolnshire Committee, 1980), p. 75; J.S. Morrill, 'The Northern Gentry and the Great Rebellion, *Northern History XV* (1979), pp. 67–8; Ann Hughes, *Politics, Society and Civil War in Warwickshire 1620–1660* (Cambridge, 1987), p. 39; R.H. Silcock, 'County Government in Worcestershire 1603–1660' (University of London Ph.D., 1974), p. 33; Hunt, *Puritan Moment*, p. 16; G.E. McPartlin, 'The Herefordshire Gentry in County Government 1625–1660' (University of Wales, University College of Aberystwyth Ph.D., 1981), p. 25.

19. Everitt, *Community of Kent*, pp. 36–7; Morrill, *Cheshire*, p. 3; Morrill, 'Northern Gentry pp. 67–8; Fletcher, *Sussex*, p. 25; Duffin, *Faction and Faith*, p. 23; Holmes, *Lincolnshire*, p. 66.

20. DRO, 1392M/L1645/29; Cynthia B. Herrup, *The Common Peace* (Cambridge, 1987), p. 98.

21. DRO, QS Rolls, boxes 28–45.

22. J.S. Morrill, *The Cheshire Grand Jury 1625–1659* (Department of English Local History, Occasional Papers, Third series, No. 6. Leicester, 1976), pp. 18–19.

23. Wanklyn, 'Landed Society and Allegiance in Cheshire and Shropshire', pp. 137, 138. Dr Wanklyn has found that many termed 'gent' as grand jurymen only claimed to be yeomen in their wills. However, if his divisions of society into different levels according to their subsidy assessment were applied to Devon grand jurymen, many of them would be at least gentlemen, if not knights or esquires. As the Cheshire grand jurymen were nearly all poorer than those in Devon, Dr Wanklyn's findings in Cheshire do not necessarily invalidate the designation of most Devon grand jurymen as 'office-holding gentlemen'.

24. DRO, QS1/6 p. 84.

25. Henrik A. Langelüddecke, 'Secular Policy Enforcement During the Personal Rule of Charles I – The Administration Work of the Parish Officers in the 1630s' (University of Oxford D.Phil., 1995), pp. 30–33. I am grateful to Dr Cust for drawing my attention to this thesis.

26. Mark Stoyle, *Loyalty and Locality* (Exeter, 1994).

27. Langelüddecke, 'Secular Policy Enforcement During the Personal Rule', pp. 30–33; DRO, Crediton 2656 A 85, 88, 90; Halberton PW2.

28. J.A. Vage, 'The Diocese of Exeter, 1519–1641: A Study of Church Government in the Age of Reformation' (University of Cambridge Ph.D., 1991), pp. 30, 59, 134, 177, 178, 189, 266–7. I am grateful to Dr Anne Duffin for drawing my attention to this thesis.

29. Vage, 'Exeter Diocese', p. 179; K. Fincham (ed.), *The Early Stuart Church, 1603–1642* (1993), p. 5 based on Professor Collinson.

30. Vage, 'Exeter Diocese' pp. 223–3, 253–262, 265; *HMC Salisbury*, X, 451; Thomas Fuller, *A History of the Worthies of England* (1811), II, p. 66.

30. Samuel Hieron, *The Dignity of Preaching in a Sermon upon I Thessalonians 5:20* (1615); Fincham (ed.), *The Early Stuart Church, 1603–1642*, p. 12.

31. Vage, 'Exeter Diocese', pp. 313, 325, 327.

32. Ibid., pp. 344, 357, 370, 401; Julian Davies, *The Caroline Captivity of the Church* (Oxford, 1992), p. 146; BL, E150 (24), *Devonshire Petition*.

Chapter 2

1. The seven peers were Edward and Henry Bourchier, 4th and 5th earls of Bath; George Carew, earl of Totnes; Viscount Edward Chichester; Thomas Ridgeway, earl of Londonderry; Francis Russell, earl of Bedford and Lord William Russell.
2. Hunt, *The Puritan Moment*, pp. 15, 167.
3. Duffin, *Faction and Faith, passim* especially pp. 74, 77, 79–82; Barnes, *Somerset, passim.*
4. Richard Cust (ed.), *The Papers of Sir Richard Grosvenor, 1st Bart (1585–1645)* (Lancashire and Cheshire Record Society, 1996); Peter Hall (ed.), *The Works of Joseph Hall DD*, VI (Oxford, 1837), pp. 98, 99.
5. Richard Cust and Peter G. Lake, 'Sir Richard Grosvenor and the Rhetoni of Magistracy', *BIHR* LIV (1981), p. 40; Cust (ed.), *Papers of Sir Richard Grosvenor*, p. xxiv.
6. C. Stephenson and F. G. Marcham, *Sources of English Constitutional History* (New York, 1937), p. 493.
7. This figure is compiled from the patent roll for 21 James I (1623) with deaths deleted and docket book entries added and so constitutes the probable commission renewed without detail on 1 April 1625; PRO C66/2310, C231/4.
8. PRO, C231/1,4,5; BL, Harl.1622, PRO, E163/18/12, SP16/212. C193/13/2, SP16/405. T.G. Barnes and A. Hassell Smith, 'Justices of the Peace from 1558–1688 – A Revised List of Sources', *BIHR*, XXXIII (1959), pp. 221–242; DRO, QS 1/5,6,7, QS Rolls boxes 28–43. See Wolffe 'Gentry Government', Appendix A for appointment, education and office holding of JPs.
9. This number includes seven peers and five clerics but excludes the national figures usually put on commissions. The gentry membership consisted of eleven baronets, thirty-seven knights and fifty-two esquires.
10. DRO, QS1/5,6, QS Rolls, box 28; PRO, C231/4. The ten were Henry Ashford, Bartholomew Berry, John Davy, Richard Cabell, Sir Edmund Fowell, Robert Haydon, John Upton, Sir Nicholas Prideaux, Walter Yonge and Sir Edward Seymour.
11. PRO, C231/4. The six newcomers were Sir James Bagg, John Bampfield, Sir John Chichester, Sir Simon Leach, Sir Henry Rosewell and Henry Walrond.
12. Anthony Fletcher, *Reform in the Provinces* (1986) p. 8.
13. BL, Add. MSS. 22474, f. 308; I am grateful to Dr Mark Stoyle for telling me that Sir John Whidden's daughters were arrested for being in company with the Jesuit, Alexander Baker.
14. Details of those dropped can be found in Wolffe, 'Gentry Government' pp. 23–4.
15. Richard Cabell and Sir Edmund Fowell were appointed on 11 May 1624 and John Upton on 29 June 1624, PRO C231/4 ff. 164v, 168v.
16. Henry Ashford from 1617, Bartholomew Berry from 1620, John Davy from 1617, Sir Nicholas Prideaux from 1617 and Walter Yonge from 1617.
17. BL, Add. MSS. 35331, f. 44.
18. PRO, C193/13/2; Fletcher, *Reform*, p. 9; SP16/335/13.
19. DRO, QS28/3.
20. Barnes and Smith, 'Sources', p. 241.
21. B. W. Quintrell, 'The Government of the County of Essex 1603–1642' (University of London Ph.D., 1965), p. 44.
22. Ibid., p. 67; Barnes, *Somerset*, p. 70.
23. DRO, QS1/7 Epiph. 1638.
24. All the *libri pacis* mark those 'of the quorum'.
25. Frances B. James, 'Sir Henry Rosewell: a Devon Worthy', *TDA* XX (1888), pp. 118–19.

26. Eight of the gentry members of the bench were not primarily Devon landowners: Sir Richard Edgecumbe, Sir Richard Grenville, Sir Robert Killigrew and Arthur Harris (Cornwall), Sir Ferdinando Gorges, Sir John Carew and Richard Warre (Somerset) and Sir Gregory Norton (Sussex). With the exception of Sir Ferdinando Gorges, they played little or no part in the county's affairs.

27. Vivian, *Visitations of Devon, passim*; four others married into these families: Sir Francis Vincent, Sir William Waller, Thomas Tuckfield, Sir Ralph Sidenham.

28. Hughes, *Politics, Society and Civil War in Warwickshire*, p. 28; Quintrell, 'The Government of Essex', p. 14.

29. *HMC, 12th Report Cowper I*, p. 213; W.G. Hoskins, 'Estates of Caroline Gentry' in H.P.R. Finberg and W.G. Hoskins (eds), *Devonshire Studies* (1952), p. 335.

30. PRO, E179/102.

31. M.J. Braddick, 'Parliamentary Lay Taxation c. 1590–1670. Local problems of enforcement and collection, with special reference to Norfolk' (University of Cambridge Ph.D., 1988), pp. 33, 160; Fletcher, *Sussex*, p. 204.

32. Duffin, *Faction and Faith* p. 24, this figure refers to the gentry; Wanklyn, 'Landed Society and Allegiance in Cheshire and Shropshire', pp. 2, 152.

33. Hoskins, *Devon*, p. 126. The South Hams were principally in the Coleridge and Stanborough hundreds.

34. Stephen K. Roberts, *Recovery and Restoration in an English County, 1646–1670* (Exeter, 1985), p. xvii.

35. Todd Gray, 'Devon's Coastal and Overseas Fisheries and New England Migration 1597–1642' (University of Exeter Ph.D., 1988), pp. 217, 233.

36. W.R. Prest, *Inns of Court 1590–1640* (1972), p. 159.

37. PRO, SP16/405; J.H. Gleason, *The Justices of the Peace in England 1558–1642* (Oxford, 1969), Appendices. Figures for MPs are adjusted to exclude those who were only members after 1640.

38. Anthony Fletcher, 'National and Local Awareness in the County Communities' in H. Tomlinson (ed.), *Before the Civil War* (1983), pp. 155–9.

39. PRO, C181/4; C193/12/2.

40. PRO, SP16/2/84, SO1/2/26 f. 45; *APC 1625–1626*, p. 93, 267–8, *September 1627–June 1628*, p. 79; DRO, QS1/7, Easter 1634.

41. PRO, E215/1383; C181/4,5; C192/1.

42. BL, Add. MSS. 35331, f. 88.

43. Dennis Rolle and Thomas Wise, though Wise was added to the commission soon after his term of office.

44. Fletcher, *Sussex*, p. 134; Peter Clark, *English Provincial Society from the Reformation to the Revolution* (1977), pp. 117, 257.

45. Barnes, *Somerset* pp. 68–9; J.S. Morrill, *Cheshire 1630–1660* (Oxford, 1974), p. 9; Joel Hurstfield, 'County Government – Wiltshire c. 1530–c. 1660' in *Freedom Corruption and Government in Elizabethan England* (1973), pp. 251–2.

46. These seventeen attended at least twenty of the fifty-three sessions with lists during these years.

47. DRO, QS1/6 p. 110, 1/7 Mich. 1633, Mich. 1639; PRO, Prob/11 132; Princes, *Worthies* p. 187; Charles Worthy, *Devonshire Wills* (1896), p. 481; Oswyn Murray typescript of Wills, 2nd Series in West Country Studies Library.

48. J. S. Cockburn, *History of English Assizes from 1558 to 1714* (Cambridge, 1972), pp. 103–4.

49. Arthur Champernowne and John Upton were shipowners; Sir Ferdinando Gorges, Sir Henry Rosewell, Sir George Chudleigh, Sir John Pole and Walter Yonge were involved in colonization.

Chapter 3

1. Langelüddecke, 'Secular Policy Enforcement During the Personal Rule', pp. 32, 33; DRO, Crediton 2656 A 81–96, Chudleigh 3944 A/PW1, Halberton PW 1-2, Acte Book of the Eight Men of Broadclyst.
2. Joan Thirsk (ed.), *The Agrarian History of England and Wales* (Cambridge, 1967), IV p. 72, 471.
3. PRO, SP12/96.
4. DRO, QS1/6, pp. 99, 136.
5. DRO, QS1/2, 23 June 1605.
6. DRO, QS1/2, 19 July 1605.
7. DRO, QS1/4, 12 January 1615; R.L. Taverner, 'The Administrative Work of the Devon Justices in the Seventeenth-Century', *TDA* C (1968), p. 60. These sub-divisions are illustrated in Map 4, p. 36.
8. DRO, QS1/8, 12 July 1642.
9. DRO, QS1/4, 13 July 1615; QS1/5, p. 281.
10. DRO, QS1/2, 2 October 1606.
11. Wolffe, 'Gentry Government', Chapter III.
12. PRO, SP14/142/37, 144/32; printed in *Harvest Failure in Cornwall and Devon* (ed.) Todd Gray, Sources of Cornish History, I (Institute of Cornish Studies, 1992).
13. Barnes, *Somerset*, p. 84–5.
14. DRO, QS Rolls, boxes 29, 30.
15. DRO QS1/6 p. 253; QS Rolls, box 30.
16. DRO, QS1/6, p. 78; QS Rolls, box 32.
17. DRO, 347A Dartington PW2 ff. 385, 395, 396, 404, 413.
18. Fletcher, *Reform*, pp. 124, 127, 128.
19. PRO, SP16/258/26.
20. PRO, SP16/252/23; DRO, Lapford 2021 A/PW 1.
21. DRO, QS Rolls, boxes 34, 35; Langelüddecke, 'Secular Policy Enforcement During the Personal Rule', pp. 67, 68, 69.
22. DRO, QS Rolls, boxes, 35, 36, 37, PRO, SP16/189/5.
23. For fuller details of meetings in sub-divisions 1631–1640, see Wolffe, 'Gentry Government', pp. 96–100.
24. Kain and Ravenhill (eds), *Historical Atlas of South West England*, Chapter VII.
25. *Historical Atlas of South West England* estimates the population of Exeter at 11,000 and that of the rest of the corporate towns at 26,050, making a total estimated population for Devon of 231,840'.

Chapter 4

1. Cynthia Herrup, *The Common Peace* (Cambridge, 1987), p. 3; *English Historical Documents* (ed.) David C. Douglas (1969), p. 541.
2. Herrup, *The Common Peace*, p. 61.
3. J.S. Cockburn, *History of English Assizes from 1558 to 1714* (Cambridge, 1972), p. 342.
4. *Joseph Hall's Works*, VI, p. 98.
5. These estimates are based on a comparison of recognizances of 1625–9 with the quarter-session calendars of those years. DRO, QS1/6; QS Rolls, boxes 28–31.

6. From 1625–1640 about 500 cases declared to be *billa vera* were brought before the Epiphany session, 220 before the Easter session, 340 before the midsummer session and 200 before the Michaelmas Session. DRO, QS 1/5, 6, 7, 8. A long gap occurred between the summer assizes in late July and the spring assizes in March.

7. See pp. 51–2. As the *ignoramus* indictments were supposed to be destroyed this percentage may underestimate the proportion of *ignoramus* decisions to *billa vera* ones. It is based on the considerable number of *ignoramus* indictments which have survived in Devon and on the note *ignor* which is marked on some recognizances during the years 1625–1630. DRO, QS Rolls, boxes 28–33.

8. DRO, QS 1/6, 1/7.

9. Herrup, *The Common Peace*, pp. 48, 143.

10. Ibid., p. 49.

11. Ibid., p. 47; J.A. Sharpe, *Crime in Seventeenth Century England* (Cambridge, 1983), pp. 92, 146.

12. DRO, QS Rolls, boxes 31, 32, provide examples of women benefiting from the statute after thefts valued at 13s and 15s 6d.

13. Herrup, *The Common Peace*, p. 142.

14. DRO, QS1/6, pp. 291, 292, 330, 368, 410; QS Rolls, box 33.

15. Herrup, *The Common Peace*, p. 112.

16. See note 7 above. From these sources evidence has been found of sixty-seven *ignoramus* returns which were not referred to the assizes compared with 152 which were.

17. DRO, QS1/5, 6, 7.

18. J.S. Cockburn, *Calender of Assize Records, Home Circuit Indictments Elizabeth and James I* (1985), Introduction p. 19.

19. PRO, SP16/250/41, 251/32, 33, 34, 257/95, 260/129, 263/74, 265/34, 274/32, 275/15.

20. This percentage is based on recognizances for 1625–7 in DRO QS Rolls, boxes 28, 29.

21. See the chapter on Richard Reynell for a more detailed discussion of comments added to recognizances.

22. Steve Hindle, 'Aspects of the Relationship of the State and Local Society in Early Modern England with Special Relationship to Cheshire c.1590–1630' (University of Cambridge Ph.D, 1991), pp. 243–248, 252, 288.

23. Ibid, p. 267.

24. See p. 35.

25. Barnes, *Somerset*, p. 177; Taverner, 'Devon JPs', *TDA* (1968), p. 61.

26. DRO, QS1/7, Easter, 1635.

27. DRO, QS1/6, pp. 97, 392, 394.

28. DRO, QS1/6, pp. 132, 392; Cockburn, *Western Circuit Assize Orders*, pp. 4–5.

29. Michael Dalton, *The Countrey Justice* (1613, reprinted 1973), pp. 34–5.

30. PRO, QS1/6, pp. 115, 178, 211, 326; Cockburn, *Western Circuit Assize Orders*, pp. 34–5.

31. DRO, QS 1/7, Easter, 1635.

32. DRO, QS 1/5, p. 642.

33. Paul Slack, 'Book of Orders: The Making of English Social Policy 1577–1634', *TRHS*, 5th series 30 (1980), p. 3.

34. DRO, QS 1/5, pp. 642, 646; Paul Slack, *The Impact of Plague in Tudor and Stuart England* (1985), pp. 209–11.

35. DRO, QS 1/6, pp. 3, 33, 45, 54, 84, 101; Slack, *Plague*, pp. 97, 258. The mayor of Exeter had fled from the plague so the notorious puritan Ignatius Jurdain filled his place and would have been the one to receive these rates.

36. Slack, *Plague*, p. 91.

37. PRO, SP14/144/32; see pp. 37–8.

38. PRO, SP14/142/37, 144/32; Gray, *Harvest Failure*.
39. *APC 1625–1626*, p. 296.
40. DRO, QS1/6, p. 235.
41. DRO, QS1/6, p. 289.
42. DRO, QS1/6, pp. 308–9.
43. DRO, QS Rolls, box 34.
44. *APC January 1627–August 1627*, p. 185.
45. DRO, QS1/6, p. 126, undated between Mid. and Mich. sessions.
46. James F. Larkin (ed.), *Stuart Royal Proclamations*, II (Oxford, 1983), p. 185–6.
47. DRO, QS1/6, p. 211.
48. Larkin, *Stuart Proclamations* pp. 233, 236.
49. See p. 42.
50. DRO, QS1/6, pp. 355, 361, 364; *CSPD April 1633–April 1634*, p. 462; DRO, QS1/7, mid. 1634.
51. DRO, QS 1/6, p. 376, 1/7 Mich. 1633, mid. 1634, Easter 1636.
52. BL. Add. MSS. 12496.
53. DRO, QS1/1, p. 87. QS1/5, pp. 601, 603, 604, 613, QS1/6 pp. 6, 17, 47–8, 65, 268.
54. DRO, QS1/6, p. 340, 409, QS1/7 Easter 1636, Epiph. 1637. Easter 1639.
55. DRO, QS1/6, p. 418; QS1/7, Mich. 1639.
56. PRO, SP16/250/41, 251/19, 26, 32, 33, 34, 252/23, 257/95, 258/26, 35, 259/86, 260/129, 263/74, 265/34, 274/32.
57. See Wolffe, 'Gentry Government', p. 82.
58. An act of 1589 prohibited the building of a cottage unless it had at least four acres of land.
59. DRO, QS1/7 Mich. 1638.
60. DRO, QS1/7 Mich. 1639.
61. PRO, SP16/251/19, 252/23, 258/26, 259/86.
62. PRO, SP16/187/91.
63. J.S. Morrill, *The Revolt of the Provinces*, (1976), p. 22.
64. Langelüddecke, 'Secular Policy Enforcement During the Personal Rule', pp. 48, 52, 53, 108.
65. PRO, SP16/259/86. This reference shows that even a JP whose son had been in prison since 1629 for opposing the King was assiduous in his duties.

Chapter 5

1. M.J. Braddick, 'Parliamentary Lay Taxation c.1590–1670. Local problems of enforcement and collection, with special reference to Norfolk' (University of Cambridge Ph.D, 1988), pp. 6–7.
2. Conrad Russell, *Parliaments and English Politics 1621–1629* (Oxford, 1979), pp. 8, 49–51.
3. David Thomas, 'Financial and Administrative Developments' in (ed.) Howard Tomlinson *Before the English Civil War* (1983). pp. 103–10.
4. PRO, SP16/522/109, DRO, 1579A/8/2, 3, 4, Dartington, 347 PW2, ff. 395, 418; Braddick, 'Parliamentary Lay Taxation', pp. 5, 32.
5. PRO, E179/102/463; Russell, *Parliaments*, p. 226.
6. Braddick, 'Parliamentary Lay Taxation', pp. 2, 8.
7. *APC 1625–6* p. 364.
8. DRO, QS 1/6 p. 22.

9. This estimate that income was 50 times subsidy rating is taken from Hughes, *Politics, Society and Civil War in Warwickshire 1620–1660* p. 30.
10. PRO, SP16/522/109.
11. See p. 100.
12. Braddick, 'Parliamentary Lay Taxation', p. 160; Fletcher, *Sussex* p. 204.
13. PRO, E401/2442.
14. PRO, E179/102/463.
15. PRO, E401/1915, 1916, 2325.
16. BL, Add. MSS. 35331, ff. 48, 51.
17. Russell, *Parliaments*, pp. 226, 236–7, 241, 259.
18. *APC 1625–6*, p. 167.
19. PRO, SP16/6/70; see pp. 105–7.
20. PRO, SP16/34/76. This letter is undated and is calendared under August 1626 but it fits the forced loan of 1625 rather than the brief abortive attempt to raise a loan in August 1626.
21. PRO, E401/2586, ff. 207–223; Richard Cust, *The Forced Loan and English Politics 1626–1628* (Oxford, 1987), p. 37. For details of those paying the loan in Devon see Wolffe 'Gentry Government', pp. 130–2.
22. BL, Add. MSS. 64884, ff. 120–1.
23. Morrill, *Cheshire*, p. 27.
24. PRO, SP16/34/76.
25. *APC 1625–6*, p. 288.
26. PRO, SP16/18/99; *APC 1625–6*, pp. 268, 298–9; see below p. 108. Sir George Chudleigh, Sir Ferdinando Gorges and Sir William Strode were concerned in both tasks.
27. Russell, *Parliaments*, p. 291.
28. Ibid, pp. 293n, 308–9.
29. Cordelia Ann Stone, 'Devon and Parliament in Early Stuart Period' (Bryn Mawr College Ph.D., 1986), p. 431.
30. PRO E401/1913 payments of £5,611 for the 2nd subsidy of 1625 made on 15 and 26 June 1626. This disproves, for Devon, the claim of Professor Russell that the subsidies granted in 1625 had been collected before the writs for this parliament of 1626 were sent out, Russell, *Parliaments*, p. 269.
31. Hughes, *Causes of The English Civil War*, p. 91.
32. PRO, SP16/31/30.
33. See pp. 59, 112.
34. Yonge *Diary*, pp.93, 97.
35. *APC 1626*, p. 167; *CSPD 1625–1626* p. 403.
36. PRO, E401/2586 f. 459. Sir Richard Buller was also listed under Devon for £200 but his influence was in Cornwall.
37. Cust, *Forced Loan* p. 38.
38. Larkin, *Proclamations*, p. 108.
39. PRO E401/1914, Drake was not a collector for the loan initiated in the autumn of 1626.
40. *APC 1626*, p. 47; Yonge, *Diary*, p. 93.
41. BL, Add. MSS. 64889, f. 75.
42. *APC 1626*, p. 163; *CSPD 1625–1626*, p. 418; *1627–1628*, pp. 29, 31; *HMC 12th Report Cowper I*, pp. 276, 279.
43. See pp. 80–1.
44. Larkin, *Proclamations*, p. 110.
45. Cust, *Forced Loan*, pp. 99–103.
46. PRO, SP16/53/96; Yonge, *Diary*, p. 99.
47. PRO, SP16/526/10; SP16/53/96.

48. PRO, E163/18/12 (*liber pacis*), C193/12/1, 2; Richard Cust, 'A List of Commissioners for the Forced Loan 1626–7', *BIHR*, LI (1978).
49. BL, Add. MSS. 64889 f. 133; see p. 115.
50. The source has not been found for this commendation.
51. PRO, SP16/53/96; *APC 1626* pp. 383–4, 388. Essex, Dorset and Berkshire were permitted to use the loan for billeting costs on 29 Nov 1626. The Devon commissioners would have been well informed of events in Dorset as one of them, Sir Francis Fulford, was also a Dorset loan commissioner (PRO, C193/12/2).
52. *APC 1627*, p. 107.
53. PRO, E351/288.
54. See pp. 118–19, 120.
55. PRO 30/26/59; E179/102/403.
56. See p. 74.
57. *APC 1627*, p. 160.
58. DRO, QS1/6 p. 99; Yonge, *Diary*, p. 105.
59. PRO, SP16/60/72.
60. *CSPD 1627*, pp. 141, 147.
61. Cust, *Forced Loan*, pp. 245–6.
62. Yonge, *Diary*, p. 99.
63. *APC 1627*, pp. 272, 387, 492.
64. PRO, SP16/70/79.
65. PRO, SP16/72/35. The rest seem insignificant: two esquires, Alexander Walker and George Rowe, the rest gentlemen, Hugh Prust, John Moltin, James Day, Humphrey Turner, George Fursdon, Gawyn Glass, Humphrey Coish, John Soper, Frances Giles, Thomas Cruse, Maximilian Comyn, William Courts, George Westcombe.
66. *CSPD 1627–1628*, p. 31.
67. PRO, SP16/77/8; DRO QS 1/6 p. 136; BL, Sloane MSS. 1775, f. 72.
68. Yonge, *Diary*, p. 105.
69. PRO, SP16/85/76.
70. BL, Sloane MSS. 1775, f. 72, see p. 84.
71. Russell, *Parliaments*, p. 334; its full yield was £264,000 compared with £275,000 for five subsidies in 1628.
72. Cust, *Forced Loan*, pp. 49, 78.
73. *CSPD 1627–1628*, p. 555; *APC 1627–1628*, pp. 284–6; PRO, SP16/92/93.
74. Yonge, *Diary*, p. 111. He recorded it as £17,400.
75. Cust, *Forced Loan*, p. 84.
76. See p. 82.
77. BL, Add. MSS. 30926, also BL, Sloane MSS. 1775, f. 72 (Miscellaneous Separates) but in that document reference was to Sir Thomas Wise. Thomas Wise was a more likely envoy than his father, as he and William Strode were members of the parliament which assembled on 17 March 1628. Cust refers to a third copy in Grays Inn MS no. 31 (*Forced Loan*, p. 84).
78. J.P. Kenyon, *The Stuart Constitution* (Cambridge, 1966), p. 81.
79. SRO, DD/PH 221/40.
80. Cust, *Forced Loan*, p. 80.
81. For a fuller account of the knighthood composition in Devon see Wolffe, 'Gentry Government', pp. 148–58.
82. Yonge, *Diary*, p. 89.
83. H.H. Leonard, 'Distraint of Knighthood: The Last Phase 1625–41', *History*, 63 (1978), p. 24.

84. BL, Add. MSS. 35331, f. 17.

85. Ibid., f. 29.

86. *CSPD* 1629–1631, p. 302.

87. PRO SP16/172/16.

88. Edward Stephens, a Gloucestershire gentleman, did not question the King's right to knighthood composition, but contended that it only applied to those summoned by writ in January 1626. Yonge recorded the decision of the Court of the Exchequer on 8 February 1631 that all ordered to attend must do so, regardless of any particular summons. BL. Add. MSS. 35331 f. 76.

89. PRO SP16/187/18. In addition to Fulford and Bagg, the commissioners were Sir Edward Seymour, Sir Francis Glanvill, Sir Thomas Drew, Sir Nicholas Martin and Sir George Chudleigh.

90. PRO E178/5153, 5614, 7154, 7161.

91. PRO, E401/1917–1921; E407/35.

92. In Fulford's area no one was charged who had a subsidy rate of less than £4 whereas a few with a rate of £3 and one with a £2 rate were charged in Bagg's area.

93. PRO, E407/35; E401/1918–1921. After his death Bagg was said to have embezzled knighthood composition; Duffin, *Faction and Faith*, p. 107.

94. *APC 1630–1631*, p. 266.

95. PRO, E401/1920.

96. Fletcher, *Sussex*, p. 212; Quintrell, 'The Government of Essex', p. 334.

97. See Chapter 6.

98. PRO, SP16/24/26.

Chapter 6

1. See genealogical table p. 94 based on Vivian, *Visitations,* pp. 159, 190, 598, 719. The JPs from Chudleigh's accession to the bench until 1642 are italicised; C.J. Tyldesley, 'The Crown and the Local Communities in Devon and Cornwall from 1377 to 1422' (University of Exeter Ph.D., 1978), p. 84; J.C. Roberts, 'Parliamentary Representation of Devon and Dorset 1559–1601 University of London MA, 1958), biographical appendices.

2. Prince, *Worthies*, p. 217. Broadclyst was the main estate sold.

3. Vage, 'Exeter Diocese', p. 217.

4. J. Foster (ed.) *Alumni Oxonienses* (Oxford, 1891–2), p. 275.

5. Prince, *Worthies*, p. 217; Pole, *Collections*, pp. 210–11.

6. Vage, 'Diocese of Exeter', p. 254.

7. Samuel Hieron, *Sermon upon I Thessalonians 5:20*, pp. 1, 22.

8. John Barlow, *The True Guide to Glory – A Sermon preached at Plympton Mary at the Funeral of the Right Worshipful and truly religious Lady, the Lady Strode of Newington* (1619), p. 50. Lady Stroke took down sermons with a goose-quill and then repeated them to her maidservants in her chamber, catechizing them on the principles of religion.

9. Ian W. Gowers, 'Puritanism in the County of Devon between 1570 and 1641' (University of Exeter MA, 1970), pp. 163, 164, 217; *HMC 9th Report Part I*, p. 283.

10. Vage, 'Diocese of Exeter, pp. 325, 327.

11. BL, Add. MSS 64887 f. 45.

12. Vage, 'Diocese of Exeter', p. 340.

13. SRO, DD/PH 221/40.

NOTES

14. Peter Hall (ed.) *Joseph Hall's Works,* p. 98.
15. DRO, QS1/7, Mid. 1637; Epiph. 1638.
16. See Wolffe, 'Gentry Government' pp. 241–5 for detail on Chudleigh as a JP.
17. Gray, 'Devon's Coastal and Overseas Fisheries', p. 202.
18. PRO, E403/2590 Privy Seal Books (Auditors) Supplementary series 1620–32, f. 143.
19. He sat for Mitchell in 1601 (his sister Bridget had married into the family who owned Mitchell); for East Looe in 1604, 1614, 1625 and for Lostwithiel in 1621, probably due to Sir Reginald Mohun, his fellow MP and married of another sister, Dorothy. In 1624 he was MP for Tiverton in Devon.
20. Robert Zaller, *The Parliament of 1621* (1971), pp. 39–40; Stone, 'Devon and Parliament', p. 360.
21. Zaller, *Parliament of 1621,* p. 134.
22. I am most grateful to Mr J.P. Ferris for this information. PRO, SP14/166/39.
23. Russell, *Parliaments,* pp. 172–3.
24. Russell, *Parliaments,* p. 186.
25. *Commons Journal, I, 1547–1628,* pp. 741–2; Robert E. Ruigh, *The Parliament of 1624* (Cambridge, Mass., 1971), p. 218.
26. Russell, *Parliaments,* p. 189.
27. *CJ* I, *p. 762.*
28. Ruigh, *1624 Parliament,* p. 241.
29. *CJ* I, pp. 694, 779.
30. Ruigh, *1624 Parliament,* p. 252.
31. Stone, 'Devon and Parliaments', Chap. XII, note 22; *CJ* I, p. 775.
32. I owe this quotation to Mr J.P. Ferris. It is taken from a transcription by the Yale Parliamentary Studies Center of Sir William Spring's diary.
33. *CJ* I, pp. 698, 736, 737, 773.
34. *CJ* I, pp. 684, 687, 737, 736, 766; Stone, 'Devon and Parliament', p. 398.
35. Ruigh, *1624 Parliament,* pp. 88, 183, 257.
36. Harold Hulme (ed.) 'Sir John Eliot and the Vice-Admiralty of Devon', *Camden Miscellany,* XVII, (3rd Series, 64, 1940) p. x. Chudleigh was appointed to this commission and attended four meetings during October 1627 but no detail has been found of his part in these proceedings (ibid., pp. 29–40).
37. Duffin, *Faction and Faith,* p. 77.
38. *HMC 12th Report Cowper I,* p. 252. Chudleigh's informant was Bishop Carey of Exeter whose wife was Coke's sister.
39. *HMC 12th Report Cowper I,* p. 238. Mohun's offer of a blank burgesship to Chudleigh on this occasion supports the view that Mohun had probably influenced Chudleigh's earlier elections to parliament.
40. Yonge, *Diary,* pp. 86, 111; PRO, SP16/84/4. I am grateful to Mr Roger Lockyer for informing me that he found no reference to Chudleigh in his study of Buckingham.
41. See p. 132; Fletcher, *Reform,* p. 297.
42. Wolffe, 'Gentry Government', pp. 210–238 for a detailed examination of the response of the leaders of the gentry as a whole to these demands.
43. *APC 1623–1625,* pp. 498–500; BL, Add. MSS 64883, f. 13; *HMC 12th Report Cowper I,* p. 190.
44. PRO, SP 16/2/84; *APC 1625–1626,* p. 55; Wallace T. MacCaffrey, *Exeter 1540–1640* (Cambridge, Mass., 1958), p. 12; Hoskins, *Devon,* p. 114.
45. PRO. SP16/3/18.
46. PRO, SP16/3/54.
47. PRO, SP16/3/55, 59, 67, 83; /4/3, 50.

48. PRO, SP16/3/101.
49. PRO, SP16/2/65; /4/129; BL, Add. MSS 64884, f. 57.
50. PRO, SP16/5/35. 47; *APC 1625–1626*, p. 99.
51. Russell, *Parliaments*, p. 359.
52. PRO, SP16/6/3.
53. A.B. Grosart (ed.), *John Glanvill's Account of the Expedition to Cadiz in 1625* (Camden Society, 2nd series, 32, 1883); P.Q. Karkeek, 'First visit of Charles I to Devon', *TDA*, X (1878), p. 233.
54. See p. 74.
55. PRO, SP16/11/29.
56. BL, Add. MSS. 64886 f. 52; 64887 f. 45.
57. PRO, SP16/11/71; /12/35. 101; /18/99; /19/88; *APC 1625–1626*. pp. 261, 267–8, 298–9, 305, 332.
58. SP16/18/23. 99; /20/57; *APC 1625–1626*, p. 305. Sir William St Leger commanded the troops after their return from Cadiz.
59. PRO, SP16/19/60; /20/63; /23/10; C231/4 f. 194v.
60. PRO, E351/288; no date is given for Chudleigh's appointment but his account is headed from 19 January 1626; SP16/18/99.
61. He signed 10 letters from the commissioners between 16 March and 15 July compared with 7 signed by Sir Ferdinando Gorges, governor of Plymouth and the next most active commissioner.
62. PRO, SP16/23/51.
63. PRO, SP16/24/26.
64. *APC 1625–1626*, pp. 415–6; PRO, SP16/25/13.
65. PRO, SP16/25/71; /29/41.
66. PRO, SP16/30/67.
67. PRO, SP16/31/33.
68. See p. 109.
69. PRO, SP16/31/62.
70. PRO, SP16/31/80.
71. BL, Add MSS. 64889 f. 51.
72. Ibid., f. 79. Part of this letter is printed in *HMC 12th Report Cowper I*, p. 276, but incorrectly said to be from the commissioners. Yonge, *Diary* p. 94 gives the date of the meeting as 28 July but he was not a signatory.
73. BL, Add. MSS. 64889. f. 151; *APC 1626*, p. 216.
74. BL, Add. MSS. 64889, f. 133.
75. *APC 1627*, p. 75.
76. BL, Add. MSS. 64889, f. 151.
77. DRO, QS1/6. p. 65.
78. PRO, SP16/38/68.
79. BL, Add. MSS. 64890 f. 34.
80. I am grateful to Professor Russell for this suggestion.
81. PRO, C193/12/2; see p. 78.
82. PRO, SP16/53/96.
83. PRO, E351/288.
84. BL, Add. MSS. 64891, ff. 47, 48; PRO, E351/288.
85. PRO, SP16/77/8i.
86. DRO, Exeter Ancient Letters 60D no. 295; PRO, C193/12/2.
87. Roger Lockyer, *Buckingham* (1981), p. 381–2, 387.
88. PRO, SP16/77/1; BL, Add. MSS. 64893, f. 44; *APC 1627*, p. 509.

89. PRO, SP16/77/8.
90. PRO, SP16/79/32.
91. PRO, SP16/81/4.
92. DRO, QS 1/6 pp. 137, 148.
93. *APC 1627–1628*, p. 60; *HMC Exeter, 73* p. 17.
94. PRO, SP16/82/82 states that the letter is from deputy lieutenants; DRO Ancient Letters 60D L.297 more accurately states that it is from JPs.
95. PRO, SP16/88/46.
96. PRO, SP16/84/12; 85/56; *APC 1627–1628*, pp. 126–7.
97. Lockyer, *Buckingham,* pp. 395, 396, 402.
98. PRO, SP16/85/8. Chudleigh was on the martial law commission drawn up at this time, *CSPD 1627–1628.*
99. *HMC Exeter, 73,* p. 182; *APC 1627–1628,* p. 147.
100. PRO, SP16/86/75; 87/12i, 27.
101. PRO, SP16/90/43.
102. PRO, SP16/93/41; *APC 1627–1628,* p. 299.
103. PRO, SP16/100/54; Lockyer, *Buckingham,* pp. 419–20.
104. Yonge, *Diary,* p. 112.
105. PRO, SP16/98/26. 26i, 31, 35, 36.
106. PRO, Prob. 11/154.
107. *APC 1627–1628,* p. 363; PRO, SP16/100/54, 103/1.
108. Russell, *Parliaments,* p. 359.
109. *APC 1627–1628,* pp. 299, 393; PRO, SP16/100/54.
110. DRO, 1/6 f. 161.
111. PRO, SP16/102/16.
112. PRO, SP16/103/1.
113. PRO, E351/288.
114. PRO, SP16/105/40, 46; BL, Add. MSS. 35331, ff. 28, 32; *APC 1627–1628,* p. 435; Birch, *Times of Charles I,* p. 355.
115. *CJ* I, 741; see p. 117.

Chapter 7

1. DRO, LXXXII, LXXXVI; PRO, C231/4, f. 186; *APC 1625–6,* p. 24.
2. Deputy lieutenants who were JPs are identified in Wolffe, 'Gentry Government' Appendix A. The others were Francis Courtenay, Hugh Pollard and Sir John Yonge.
3. PRO, SP16/3/55. See p. 104.
4. Lindsay Boynton, *The Elizabethan Militia 1558–1638* (1967), pp. 208, 210, 212.
5. *CSPD 1611–1618,* p. 182.
6. *CSPD 1619–1623,* p. 264; Fletcher, *Reform,* p. 283, quoting the earl of Hertford.
7. *APC 1623–1625,* p. 8.
8. *APC 1625–1626,* p. 141.
9. Barnes, *Somerset,* p. 245.
10. DRO, 1148M/add/18/1; PRO, SP16/8/4.
11. *CSPD 1625–1626,* p. 149.
12. Ibid., p. 229.
13. *APC 1625–1626,* p. 323.

14. Ibid., p. 484.
15. PRO, SP16/31/62.
16. PRO, SP16/31/80; *APC 1626*, pp. 72–4.
17. *APC 1626*, p. 87.
18. BL, Add. MSS. 64889, f. 79.
19. PRO, SP16/70/18; /72/16; /147/3; *APC 1627–1628*, p. 227.
20. L.J. Reeve, *Charles I and the Road to Personal Rule* (Cambridge, 1989), pp. 134–5.
21. PRO, SP16/147/3.
22. SRO, DD/PH 221/4. It is Hall's reference to Devon responding better to recent financial demands than any other part of the kingdom which suggests that this letter should be dated soon after the second forced loan.
23. PRO, SP16/147/3; /150/43, 76(i–iv).
24. Duffin, *Faction and Faith*, p. 121.
25. DRO QS1/6 pp. 308–11, 427, 435.
26. Fincham, 'Episcopal Government 1603–1640' in *The Early Stuart Church 1604–1642*, pp. 86; Davies, *The Caroline Captivity*, pp. 188–9, 194.
27. PRO, SP16/187/91; see p. 66.
28. BL, ADD 35,331, f. 48; PRO, SP16/199/29, 32, 33, 202/53, 241/55; PC/42, f. 320; PC2/44, f. 181; DRO, 1180 A add 2/PW 15 East Budleigh f. 44; Simon Adams, 'Spain or the Netherlands? The Dilemmas of Early Stuart Foreign Policy', in (ed). Harold Tomlinson *Before the English Civil War*, pp. 83–4, 100.
29. PRO, SP16/291/14.
30. DRO, QS1/7 Epiph. 1635; Lady E.F. Eliot-Drake, *The Family and Heirs of Sir Francis Drake* (1911), p. 240; PRO, PC2/44, f. 439. See Chapter 10.
31. PRO, PC2/44, f. 356.
32. PRO, SP16/291/14.
33. BL, H1 6804, ff. 60–1.
34. Conrad Russell, *The Fall of the British Monarchies 1637–1642* (Oxford, 1991) p. 55; BL, Add. MSS. 35331 f. 69; PRO, PC2/49 f. 542.
35. PRO, SP16/402/69,69i. Lord William Russell had now joined his father in a joint lieutenancy. See pp. 231–2 for details of the orders received by John Willoughby for this muster.
36. PRO, SP16/410/163; /413/65, 69, 70, 132.
37. *CSPD 1638–1639*, pp. 277, 323; SP16/413/111.
38. PRO, SP16/421/23.
39. PRO, SP16/429/95; 430/19.
40. PRO, PC2/50 f. 299; John Rushworth, *Historical Collections*, III (1721) p. 911.
41. Russell, *Fall of Monarchies*, p. 92.
42. BL, H1 2217 is undated but H1 2305 refers to it as 2 May 1628.
43. *Joseph Hall's Works*, I, p. xxxvi; R.N. Worth (ed.), *The Buller Papers* (1895), pp. 136–7.
44. BL, Add. MSS. 4931 ff. 58–60; Rushworth, *Historical Collections* III, pp. 1205–7.
45. PRO, SP16/462; PC2/52 f. 727; SRO WO 56/6/52.1; CSPD, 1640, p. 657.
46. PRO, SP16/469/54.
47. Worth. (ed.), *Buller Papers*, pp. 139–40.
48. DRO, QS 1/7, Epiph. 1641; John Jones, *Bishop Hall, His Life and Times* (1826), p. 114; Davies, *Caroline Captivity*, pp. 255, 259.
49. Russell, *Fall of Monarchies* p. 292.
50. *Joseph Hall's Works*, V, pp. 454, 457, 459.
51. DRO, QS1/8 Mich. 1641.
52. DRO, QS1/8 Epiph. 1642; BL, E.181 (27) *Petition of Knights, Gentlemen and Yeomanry*

of the County of Devon (1642); *HMC 4th Report, House of Lords MSS.* p. 143; *HMC 5th Report*, pp. 4–5; A. Fletcher, *The Outbreak of the English Civil War* (1981), pp. 191–2.

53. *Lords Journal*, IV, p. 536–7, QS1/8, Epiph. 1642.

54. Fletcher, *Outbreak*, p. 226.

55. *CJ*, II, p. 391; *LJ*, IV, pp. 536–7; *The Private Journals of the Long Parliament, 3 January to 5 March 1642*, (ed.), William H. Coates, Anne Steele Young, Vernon F. Snow (Newhaven and London, Yale University Press, 1982), p. 145; Russell, *Fall of Monarchies*, p. 457.

56. Fletcher, *Outbreak*, p. 223–226; Russell, *Fall of Monarchies*, pp. 449–50, 454.

57. Ibid., p. 464; *CJ*, II, p. 424.

58. *LJ*, V, p. 79.

59. *LJ*, V pp. 94, 144; *CJ* II, p. 651. E.A. Andriette, *Devon and Exeter in the Civil War* (Newton Abbot, 1971), p. 56; *The Constitutional Documents of the Puritan Revolution* (ed.), S.R. Gardiner (Oxford, 1899), pp. 245–7, 248–254.

60. DRO, QS1/8 Mid. 1642; *LJ*, V 295–7, partly printed in Morrill, *Revolt of the Provinces*, pp. 162–3.

61. SRO, W056/6/52.2.3.

62. BL (Thomason Tract), E112/23; I.R. Palfrey, 'Devon and the Outbreak of the English Civil War, 1642–43' in *Southern History*, 10, (1988), p. 31.

63. PRO, C231/5 f. 530.

64. DRO 1392/1645/29; SP16/491/113, 116.

65. (ed.) Gardiner, *Constitutional Documents*, pp. 247–8, 249–254; *A Declaration published in the County of Devon by that Grand Ambo-dexter, Sir George Chudleigh Baronet. To delude his Country-men in their Judgement and Affection, touching the present difference between his Majestie and the Parliament. Together with a full and satisfactory Answer thereunto, transmitted from thence under the Hand of a Judicious and well affected Patriot* (1644). 1644 has been deleted and 14 March 1643 inserted by hand; *LJ*, V p. 94.

66. BL, E.18 (5). I am grateful to Dr Stoyle for this reference; Vivian, *Cornwall*, p. 69. In 1644 Carew planned to betray the island to the royalists and was executed on 23 December 1644.

67. (ed.) C.E.H. Chadwyck-Healey, 'Sir Ralph Hopton's Campaign in the West 1642–1644' *Somerset Record Society*, 18 (1902) pp. 11–13, 22; *Buller Papers*, p. 79; E. Hyde, earl of Clarendon, *The History of the Rebellion and Civil Wars in England* (Oxford, 1839), III, p. 398; BL, E.126 (2), *Reply by Parliament to petition presented to said Houses by inhabitants of Devon and Cornwall October 22 1642* (1642). Chudleigh is referred to as Sir George Studley.

68. BL (Thomason Tract), 669 f. 5 (99); E.83 (43), p. 6. The others were Sir John Northcott, Sir Samuel Rolle and Sir Nicholas Martin.

69. BL, E.244 (30) I am grateful to Dr Stoyle for this reference. BL, E.244 (42); BL, *Mercurius Aulicus* 7 Jan. 1643 (Burney Collection 13); *CJ*, II, p. 932.

70. Hopton, 'Campaign' pp. 31–3; DRO, 1392 M/L1645/30–3.

71. *HMC 13th Report, Appendix I, Portland*, p. 100.

72. DRO, 1392M/L1645/29.

73. *CJ*, II, p. 999; BL, E.93/19, E.99/15; *Mercurius Aulicus* 21 April 1643 (Burney Collection 13); SRO, W056/5/59; Palfrey, 'Devon and the Outbreak of the English Civil War, pp. 40–1.

74. *CJ*, III p. 57; F.T.R. Edgar, *Sir Ralph Hopton* (1968), p. 76.

75. Clarendon, *Rebellion*, IV, p. 425; Edgar, *Hopton*, pp. 64, 73; DRO, 1392M/L1645/32.

76. Andriette, *Devon and Exeter in the Civil War*, p. 87; Clarendon, *Rebellion*, IV, p. 94; BL, Add. MSS. 35297 f. 15. I owe this reference to Dr Stoyle.

77. Clarendon, *Rebellion*, IV p. 95.

78. Hopton, 'Campaign', p. 45.

79. BL, E.249 (12); *Mercurius Aulicus*, 5 June 1643 (Burney Collection 13); S.R. Gardiner, *History of the Great Civil War* (1987), I, pp. 135, 138, 139.

80. DRO, 1392M/L1645/32; Gardiner, *Great Civil War* I, pp. 173, 182; *CJ*, III, p. 216.

81. BL, *Mercurius Aulicus*, 2 Nov. 1643 (Burney Collection 17); *A Declaration published by Sir George Chudleigh Baronet*.

82. Gardiner, *Great Civil War* I, p. 181; Gardiner (ed.), *Constitutional Documents*, p. 267–71.

83. Stoyle, *Loyalty and Locality*, p. 214.

84. PRO, SP19/142/33. Junto was a term for the royalist parliament which met at Oxford from 22 January to 16 April 1644.

85. BL, Add. MSS. 18980; E.71 (32), I owe this reference to Dr Stoyle; E.266 (37).

86. PRO, SP19/9/407; 142/33, 34, 36, 37, 38; Kenyon, *Stuart Constitution*, p. 341.

87. PRO, SP23/152/29; SP19/86/29; /11/275.

88. DRO, QS28/3–7, QS Rolls, box 52, Epiph. 1646/7.

Chapter 8

1. Vivian, *Visitations*, p. 643.

2. See genealogical table p. 166 compiled from Vivian, *Visitations*, pp. 603, 643–4. The JPs from Reynell's accession to the bench until 1642 are italicised. Two positions assigned to Richard Reynell of Creedy in P.W. Hasler, *History of Parliament The Commons 1558–1603* (1981), p. 285, were more likely to have been held by Reynell of Ford. One was as a clerk in the office of the Lord Treasurer's Remembrancer in 1593 (Reynell of Ford was a Secondary in the Lord Treasurer's Remembrancer's office later in his life. PRO, E403/2750–2753 Order Book Pells). The other was as MP for the Cornish constituency of Mitchell in 1593. I am grateful to J.P. Ferris, a later editor of *The History of Parliament*, for his assistance over this entry and his agreement that Reynell of Ford was the more likely member of parliament.

3. *Register of Admissions to the Middle Temple* I (ed.) H.A.C. Sturgess (1949) p. 55; W.R. Prest, *The Inns of Court 1590–1640* (1972) p. 9.

4. *DNB*, Sir William Periam died in 1604.

5. DRO, 1579A/10/20. I am grateful to George Yerby for this reference; Pole, *Collections*, pp. 175, 177, 178.

6. PRO, C66/1620; Charles Crosleigh, *History of Bradninch* (1911), p. 130; DRO 1310 F/A, Acte Book of Eight Men of Broadclyst.

7. Richard Polwhele, *The History of Devonshire* (1977, Dorking), II, p. 47; DRO, Z1/27/1/26; Z1/15/14, 18; Z1/48/26/1; Z1/48/26/3; Z1/15/14, 16; Z1/48/26/5.

8. Signifies session without a list of those present.

9. Richard Reynell of Ogwell became a JP on 13 June 1618 (PRO, C231/4 p. 64), but the two Richard Reynells were not identified by their residences until Easter 1619. Either of them may have attended the three sessions marked '*?'.

10. See above p. .

11. DRO, QS Rolls, box 28, Epiph. 1625; box 29, Easter 1626; box 32, Epiph. 1629.

12. Ibid., box 28, Mid. 1625; box 29, Epiph. 1626.

13. Ibid., box 30, Mich. 1627.

14. Ibid., box 21, Easter 1617.

15. Ibid., box 23, Epiph. 1619.

16. Ibid., box 31, Epiph. 1628; box 29, Epiph. 1626.

17. Ibid., box 31, Epiph. 1628; box 28, Mich. 1625.
18. Ibid., box 30, Easter 1627.
19. Ibid., box 13, Easter 1607; box 12, 1605; box 13, Epiph. 1608; box 22, Mich. 1615; box 19, Mich. 1613.
20. Ibid., box 31 Epiph. 1628; box 26, Mich. 1622.
21. Ibid., box 31 Mich. 1627.
22. Ibid., box 22, Easter 1618.
23. Ibid., box 32, Epiph. 1629.
24. Ibid., box 19, Easter 1613.
25. Ibid., box 17, Mich. 1611.
26. Ibid., box 20, Easter 1615; box 22, Easter 1619.
27. Ibid., box 19, Epiph. 1613.
28. Ibid., box 21, Easter 1617; thirty-two orders against forestalling, regrating and ingrossing have been found between 1625 and 1640, QS 1/5, 6, 7.
29. See p. 40.
30. PRO, C231/1, p. 114; C231/4, ff. 45, 59v.
31. PRO, C66/1988; C231/4, p. 225.
32. DRO, QS Rolls, boxes 22, 23.
33. DRO, QS1/5 p. 602.
34. Margery M. Rowe and Andrew M. Jackson (eds), *Freemen of Exeter 1266–1947* (Devon and Cornwall Record Society, Extra series I, 1973), p. 113; *HMC Exeter 73*, pp. 110–1.
35. DRO, QS 1/7, Epiph. 1638.
36. DRO, Exeter Ancient Letters 60 C, nos. 211, 212.
37. DRO, Exeter Chamber Act Book VII, 1616–34, p. 241; *HMC Exeter 73*, p. 252; DRO, Exeter quarter session C1/62, pp. 148, 364.
38. *HMC 12th Report Cowper I*, p. 276; see pp. 77–8.
39. DRO, 1579A/7/1/20; I am grateful to George Yerby for this reference. All were JPs except Ambrose Bellot who had been dropped from the commission earlier in 1626; *HMC 12th Report Cowper I*, p. 276; see above p. .
40. DRO, 4652M/F5/1.
41. Yonge, *Diary*, p. 6.
42. Vage, 'Diocese of Exeter' pp. 166–70, 235.
43. Hasler (ed.), *Commons 1558–1603*, p. 209; *HMC Exeter 73*, p. 93.
44. PRO, Prob. 11/159.
45. The evidence for Reynell acting as deputy *custos rotulorum*, has been considered in Part I, see p. 21.

Chapter 9

1. DNB; *Alumni Oxonienses*, p. 1705; *Register of Middle Temple*, Vol. I, p. 77; Yonge, *Diary*, pp. ix. There is no evidence that he was a barrister-at-law as claimed (ibid. p.x); that would have debarred him from being sheriff: Myron C. Noonkester, 'Kings of their Counties. The Shrievalty in England form Elizabeth I to Charles I', (University of Chicago Ph.D, 1984), p. 13.
2. Polwhele. *Devonshire* p. 47.
3. See genealogical table p. 181.
4. PRO, C231/4, f. 141v.
5. PRO, E179/102/463.

6. PRO, C231/4 f. 200; C231/5, f. 530; DRO, QS 28/3, 4, 5; *APC 1625–1626*, p. 371; David Underdown, *Pride's Purge* (Oxford, 1971) p. 390.

7. See p. 169.

8. Signifies session without list of those present.

9. BL, Add. MSS. 35331, ff. 74–5.

10. Yonge, *Diary*, p. x. It was reprinted in 1660 when it was stated that it was 'intended only to help the memory'. Its practical value stood the test of time and was the basis of a book published by Samuel Blackersby of Grays Inn in 1719, but without any acknowledgement to Yonge.

11. PRO, SP16/8/14; see p. 140; Yonge, *Diary*, p. 106; PRO, SP16/291/14ii.

12. BL, Add. MSS. 28032 f. 123; PRO, SP16/82/82; /84/12; /85/56.

13. PRO, SP16/85/56. 107/52. Only one of the eight signatories to the first letter and only one of the four to the second have been found elsewhere referred to as deputy lieutenants at this period.

14. BL, Add. MSS. 35331. ff. 40; Yonge, *Diary*, p. 111; PRO, E401/1915, 1916, 1917.

15. Yonge, *Diary*, pp. 19, 49, 52, 53.

16. Peter Lake, 'The moderate and irenic case for religious war: Joseph Hall's Via Media in context' in Susan D. Amussen and Mark A. Kishlansky (eds), *Political Culture and Cultural Politics in Early Modern England*, p. 62.

17. Yonge, *Diary*, p. 118; Vage, 'Exeter Diocese', p. 348; *DNB*.

18. Yonge, *Diary*, p. 93; SRO, DD/PH 221/40.

19. Yonge, *Diary*, pp. 64, 106.

20. Yonge, *Diary*, p. 84; BL, Add. MSS. 35331, f. 118, with a drawing of a head in the margin.

21. Yonge, *Diary*, pp. 59, 96.

22. BL, Add. MSS. 28032, ff. 2v, 37v, 64.

23. R. Cust, 'News and Politics in Early Seventeenth-Century England', *Past and Present*, 112 (August 1986); F.J. Levy, 'How Information Spread among the Gentry 1550–1640 in *Journal of British Studies*, XXI (1982).

24. PRO, C193/12/2; SP16/53/96, 102/16.

25. BL, Add. MSS. 35331, ff. 1–9.

26. Ibid., ff. 15, 17, 20, 30, 33–34, 38.

27. Yonge was not present at the Epiphany quarter session and was in London on 7 and 17 February 1629. BL, Add. MSS. 35331, f. 48. PRO, E401/1916.

28. Russell, *Parliaments*, p. 405; BL, Add. MSS. 35331 f. 48.

29. Kenyon, *Stuart Constitution* p. 85.

30. BL, Add. MSS. 35331, f. 48.

31. Ibid., ff. 48, 51. January 1640 he recorded the release of Mr Strode and Mr Valentyne, ibid., f. 143.

32. Larkin, *Proclamations*, pp. 226–7; Birch, *Court and Times of Charles I*, II, p. 389.

33. BL, Add. MSS. 35331, f. 121.

34. Charles M. Andrews, *The Colonial Period of American History The Settlements* I (New Haven, 1934), pp. 347, 348, 352, 354, 420; F. Rose-Troup, *John White, Founder of Massachusetts*, (New York, 1930), p. 263, Appendix III; F. Rose-Troup, 'A Forgotten Page of the Ecclesiastical History of Seaton', *TDA*, XXX (1898), pp. 336–7.

35. BL, Add. MSS. 35331, ff. 79, 84; PRO, E401/1917; see above pp. .

36. BL, Add. MSS. 35331, f. 16, 150.

37. Ibid., ff. 53, 125.

38. Ibid., f. 89. News of action against the Dutch fishing fleet may have reached Yonge through Chudleigh's contact with Coke, who had been suggesting this since 1628 or earlier. I am grateful to Professor Russell for this comment. Adams, 'Spain or the Netherlands', pp. 84, 100.

39. BL, Add. MSS. 35331, ff. 120, 131, 140.
40. Ibid., ff. 129–131; PRO, SP16/435/33i.
41. BL, Add. MSS. 35331, f. 142.
42. Ibid., f. 89.
43. Ibid., f. 97; Russell, *Fall of British Monarchies*, p. 46.
44. BL, Add. MSS. 35331, f. 128–9, Yonge noted that he copied this from Sir John Pole's copy f. 131; David Stevenson, *The Scottish Revolution 1637–44* (Newton Abbot, 1973), p. 72–3.
45. BL, Add. MSS. 35331, ff. 130, 131, 135; Stevenson, *Scottish Revolution*, p. 97.
46. BL, Add. MSS. 35331, f. 136; SRO, DD W053/1/115.
47. BL, Add. MSS. 35332, ff. 137, 138.
48. Sir Peter and Edmund Prideaux; Gowers 'Puritanism in Devon', p. 186; *CSPD April 1635–December 1635*, pp. 190, 198; *1639–1640*, p. 403; James, 'Sir Henry Rosewell', pp. 118–9; DRO, QS 28/1.
49. BL, Add. MSS. 35331, f. 1; *Mercurius Aulicus*, 4 and 24 April 1644, (Burney Collection 13).
50. J.T. Cliffe, *Puritans in Conflict* (1988), p. 116.
51. *CJ*, III p. 29.
52. BL, Add. MSS. 18777–18780. He continued the practice of adding roses against comments in these diaries. I am informed by Dr Cust that Christopher Thompson has deciphered Yonge's code and that his transcript of these diaries are in the Institute of Historical Research.
53. J.H. Hexter, *The Reign of King Pym* (Harvard University Press, 1961), p. 52.
54. BL, Add. MSS. 18778 f. 3.
55. *CJ*, III, p. 569.
56. Kenyon, *Stuart Constitution*, p. 262; *CJ*, III, pp. 118, 144; Cliffe, *Puritans in Conflict*, pp. 95, 116.
57. Underdown, *Pride's Purge*, p. 390, Yonge marked as an abstainer.

Chapter 10

1. Noonkester, 'Kings of their Counties. The Shrievalty in England from Elizabeth I to Charles I' p. 44.
2. Michael Dalton, *The Office and Authority of Sheriff* (1623), p. 119, 125, 143–4; J.S. Cockburn (ed.), 'Memorandum Book of Robert Hunt, Sheriff of Somerset 1654–1656' in *Somerset Assize Orders*, Appendix II (Somerset Record Society LXXI, 1971). For an account of the Devon sheriff from 1625–1640 see Wolffe, 'Gentry Government', Chapter IV.
3. Princes, *Worthies*, p. 235.
4. See p. 102 for Sir George Chudleigh, p. 235 for John Willoughby.
5. *DNB*; Inner Temple; AO; Vivian, *Visitations*, p. 307.
6. DRO, QS1/2–7 (1604–1640); between 1625–40 he signed about eighteen recognizances or examinations each year, QS, Rolls boxes 28–43.
7. BL, Add. MSS 35331, ff. 114, 115. For a detailed account of the ship money collection in Devon see Wolffe, 'Gentry Government', pp. 158–191.
8. PRO, PC2/44, ff. 260–1.
9. PRO, PC2/44, f. 293.
10. PRO, SP16/282/10.
11. PRO, SP16/297/35; BL, Add. MSS. 35331, f. 61.
12. Ibid.

13. DRO, QS1/7, Epiph. 1635; DRO, Exeter City Chamber Act Book VIII (1634–1647), 20 January 1635.
14. See p. 139.
15. PRO, PC2/44 ff. 473, 517.
16. PRO, PC2/44, f. 513.
17. PRO, PC2/44, f. 659.
18. M.D. Gordon, 'The Collection of Ship Money in the Reign of Charles I', *TRHS* 3rd Series IV (1910), pp. 156–162, for comparative payments of the counties; Fletcher, *Sussex* p. 208; Duffin, *Faction and Faith*, pp. 158, 163–4; Gardiner, *Constitutional Documents*, p. 105.
19. DRO, 1579A/8/8.
20. 1635: PRO, SP16/295/54, PC2/45, ff. 77, 78; 1636: DRO, 1579A/8/14; PRO, PC2/46, ff. 378, 379; 1637: PRO, PC2/48, f. 236.
21. PRO, PC2/45, f. 249.
22. There was considerable variations in the way different counties assessed ship money, see Kevin Sharpe, *The Personal Rule of Charles I* (Yale, 1992) pp. 569–70. The only other county known to have assessed areas equally, though of variable size, was Cheshire: G. A. Kerby, 'Inequality in a Pre-Industrial Society. A Study of Wealth, Status, Office and Taxation in Tudor and Stuart England with Particular Reference to Cheshire' (University of Cambridge Ph.D, 1983), p. 60.
23. PRO, SP16/302/57, 87.
24. PRO, SP16/297/35, 301/77.
25. *CSPD 1635–1636*, p. 137; PRO, SP16/305/64; DRO, 1579A/8/12; PRO, SP16/313/107.
26. PRO, SP16/297/35.
27. PRO, PC2/45, f. 110.
28. PRO, PC2/45, f. 249, SP16/301/76, 77.
29. Langelüddecke, 'Secular Policy Enforcement During the Personal Rule of Charles I' p. 162.
30. PRO, SP16/303/127, DRO, 32428A/9/20, 1579A/8/10.
31. PRO, SP16/305/64, 313/79, 80, 107, 314/42, 104, 250/80. Barnes, *Somerset*, p. 207.
32. Langelüddecke, 'Secular Policy Enforcement During the Personal Rule of Charles I', p. 181.
33. PRO, SP16/325/80.
34. Barnes, *Somerset*, pp. 212, 214–5, 233–5.
35. PRO, SP16,329/75.
36. PRO, PC2/50 f. 299, Rushworth, *Historical Collections*, III, 910–2.
37. PRO, SP16/462/15–26, 41; 460/28; for an account of the mutiny see Stoyle, *Loyalty and Locality*, pp. 168–9.
38. SRO, W056/6/52.1; See pp. 146–7.
39. BL, Thomason Tract E114/24; *CJ*, II 813.
40. SRO, W056/6/59; DRO, QS28/1.
41. PRO, SP19/9/308, 21/271.
42. Prince *Worthies*, p. 707.
43. DRO, 1579A/8/13, 14.
44. *CSPD 1635–1636*, p. 137; PRO, SP16/376/138.
45. PRO, SP16/338/8. 8i.
46. PRO, SP16/346/5, 77, 87.
47. PRO, SP16/344/60.
48. PRO, SP16/351/2, 20.

49. BL, Add. MSS. 35331, ff. 125, 126; DRO, QS1/7, Mich. 1636. In spite of the pirates being termed 'Turkish', they normally came from North Africa.
50. PRO, SP16/372/3, 7.
51. Duffin, *Faction and Faith*, p. 57.
52. PRO, SP16/370/55, 401/38.
53. DRO, 1499 Madd 3/E15, ff. 675, 678, 681–3.
54. Langelüddecke, 'Secular Policy Enforcement During the Personal Rule of Charles I', p. 182.
55. DRO, 1499 Madd 3/E15, f. 699; in February 1641 Wise was told that the vicar of Ilsington had termed him 'a factious man who ought not to be elected for a knight from this county and whosoever did take your part he would denounce him a factious man in his pulpit because you did not levy the ship money.' R.N. Worth, (ed.), *Buller Papers* (1895), p. 33.
56. BL, Add. MSS. 35331, f. 127; Duffin, *Faith and Faction*, p. 139.
57. DRO, Chanter 57, Patent Book No. I, ff. 31–32.
58. BL, Add. MSS. 35331, ff. 129, 130, 131.
59. PRO, PC2/45 f. 249; SP16/338/8.
60. PRO, PC2/47 f. 472, PC2/48 f. 295.
61. PRO, SP16/391/12, PC2/49, f. 307.
62. DRO, QS1/7 Mich. 1637; PRO, PC2/48 f. 596; SP16/391/13. Comparison in PRO, SP16/338/8i and SP16/449/61 of nine parishes named in DRO, QS1/7 Mich. 1637.
63. PRO, PC2/49, ff. 308, 353.
64. PRO, SP16/405/54; 410/128, PC2/50, f. 64.
65. PRO, SP16/402/69 (i).
66. PRO, SP16/418/93.
67. PRO, C231/5, f. 349.
68. PRO, SP16/435/33.
69. PRO, SP16/435/33i. The figure of arrears given by Gordon is £611 4s 8d. 'Ship Money', p. 155.
70. Langelüddecke, 'Secular Policy Enforcement During the Personal Rule of Charles I', p. 260.
71. Worth (ed.), *Buller Papers*, pp. 139–40.
72. Vivian, *Visitations*, p. 603.
73. PRO C66/2449; C231/4 f. 256; E163/14/8. Prince, *Worthies*, p. 637.
74. PRO, SP16/401/36, 37, 38.
75. PRO, SP16/417/43. Pole returned assessments of the clergy on 25 May 1639.
76. Morrill, *Revolt of the Provinces*, p. 28.
77. PRO, SP16/427/31. Richard Strode, eldest son of Sir William, was not a county JP, only one for Plympton St Mary.
78. PRO, SP16/432/78.
79. PRO, SP16/441/26.
80. PRO, SP16/460/28, 462/15, 16, 20, 21, 26.
81. BL, Add. MSS. 35331 f. 128; F.R. Troup, *John White*, Appendix; notice on tomb in Colyton church; DRO, QS 1/8, Epiph. 1640.
82. DRO, QS1/8 Epiph. 1642; pp. 149–50.
83. DRO, QS1/8 Mid. 1642; *LJ*, V, 94.
84. SRO, W056/6/52.2.
85. SRO, W053/1/129.
86. DRO, 1392M/L1645/28, 30–3; BL, Thomason Tract, E94/21; E99/15.
87. BL, *Mercurius Aulicus*, 20 May 1643, Burney Collection 13.

88. PRO, SP23/109/181, 191, 195.
89. Steven Pugsley, 'Landed Society and the Emergence of the Country House in Tudor and Early Stuart Devon' in Todd Gray, Margery Rowe and Audrey Erskine (eds), *Tudor and Stuart Devon*, (Exeter, 1992) pp. 111–112.
90. DRO, QS Rolls, box 51; QS28/1, 3–8; Vivian, *Visitations*, p. 603.
91. Vivian, *Visitations*, pp. 553–4; Wallace T. MacCaffrey, *Exeter 1540–1640* (Cambridge, 1958), pp. 253, 255; W.G. Willis Watson, *The House of Martin* (Exeter, 1906), p.125; PRO, C231/5 f. 38.
92. PRO, PC2/51, ff. 38, 101–4; *CSPD 1639–1640*, p. 498.
93. PRO, SP16/338/8i compared with SP16/449/61.
94. PRO, PC2/51, ff. 481–2; *CSPD 1640*, p. 352.
95. *CSPD 1640* p. 563. The total collection was stated to be £4,496 4s 1d, leaving arrears of £4,503 15s 11d; no evidence has been found for the lower arrears of £3,901 8s cited by Gordon 'Ship Money', p. 157.
96. Barnes, *Somerset*, p. 322.
97. Morrill, *Revolt of the Provinces*, p. 25.
98. SRO, W053/1/129, 131; BL, Thomason Tract, 669 f. 5 (99); E83 (43).
99. BL, Thomason Tract E94/21; E96/18; DRO, 1392M/L1645/32. QS28/1; Mark Stoyle, *Documentary Evidence for the Civil War Defences of Exeter, 1642–43* (Exeter Museums Archaeological Field Unit Report No 92. 10, 1992), p. 19.
100. DRO, QS1/8; QS Rolls, box 51.
101. Andriette, *Devon and Exeter in the Civil War*, p. 184; DRO, QS28/3–10.
102. Underdown, *Pride's Purge*, pp. 139, 141, 147, 159.
103. Roberts, *Recovery and Restoration*, p. 180.
104. Langelüddecke, 'Secular Policy Enforcement During the Personal Rule of Charles I', p. 183.
105. Sharpe, *The Personal Rule*, p. 593–4.
106. Ibid., pp. 578–81.
107. Quintrell, 'The Government of Essex', p. 92; McPartlin, 'Herefordshire', p. 19; Holmes, *Lincolnshire*, p. 132; Silcock, 'Worcestershire', p. 60.

Chapter 11

1. I am most grateful to Dr Mark Stoyle for drawing my attention to the Willoughby papers in the Somerset Record Office.
2. Youings (ed.), *Devon Monastic Lands*, p. 120. I am grateful to the current owners of Leyhill, Mr & Mrs Garvey, for showing me over their house.
3. R. Troup, *TDA*, 1898; SRO, W019/1/1; 45/5; PRO, E179/102/463 in 1624.
4. See genealogical table p. 229 based on Vivian, *Visitations* p. 790, Charles E.H. Chadwyck Healey, *The History of the Part of West Somerset Comprising the Parishes of Luccombe, Selworthy Stoke Pero, Porlock, Culbone and Oare* (1901) p. 192. The italic identifies JPs who were on the bench with Willoughby.
5. SRO, W053/1/125; PRO SP14/142/32.
6. *Trevelyan Papers*, pp. 34n, 44, 47, 52, 55, 58, 63, 68, 106.
7. SRO, W056/5/37.1; DRO, QS1/5 p. 251.
8. *Trevelyan Papers*, pp. 130, 186.
9. SRO, W056/1/7.1, .2, .3.

10. SRO, W056/6/42.3, .4.

11. PRO, PC2/47 f. 269; SRO W056/6/44, 45, 47.3, .4; 53/1/149;

12. SRO, W053/1/115; SRO, W056/6/47.1,.2; PRO, SP16/410/163.

13. SRO, W053/1/115, 56/6/16.1–16.

14. SRO, W056/6/49.3.

15. SRO, W056/6/29; printed in *Devon Documents* (ed.) Todd Gray, *DCNQ* Special Issue (Exeter, 1996). pp. 204–5.

16. SRO, W056/6/16.13, .14, .15, /23.2; 56/1/7.3.

17. PRO, SP16/462.

18. SRO, W056/6/51.1, .3; Stoyle, *Loyalty and Locality* pp. 168–9; see pp. 205–6.

19. SRO, W053/1/121, 122, 123, 56/5/56; 56/6/51.1, 12.

20. Larkin, *Proclamations*, pp. 731, 732. This confusion was also raised by the deputy lieutenants in their letter to the Earl Marshal on 2 September 1640, PRO, PC52 f. 727.

21. SRO, W054/5/2.4, printed in *Trevelyan Papers*, pp. 193–4.

22. Sharpe, *Personal Rule*, p. 563.

23. *Trevelyan Papers*, pp. 195–6.

24. SRO, W054/7/11.1, .2; *Trevelyan Papers*, pp. 213–4.

25. Ibid., pp. 192–204, 205–220.

26. Ibid., p. 217; Larkins *Proclamations*, p. 745; SRO, W053/1/125.

27. *Trevelyan Papers*, pp. 214, 218, 221.

28. Ibid., p. 216; PRO, C231/5, p. 507, appointed 24 February 1642.

29. SRO, W054/5/2.8.

30. DRO, QS Rolls, box 46.

31. BL, Thomason Tract E121/4, 34.

32. BL, Thomason Tract E84/36.

33. DRO, QS1/8, QS Rolls, 12 September 1643; 13 December 1643.

34. DRO, QS1/8; QS Rolls boxes 47–50; Humphrey Prouz 88, John Courtenay 78, John Were of Silverton 71, Peter Sainthill 67, John Davy of Ruxford 60, William Tothill 56, John Willoughby 50, Thomas Wood 55, Gregory Hockmore 45, Richard Cabell 42, Henry Rolle and Henry Ashford 33, John Gifford 29, Sir Amias Ameridith and Edward Yard 27.

35. SRO, W053/1/136, 53/7/13, 56/6/56, 57, DRO, QS Rolls, box 47.

36. SRO, W056/6/52.2, .3.

37. BL, Thomason Tract E114/24.

38. M. Coate, 'An Original Diary of Colonel Robert Bennett of Hexworthy', *DCNQ*, Vol. 18, p. 252.

39. *Trevelyan Papers*, pp. 228–9.

40. SRO, W053/1/129; 57/9/24.6; *Trevelyan Papers*, p. 230.

41. BL, Thomason Tract, E60/17, 62/9. 105/27.

42. BL, Thomason Tract E105/13; DRO, QS Rolls, box 47.

43. *Trevelyan Papers*, p 239; SRO, W054/1/94.

44. DRO, QS Rolls, box 47.

45. Ronald Hutton, *The Royalist War Effort 1642–1646* (1982) p. 87. Devon Commissioners identified: John Acland, Henry Ashford, Peter Ball, Arthur Basset, Sir John Berkeley, Richard Cabell, Sir John Chichester, Richard Cholmeley, John Davy of Ruxford, Sir Edmund Fortescue, Sir Francis Fulford, Sir John Hele, Sir Thomas Hele, Dr George Parry, Humphrey Prouz, Peter Sainthill, Edward Seymour, Sir Ralph Sidenham, George Southcott, William Tothill, John Were of Silverton, Thomas Wood, (all county JPs). John Digby, Thomas Modiford, Gilbert Yard, Sir Hugh Pollard.

46. SRO, W053/3/40. BL, Thomason Tract, E60/18; E63/2.

47. SRO, W056/6/52.12, .13.
48. SRO, W056/6/52.10.
49. DRO, QS1/8 Mich. 1643.
50. SRO, W056/6/61.
51. DRO, QS Rolls, boxes 48, 49; SRO W056/6/52.6, .7, .9.
52. SRO, W057/12/1, 2, undated rough copies of his petition received by commission by 6 January 1646, PRO, SP23/174/754.
53. SRO, W053/1/146, 147.
54. DRO, QS1/8; SRO, W054/4/15.
55. SRO, W057/12/1.1. Another JP, Richard Cabell, claimed he was 'compelled to sit with the King's Commissioners', *CCC*, 1352.
56. SRO, W053/1/149, 56/6/52.5.
57. Stoyle, *Loyalty and Locality*, p. 51.
58. SRO, W056/6/52.16.
59. PRO, SP23/174/761. The John Davy signing this letter would have been the commissioner John Davy of Ruxford.
60. *Trevelyan Papers*, p. 249.
61. SRO, W057/12/1.1.
62. SRO, W056/8/20.61.1.
63. D. Underwood, *Somerset in the Civil War and Interregnum* (Newton Abbot. 1973), p. 140.
64. SRO, W056/8/20.61.2. Willoughby's accounts have been published in, Todd Gray (ed.), *Devon Household Accounts, 1627–59* (Devon and Cornwall Record Society, 1996).
65. PRO, SP23/174/751, 174/755; SRO, W055/6/8.
66. SRO, W054/4/15, 56/8/20.61.2; PRO, SP23/174/751, 757.
67. SRO, W057/12/1, 2.
68. Ibid., PRO, SP23/174/751, 754, 758, 764, SP19/71/69; SP19/11/9, 275.
69. Underdown, *Somerset in the Civil War and Interregnum*, p. 158
70. Stoyle, *Loyality and Locality*, pp. 201, 223.
71. SRO, W055/2/39.1; W055/6/15. This list of books has considerable additions in different hands, only those in the same hand as the heading referring to 1643 are mentioned here.
72. PRO, Prob 11, 281:497.
73. Sir Thomas Prideaux, Thomas Risden, Sir John Speccot, Thomas Tuckfield, John Upton, Thomas Wise, Leonard Yeo.

Chapter 12

1. BL, Add. MSS. 30926.
2. PRO, SP16/147/3.
3. PRO, SP16/82/82, *HMC Exeter*, p. 17.
4. See pp. 79–80, 120, 124.
5. PRO, SP16/34/76; 53/96.
6. BL, Add. MSS. 30926; see p. 123.
7. *HMC 15th Report, Appendix 7*, p. 64.
8. The eight dropped were, John Bampfield, Sir Shilston Calmady, Sir George Chudleigh, Sir John Davy, Sir Nicholas Martin, Sir John Pole, Sir Peter Prideaux, Edmund Prideaux. The six future commissioners were, John Acland, Richard Cabell, Sir Thomas Hele,

Humphrey Prouz, Peter Sainthill, William Tothill. In addition, Edmund Arscott remained on the bench but there is no evidence of him being a commissioner.

9. *CJ*, II, p. 424; *Lords Journal*, V, pp. 94, 144; Andriette, *Devon and Exeter in the Civil War*, p. 56; Palfrey, 'Devon and the Outbreak of the English Civil War, p. 30.

10. DRO, QS1/8 Mid. 1642. Sir John Northcott who was only on the bench from August 1641 to July 1642. PRO C231/5 ff. 478, 530.

11. DRO, QS1/8 Mid. 1642; *LJ*, V p. 295–7, partly printed in Morrill, *Revolt of the Provinces*, pp. 162–3.

12. PRO, C231/4 f. 42v, 239; Westcote, *Devonshire*, p. 114; SP16/70/18; 150/76i/; 291/14; 402/69.

13. *Somerset Record Society*, 18 (1902), pp. 103–4; SRO, W056/6/52.4; PRO, SP23/182 f. 839.

14. PRO, SP23/174/761; /182/829; SRO, W056/52.5; BL, Harl. 6852 f. 179; DRO, 1392M/L1645/7, 16.

15. BL, Harl. 6852. f. 179; Andriette, *Devon and Exeter in the Civil War*, p. 121.

16. PRO, Prob 11/214.

17. PRO, C66/1988, E163/18/12; C193/12/2, 13/2.

18. BL, E245/16 (Thomason Tract); *CSPD 1640*, p. 291; Andriette, *Devon and Exeter in the Civil War*, p. 78; Stoyle, *Loyalty and Locality*, p. 78. DRO, QS1/8 Mich. 1643. Vivian, *Visitations*, p. 379.

19. BL, Burney Collection 13; 22, *Perfect Diurnell*, 16 Dec. 1645. DRO, QS Box 50, QS1/8 Epiph. Easter 1645; 1392M/L1645/7.

20. PRO, SP23/213/f. 673.

21. *HMC 13th Report, Portland*, p. 100.

Bibliography

Unpublished Primary Sources

PUBLIC RECORD OFFICE

C66, Patent Rolls.

C181/3.4.5, Crown Office Entry Books.

C192/1, Commission of Charitable Uses.

C193/12/2, Commissioners for the forced loan.

C193/13/2, *Liber pacis*, 1634.

C227/27–30, Sheriffs Rolls.

C231/1, 4, 5, Crown Office Docquet Books.

E163/14/8, *Liber pacis*, 1584.

E163/18/12, *Liber pacis*, 1626.

E178/5153, 5614, 7154, 7161, Instructions and reports on knighthood composition.

E179/102/450–559, Lay subsidy rolls for Devon, 1624–41.

E179/172/413, Lay subsidy roll for Devon, 1640–1.

E215/1328,1383, Commissions on exacted fees.

E351/282, 283, 284, 288, Accounts for billeting soldiers.

E401/1912–1926, Exchequer receipt books.

E401/2330–3, Abbreviate of receipts (Pells).

E401/2586, Account of 1625 forced loan.

E403/2590 Privy Seal Books (Auditors) Supplementary series 1620–32.

E403/2750–2753, Pells Order Books.

E407/35, Composition for not taking knighthood.

PC2/41–52, Acts of the Privy Council, 1631–1640.

PRO 30/26/59, Return of Coleridge hundred for the forced loan. PROb. 11. Wills.

SO1/2/26, Commissions for knighthood composition.

SP12, State Papers, Elizabeth I.

SP14, State Papers, James I.
SP16, State Papers, Charles I.
SP19, Records of the Committee for the Advance of Money.
SP23, Records of the Committee for Compounding.

BRITISH LIBRARY

Additional MSS 4931, unease over Canons in Devon, 1640.
Additional MSS 12496, Book of Orders, January 1630–1.
Additional MSS 18777–18780, Parliamentary diary of Walter Yonge, 1642–4.
Additional MSS 18980, Prince Rupert's Correspondence.
Additional MSS 22474, Speeches and passages in Parliament 1626, initialled 'WY' but it is not in Walter Yonge's hand and he was in Devon at this time.
Additional MSS 28032, Diary of Walter Yonge, 1604–1628.
Additional MSS 30926, Reply to demand for ship money in 1628.
Additional MSS 35297, Diary of John Syms.
Additional MSS 35331, Diary of Walter Yonge, 1627–1641.
Additional MSS 37817, Nicholas Papers.
Additional MSS 46191, Diary of Sir Nathaniel Rich.
Additional MSS 64883–64893 Coke Papers.
Harleian 1622, *Liber pacis*.
Harleian 2217, 2305, letter of Joseph Hall, bishop of Exeter.
Harleian 6383, Account of proceedings in House of Commons in 1624 by Denzil Holles.
Harleian 6804, Command of the tinners.
Harleian 6852, Letter of Devon JPs, 1644.
Sloane MSS 1775, Reply to demand for ship money in 1628.

DEVON RECORD OFFICE

Chanter 57, Patent Book No. I, concerning the diocese of Exeter. ff. 1–48, 1628–1646.
ECAB, 7–8, Exeter Chamber Act books, 1616–1647.
EQSOB, 62–63, Exeter Quarter Sessions order books.
LXXXII, LXXXVI, Commissions of deputy lieutenants.
QSOB, 1–8, Devon Quarter Sessions order books.
QSR, Devon Quarter Sessions rolls, boxes 1–51.
QS28/1–12, Commissions of the Peace, 1643–1659.
Z1/27/1/26, Z1/48/26/1, 3, 5, Estate of Reynell of Creedy.

Z1/15/14, 16, 18, Estate of Walter Yonge.
60C, 60D, Ancient Letters, Corporation of Exeter.
347 A, Dartington PW2, churchwardens' accounts.
1148 M/add/18/1, deputy lieutenants orders, 1625.
1180 A add 2/PW 15, East Budleigh churchwardens' accounts.
1310 F/A Acte Book of the Eight Men of Broadclyst.
1392 M/L1645/29, Seymour Papers.
1499 M/add 3/E15, Thomas Wise accounts.
1579 A, Totnes records.
1700 M CP20, Colyton Drake papers.
2021 A/PW 1, Lapford churchwardens' accounts.
2656 A 81–96, Crediton headwardens' accounts.
32428 A, Okehampton records.
3944 A/PW I, Chudleigh churchwardens' accounts.
4074 A/PW 1–2, Halberton churchwardens' accounts.
4652M/F5/1, Diary of Sir Richard Reynell of Ogwell.

KENT ARCHIVES OFFICE
U269/C276, 290, 292, Papers of fifth earl of Bath, 1642–4.

SOMERSET RECORD OFFICE
DD/PH 221/40, Phelips papers.
DD/WO 19, 45, 52–57. Wolseley, MSS.

Published Primary Sources

Acts of the Privy Council, 1613–1630.
Barlow, John, *The True Guide to Glory – A Sermon preached at Plympton Mary at the Funeral of the Right Worshipful and truly religious Lady, The Lady Strode of Newington* (1619).
Barnes, T.G., *Somerset Assize Orders 1629–1640* (Somerset Record Society, LXV, 1959).
Birch, T., *Court and Times of Charles I* (ed.) R.F. Williams (1848).
Blake, William J. (ed.), 'Hooker's Synopsis Chorographical of Devonshire, *TDA*, LVII (1915), pp. 334–48.
British Library, Burney Collection, News pamphlets, 1642–1646.
British Library, Thomason Tracts, News pamphlets, 1642–1646.

Calendar of State Papers Domestic 1611–1642.

Chadwyck-Healy, C.E.H. (ed.), 'Sir Ralph Hopton's Campaign in the West 1642–1644', *Somerset Record Society*, 18 (1902).

Chudleigh, Sir George, *A Declaration published in the County of Devon by that Grand Ambo-dexter, Sir George Chudleigh Baronet. To delude his Country-men in their Judgement and Affection, touching the present difference between his Majestie and the Parliament. Together with a full and satisfactory Answer thereunto, transmitted from thence under the Hand of a Judicious and well affected Patriot* (1644).

Coates, William H., Young, Anne Steele, Snow Vernon F. (eds), *The Private Journals of the Long Parliament, 3 January to 5 March 1642* (Newhaven and London, Yale University Press, 1982).

Cockburn, J.S. (ed.), 'Memorandum Book of Robert Hunt, Sheriff of Somerset 1654–1656' in *Somerset Assize Orders*, Appendix II (Somerset Record Society, LXXI, 1971).

Cockburn, J.S. (ed.) *Western Circuit Assize Orders 1629–1648*, (Camden 4th series, 17, 1976).

Cockburn, J.S. (ed.), *Calendar of Assize Records, Home Circuit Indictments Elizabeth and James I* (1985).

Commons Journal, I–III.

Cooke, W.H. (ed.), *Students of Inner Temple 1545–1660* (1868).

Cust, Richard (ed.), *The Papers of Sir Richard Grosvenor, Ist Bart (1585–1645)* (Lancashire and Cheshire Record Society, 1996).

Dalton, Michael, *The Countrey Justice* (1619, reprinted 1973).

Dalton, Michael, *The Office and Authority of Sheriff* (1623).

Foster, J. (ed.), *Alumni Oxonienses* (Oxford, 1891–2).

Fuller Thomas, *A History of the Worthies of England*, two volumes (1881).

Gardiner, S.R., *The Constitutional Documents of the Puritan Revolution* (Oxford, 1899).

Gray, Todd (ed.), *Harvest Failure in Cornwall and Devon*, Sources of Cornish History, Vol. I (Institute of Cornish Studies, 1992).

Gray, Todd (ed.), *Devon Household Accounts, 1627–59* (Devon and Cornwall Record Society, 1996).

Gray, Todd (ed.) *Devon Documents*, DCNQ, Special Issue (1996).

Green, M.A. (ed.), *Calendar of the Committee for Compounding with Delinquents 1643–60*, five volumes, (1882–92).

Grosart, A.B. (ed.), *John Glanvill's Account of the Expedition to Cadiz in 1625* (Camden Society, 2nd series, 32, 1883).

Hall, Peter (ed.), *The Works of Joseph Hall DD*, twelve volumes (Oxford, 1837).

Hieron, Samuel, *The Dignity of Preaching in a Sermon upon I Thessalonians 5:20* (1615).

Historical Manuscripts Commission,
4th Report, House of Lords MSS;
5th Report;
9th Report Part I;
10th Report, Salisbury;
12th Report Cowper I;
13th Report, Appendix I, Portland;
15th Report, Appendix 7;
Exeter, 73.

Howard, A.J. (ed.), *The Devon Protestation Returns 1641*, two volumes (1971).

Hulme, Harold (ed.), 'Sir John Eliot and the Vice-Admiralty of Devon', *Camden Miscellany*, XVII (3rd series, 64, 1940).

Hyde, E., Earl of Clarendon, *The History of the Rebellion and Civil Wars in England* (Oxford, 1839).

Instructions for Musters and Arms and Use Thereof (1623).

Karkeek, P.Q. (ed.), 'Extract from a Memoranda Book belonging to Thomas Roberts and Family of Stockleigh Pomeroy 1621–1644', *TDA*, X (1878), pp. 315–329.

Kenyon, J.P., *The Stuart Constitution* (Cambridge, 1966).

Larkin, James E. (ed.), *Stuart Royal Proclamations*, II (Oxford, 1983).

Lords Journal, IV, V.

Myers, A.R., *English Historical Documents*, IV (1969).

Parliamentary Returns, Part I (1879).

Pole, Sir William, *Collections Towards a Description of the County of Devon* (1791).

Prince, J., *Worthies of Devon*, (Exeter, 1701).

Register of Admissions to the Honourable Society of Lincoln's Inn, I, Admissions 1420–1799 (1896).

Risdon, Tristram, *Survey of the County of Devon* (1811).

Roberts G. (ed.), *The Diary of Walter Yonge* (Camden Society Ist Series, 41, 1848).

Rowe, Margery, M and Jackson, Andrew, M. (eds), *Freemen of Exeter 1266–1947* (Devon and Cornwall Record Society, extra series I, 1973).

Rushworth, John, *Historical Collections*, seven volumes (1721).

Stephenson, C and Marcham, F.G., *Sources of English Constitutional History* (New York, 1937).

Sturgess, H.A.C. (ed.), *Register of Admissions to the Middle Temple* I (1949).

Trevelyan, Walter and Charles (eds), *Trevelyan Papers Part III 1446–1643* (Camden Society, Ist Series, 105, 1872).

Venn J and J.A. (eds), *Alumni Cantabrigiensis, Pt. I* (Cambridge, 1922).

Weinbaum, M. (ed.), *British Borough Charters 1307–1660* (Cambridge 1943).

Westcote, Thomas, *A View of Devonshire in 1630* (eds) G. Oliver and P. Jones (Exeter, 1845).

Worth, R.N. (ed.), *Buller Papers* (1895).

Worthy, Charles, *Devonshire Wills* (1896).

Yonge, Walter, *Table containing such statutes wherein one or more JPs are enabled to act as well in Session as out of Session* (1660).

Youings, Joyce, *Devon Monastic Lands: Calendars of Particulars from Grants 1536–1558* (Devon and Cornwall Record Society, New Series I, 1955).

Typescript of primary sources in West Country Studies Library, Sir Oswyn Murray, Wills, Ist Series 37 Vols. 2nd and 3rd Series.

Published Secondary Sources

Adams, Simon, 'Spain or the Netherlands? The Dilemmas of Early Stuart Foreign Policy' in *Before the English Civil War* (ed.) Harold Tomlinson (1983), pp. 79–101.

Andrews, Charles M., *The Colonial Period of American History The Settlements I* (New Haven, 1934).

Andriette, E.A., *Devon and Exeter in the Civil War* (Newton Abbot, 1971).

Aylmer, G.E., *The King's Servants* (1961).

Barnes, T.G., *Somerset 1625–1640* (Cambridge, Mass., 1961).

Barnes, T.G. and Hassell Smith A., 'Justices of the Peace from 1558–1688 – a Revised List of Sources', *BIHR* XXXIII (1959). pp. 221–242.

Boynton, Lindsay, *The Elizabethan Militia 1558–1638* (1967).

Chadwyck-Healey, Charles E.H., *The History of the part of West Somerset comprising the parishes of Luccombe, Selworthy, Stoke Pero, Porlock, Culbone and Oare* (1901).

Clark, Peter, *English Provincial Society from the Reformation to the Revolution* (1977).

Cliffe, J.T., *The Puritan Gentry* (1984).

Cliffe, J.T., *Puritans in Conflict* (1988).

Coate, M., 'An Original Diary of Colonel Robert Bennett of Hexworthy', *DCNQ* 18 (1935), pp. 251–259.

Cockburn, J.S., *History of English Assizes from 1558 to 1714* (Cambridge, 1972).

Cope, Esther S., *Politics without Parliament 1629–1640* (1987).

Cotton, R.W., *Barnstaple and the Northern part of Devonshire during the Great Civil War* (1889).

Crosleigh, Charles, *History of Bradninch* (1911).

Cust, Richard, 'A List of Commissioners for the Forced Loan 1626–7' *BIHR* LI (1978), pp. 199–206.

Cust, Richard, 'News and Politics in Early Seventeenth-Century England', *Past and Present*, 112 (August 1986), pp. 60–90.

Cust, Richard, *The Forced Loan and English Politics 1626–1628* (Oxford, 1987).

Cust, Richard and Hughes Ann (eds), *Conflicts in Early Stuart England* (1989).

Cust, Richard and Lake Peter G., 'Sir Richard Grosvenor and the Rhetoni of Magistracy', *BIHR* LIV (1981), pp. 40–55.

Davies, Julian, *The Caroline Captivity of the Church 1625–1641* (Oxford, 1992).

Dictionary of National Biography.

Duffin, Anne, *Faction and Faith* (Exeter, 1996).

Edgar, F.T.R., *Sir Ralph Hopton* (1968).

Eliot-Drake, E.F., *The Family and Heirs of Sir Francis Drake* (1911).

Everitt, Alan, *Change in the Provinces* (Leicester, 1969).

Everitt, Alan, *The Community of Kent and the Great Rebellion 1640–1660* (Leicester, 1973).

Fincham, K. (ed.), *The Early Stuart Church, 1603–1642* (1993).

Fletcher, Anthony, *A County Community in Peace and War, Sussex 1600–1660* (1975).

Fletcher, Anthony, *The Outbreak of the English Civil War* (1981).

Fletcher, Anthony, 'National and Local Awareness in the County Communities' in H. Tomlinson (ed.) *Before the Civil War* (1983), pp. 151–174.

Fletcher, Anthony, *Reform in the Provinces* (1986).

Gardiner, S.R., *History of the Great Civil War* (1987).

Gleason, J.H., *The Justices of the Peace in England 1558–1642* (Oxford, 1969).

Gordon, M.D., 'The Collection of Ship Money in the Reign of Charles I', *TRHS* 3rd Series IV (1910), pp. 141–162.

Hamilton, A.H.A., 'The Justices of the Peace of the County of Devon and the Benevolences of 1616 and 1622', *TDA* IX (1877), pp. 404–6.

Hasler, P.W. (ed.), *History of Parliament The Commons 1558–1603* (1981).

Herrup, Cynthia B., *The Common Peace* (Cambridge, 1987).

Hexter, J.H., *The Reign of King Pym* (Harvard University Press, 1961).

Holmes, Clive, *Seventeenth-Century Lincolnshire*, History of Lincolnshire, 7 (Lincoln, 1980).

Holmes, Clive, 'The County Community in Stuart Historigraphy', *Journal of British Studies* XIX (1980), pp. 54–73.

Hoskins, W.G., 'Devonshire Gentry in Carolean Times', *DCNQ* 22 (1946), pp. 317–27, 353–62.

Hoskins, W.G., 'Estates of Caroline Gentry' in H.P.R. Finberg and W.G. Hoskins, *Devonshire Studies* (1952), pp. 334–65.

Hoskins, W.G., *Devon* (1954).

Hughes, Ann, *Politics, Society and Civil War in Warwickshire*, (Cambridge, 1987).

Hughes, Ann, *The Causes of the English Civil War* (New York, 1991).

Hunt, William, *Puritan Moment* (Harvard, 1983).

Hurstfield, Joel, 'County Government in Wiltshire c.1530–c.1660 in *Freedom, Corruption and Government in Elizabethan England* (1973), pp. 236–93.

Hutton, Ronald, *The Royalist War Effort 1642–1646* (1982).

James, Frances B., 'Sir Henry Rosewell: A Devon Worthy', *TDA* XX (1888), pp. 113–122.

Jones, John, *Bishop Hall, His Life and Times* (1826).

Kain, Roger and Ravenhill, Bill (ed.), *Historical Atlas of South West England*, (Exeter, forthcoming).

Karkeek, P.Q., 'First Visit of Charles I to Devon' *TDA* X (1878), pp. 223–36.

Keeler, M.F., *The Long Parliament* (1954).

Lake, Peter, 'The moderate and irenic case for religious war: Joseph Hall's Via Media in context' in Susan D. Amussen and Mark A. Kishlansky (eds), *Political Culture and Cultural Politics in Early Modern England* (1995).

Leonard, H.H., 'Distraint of Knighthood: The Last Phase 1625–41', *History* 63 (1978), pp. 23–37.

Levy, F.J., 'How Information Spread among the Gentry 1550–1640', *Journal of British Studies* XXI (1982), pp. 11–34.

Lockyer, Roger, *Buckingham* (1981).

MacCaffrey, Wallace T., *Exeter 1540–1640* (Cambridge, Mass., 1958).

Morrill, J.S., *Cheshire 1630–1660* (Oxford, 1974).

Morrill, J.S., *The Revolt of the Provinces* (1976).

Morrill, J.S., *The Cheshire Grand Jury 1625–1659* (Department of English Local History, Occasional Papers, Third series, No. 6. Leicester, 1976).

Morrill, J.S., 'The Northern Gentry and the Great Rebellion', *Northern History* XV (1979), pp. 66–87.

Morrill, J.S., *The Nature of the English Revolution* (1993).

Palfrey, I.R., 'Devon and the Outbreak of the English Civil War, 1642–43', *Southern History*, 10 (1988), pp. 29–46.

Polwhele, Richard, *The History of Devonshire* (1977, Dorking).

Prest, W.R., *The Inns of Court 1590–1640* (1972).

Pugsley, Steven, 'Landed Society and the Emergence of the Country House in Tudor and Early Stuart Devon' in Todd Gray, Margery Rowe and Audrey Erskine (eds), *Tudor and Stuart Devon* (Exeter, 1992).

Quintrell, B.W., 'The Making of Charles I's Book of Orders', *EHR*, XCV (1980), pp. 553–72.

Reeve, L.J., *Charles I and the Road to Personal Rule* (Cambridge, 1989).

Roberts, Stephen, K., *Recovery and Restoration in an English County, 1646–1670* (Exeter, 1985).

Ruigh, Robert E., *The Parliament of 1624* (Cambridge, Mass., 1971).

Russell, Conrad, *Parliaments and English Politics 1621–1629* (Oxford, 1979).

Russell, Conrad, *The Fall of the British Monarchies 1637–1642* (Oxford, 1991).

Sharpe, J.A., *Crime in Seventeenth Century England* (Cambridge, 1983).

Sharpe, Kevin, *The Personal Rule of Charles I* (Yale, 1992).

Sharpe, Kevin, 'Crown, Parliament and Locality: Government and Communications in Early Stuart England', *EHR*, CI (1986), pp. 321–50.

Slack, Paul, 'Mortality Crises and Epidemic Disease in England 1485–1610', reprinted from Charles Webster (ed.), *Health, Medicine and Mortality in the Sixteenth Century* (Cambridge, 1979).

Slack, Paul, 'Book of Orders: The Making of English Social Policy 1577–1634', *TRHS* 5th series (1980), pp. 1–22.

Slack, Paul, *The Impact of Plague in Tudor and Stuart England* (1985).

Stevenson, David *The Scottish Revolution 1637–44* (Newton Abbot, 1973).

Stoyle, Mark, *Loyalty and Locality* (Exeter, 1994).

Stoyle, Mark, *Documentary Evidence for the Civil War Defences of Exeter, 1642–43* (Exeter Museums Archaeological Field Unit Report No. 92. 10, 1992).

Taverner, R.L., 'The Administrative Work of the Devon Justices in the Seventeenth-Century' *TDA*, C (1968), pp. 55–84.

Thirsk, Joan (ed.), *The Agrarian History of England and Wales*, IV (Cambridge, 1967).

Thomas, David, 'Financial and Administrative Developments' in Howard Tomlinson (ed.), *Before the English Civil War* (1983), pp. 103–22.

Troup, F.R., *John White, Founder of Massachusetts* (New York, 1930).

Troup, F.R., 'A Forgotten Page of the Ecclesiastical History of Seaton, *TDA*, XXX (1898), pp. 331–49.

Underdown, David, *Pride's Purge* (Oxford, 1971).

Underdown, David, *Somerset in the Civil War and Interregnum* (Newton Abbot, 1973).

Vivian, J.L., *The Visitations of the County of Devon, Comprising the Heralds Visitations of 1531, 1564 and 1620* (Exeter, 1895).

Vivian, J.L., *The Visitations of the County of Cornwall* (1887).

Watson, W.G. Willis, *The House of Martin* (Exeter, 1906).

Zaller, Robert, *The Parliament of 1621* (1971).

Theses

Braddick, M.J., 'Parliamentary Lay Taxation c.1590–1670. Local problems of enforcement and collection, with special reference to Norfolk' (University of Cambridge Ph.D., 1988).

Dias, Jill R. 'Politics and Administration in Nottinghamshire and Derbyshire 1590–1640' (University of Oxford D.Phil., 1973).

Gowers, Ian W., 'Puritanism in the County of Devon between 1570 and 1641' (University of Exeter MA, 1970).

Gray, Todd, 'Devon's Coastal and Overseas Fisheries and New England Migration 1597–1642 (University of Exeter Ph.D., 1988).

Hindle, Steve, 'Aspects of the relationship of the State and Local Society in early modern England with special relationship to Cheshire c.1590–1630' (University of Cambridge Ph.D., 1991).

Kerby, G.A. 'Inequality in a Pre-Industrial Society. A Study of Wealth, Status, Office and Taxation in Tudor and Stuart England with Particular Reference to Cheshire' (University of Cambridge Ph.D., 1983).

Langelüddecke, Henrik A., 'Secural Policy Enforcement During the Personal Rule of Charles I – The Administrative Work of the Parish Officers in the 1630s' (University of Oxford, D.Phil, 1995).

McPartlin, G.E., 'The Herefordshire Gentry in County Government 1625–1660' (University of Wales, University College of Aberystwyth Ph.D., 1981).

Noonkester, Myron C, 'Kings of their Counties. The Shrievalty in England from Elizabeth I to Charles I' (University of Chicago Ph.D., 1984).

Quintrell, B.W., 'The Government of the County of Essex 1603–1642' (University of London Ph.D., 1965).

Roberts, J.C., 'Parliamentary Representation of Devon and Dorset 1559–1601' (University of London MA, 1958).

Silcock, R.H., 'County Government in Worcestershire 1603–1660' (University of London Ph.D., 1974).

Stone, Cordelia Ann, 'Devon and Parliament in Early Stuart Period' (Bryn Mawr College Ph.D., 1986).

Tyldesley, C.J., 'The Crown and the Local Communities in Devon and Cornwall from 1377 to 1422' (University of Exeter Ph.D., 1978).

Vage, J.A., 'The Diocese of Exeter, 1519–1641: A Study of Church Government in the Age of Reformation' (University of Cambridge Ph.D., 1991).

Wanklyn, M.D.G., 'Landed Society and Allegiance in Cheshire and Shropshire in the First Civil War' (University of Manchester Ph.D., 1976).

Wolffe, A.M., 'The Gentry Government of Devon, 1625–1640' (University of Exeter Ph.D., 1992).

Index

INDEX

Poulett, baron, 17, 207
Prideaux family, 8, 180
Prideaux, Sir Edmund, JP, 1st baronet, of
    Netherton, 20, 26, 31, 181
Prideaux, Edmund, JP, 31, 156, 181, 194, 288n8
Prideaux, Sir Nicholas, JP, of Soldon, 30, 267n10,
    n16
Prideaux, Sir Peter, JP, 2nd baronet, of Netherton,
    20, 31, 151, 152, 181, 194 288n8; clerk of, 171
Prideaux, Sir Thomas, JP, of Nutwell, 31, 288n73
Pride's Purge, 195, 223
Privy Council, 83, 107, 133; Council orders of
    1605, 35, 43, 55; of 1623 to produce grain
    certificates, 37–8, 43; over militia, 132, 133,
    134, 135–6, 137, 140, 141, 146–7; over ship
    money, of 1634, 199–200; of 1635, 202;
    207–8, 209; of 1637, 211–12, 213; petition to
    Council against Canons of 1640, 145–6;
    petition over costs of trained bands against
    Scots, 147
Prouz, Humphrey, JP, of Chagford, 31, 140, 152,
    257, 287n34, n45, 288n8
Protestation Returns, 7, 149
Puritan writers, 185
Putt, Nicholas, JP, 235, 249
Pym, John, 24

Quarter Sessions, 4, 48, 49. 212, 257; deputy *custos
    rotulorum*, 21; during Civil War, 237–8, 243,
    244, 261; juries, grand, 10, 11, 49, 52; petty,
    49–50; orders from the Commons, 147;
    quorum, 21; petititions to, 64, 65, petition
    from, in 1634, 139, 201; in 1642, 149–50, 152,
    257

Rackenford, 170
Raleigh, Sir Walter, 95
Recusancy, 149; rumours of popish plots, 149
Reynell, Periam, JP, of Creedy, 31, 166
Reynell, Richard, JP, of Creedy, 8, 31, 179, 180,
    185; Bradninch, recorder of, 167; Broadclyst,
    one of Eight Men of, 167; career at bar, 167;
    Creedywiger, manor of, 168; family
    background, 165–7; relations with the
    Reynells of Ogwell, 175
—, Exeter, house in, 21, 27; freedom of city, 174;
    acting recorder of, 174; negotiations over
    royal demand for ships from, 175; support
    against recusants of, 174, 175
—, JP, out-of-Sessions work, 168–73; development
    of Crediton sub-division, 173–4; possibly
    deputy *custos rotulorum*, 21; Totnes, asked for
    aid over billeting, 175
Reynell, Sir Richard, JP, of Ogwell, 27, 31, 166,
    175, 181, 239
Reynell, Sir Thomas, JP, 31, 166
Rich, Henry, earl of Holland, 123, 124, 183
Rich, Robert, earl of Warwick, 17
Richards, William, JP, 30
Ridgeway, Thomas, earl of Londonderry, 31,
    267n1
Risden, Thomas, JP, of Sandwell, 31, 288n73
Roborough Down, 107
Robinson Ralph, pursuivant, 82, 120
Rolle, Dennis, 207, 214, 223, 268n43; ship money
    collection of 1636, 207–9, 211

Rolle, Sir Henry, JP, of Stevenstone, 22, 30, 207
Rolle, Henry, JP, 287n34
Rolle, Sir Samuel, JP, 30, 214, 222, 240, 279n68
Rosewell, Sir Henry, JP, of Ford, 21, 31, 194,
    267n11, 268n49
Roundaway Down, battle of, 159
Royal commissioners, 241–2, 243, 244, 245, 246,
    261, 287n45
Russell, John, 1st earl of Bedford, 13, 95
Russell, Francis, 2nd earl of Bedford, 13
Russell, Francis, Lord Russell of Thornhaugh, 4th
    earl of Bedford, lord lieutenant 1625–41, 17,
    74, 75, 78, 95, 124, 128, 131–2, 134, 135, 137,
    140, 141, 190, 256, 267n1
Russell, William, 5th earl of Bedford, 95, 141, 150,
    151, 152, 159, 240, 257, 261n1
Russell, Sir William, treasurer of the navy, 198,
    201, 204, 209, 213, 217

Sainthill, Peter, JP, of Bradninch, 31, 238, 239, 240,
    241, 245, 246, 287n34, n45, 288n8
St John, Sir Alexander, JP, 25
St Leger, Sir William, 276n58
Salcombe, 209
Sampford Peverell, 247
Sanders, Mr Humphrey, parson of Hemyock, 246
Savery Robert, JP, of Rattery, 31, 140
Scilly Isles, 125
Scotland, Charles in Edinburgh, 148, 192;
    imposition of prayer book, 192; steps towards
    war, 193, 215; war, 141, 193, 234; trained
    bands for, 142, 143, 231, 232–3, 234
Seaton, 183, 228, 235
Seymour, Sir Edward, JP, 2nd baronet, 20, 23, 31,
    267n10, 274n89
Seymour, Edward, 144, 223, 256, 257, 287n45
Sherborne, 154, 237
Sheriff, 25, 197–8, 224–5, 235. See also Drew, Sir
    Thomas; Fry, Nicholas; Martin, Sir Nicholas;
    Pole, Sir John; Rolle, Dennis; Wise, Thomas;
    Yonge, Walter; Undersheriffs, 184, 204, 217;
    sheriff's bailiffs, 204
Shipley, Archillis, 222
Ship money, 198, in 1628, 83–4, 198; writ of 1634,
    191, 199–201; of 1635, 202–5; of 1636, 207–9;
    of 1637, 210–14; of 1638, 215–18; of 1639, 221
Ships, demand for in 1626–7, 77–8, 80–1
Shropshire, 22
Shute, 215, 220
Sidenham, Sir Ralph, JP, 30, 259, 268n27, 287n45
Slanning, Sir Nicholas, JP, 31
Somerset, 4, 9, 17, 24, 26, 40, 75, 125, 127, 136,
    156, 191; ship money, 204, 205, 222
Sourton Down, battle of, 157
South Hams, 23, 26, 34
South Molton, 6; ship money, 200
Southcott, Sir Edward, JP, 30
Southcott, Sir George, JP, 31
Southcott, George, JP, 287n45
Southcott, Sir Popham, JP, 31
Spanish alliance, 138–9, 191
Spanish war, 70, 71, 100, 102, 131; effects on
    trade, 23, 76, 78
Speccot, Sir John, 30, 181, 288n73
Stamford, earl of, see Grey
Starr, Robert, 235

305

INDEX